The International Library of Sociology

THE IDEAL FOUNDATIONS
OF ECONOMIC THOUGHT

Founded by KARL MANNHEIM

The International Library of Sociology

ECONOMICS AND SOCIETY
In 11 Volumes

THE IDEAL FOUNDATIONS OF ECONOMIC THOUGHT

Three Essays on the Philosophy of Economics

by

WERNER STARK

First published in 1943
by Routledge

Reprinted in 1998, 2002
by Routledge
2 Park Square, Milton Park, Abingdon, Oxon, OX14 4RN
or
270 Madison Avenue, New York, NY 10016

First issued in paperback 2010

Routledge is an imprint of the Taylor & Francis Group

The publishers have made every effort to contact authors/copyright holders
of the works reprinted in *The International Library of Sociology*.
This has not been possible in every case, however, and we would
welcome correspondence from those individuals/companies
we have been unable to trace.

British Library Cataloguing in Publication Data
A CIP catalogue record for this book
is available from the British Library

The Ideal Foundations of Economic Thought
ISBN 978–0–415–17529–6 (hbk)
ISBN 978–0–415–60519–9 (pbk)
Economics and Society: 11 Volumes
ISBN 978–0–415–17819–8
The International Library of Sociology: 274 Volumes
ISBN 978–0–415–17838–9

Publisher's Note
The publisher has gone to great lengths to ensure the quality
of this reprint but points out that some imperfections
in the original may be apparent

CONTENTS

v

To
LORD KEYNES OF TILTON,
the great heir of a great tradition

PREFACE

THIS is, and at the same time is not, an historical book. In its essence it is indeed an investigation and description of past developments, but in its result it has important bearings on the discussions of the present day.

What I have tried to understand, and what I am endeavouring to make understood, is the social philosophy behind modern economic thought—that body of social ideas and ideals from which the science of political economy originally sprang and to which it is ever leading back. It is here presented in three distinct essays, each dealing with one of the crucial stages through which economics has passed in its evolution. These stages or phases are characterized by three pairs of thinkers who, as it were, sum up the creed of their various ages : Locke and Leibniz, the philosophers of classical economics ; Gossen and Jennings, the pioneers of the modern doctrine ; and, lastly, Thompson and Hodgskin, in whose thought the great crisis which led from the one to the other found its clearest expression.

Thus far, then, the present book is an historical investigation. But, in writing it, the author could not but constantly compare the two great systems of ideas which comprise and divide modern economic thought. Comparison naturally led to judgment, and thus a critical conclusion forced itself upon the historian which could not possibly be suppressed or withheld.

Hence it is that I cannot expect for this treatise willing acceptance in all quarters. I am confident, however, that even those who disagree with my final result will not find it difficult to do me justice. Let them disregard the confession set forth in my postscript, and judge the book solely upon its merits or demerits as an historical investigation. They will, I trust, find it an unprejudiced account.

I gladly take this opportunity to express my thanks to all those who, in the difficult years that lie behind us, have been of help to me. I mention first the Graduate Faculty of Political and Social Science in New York who, shortly after the military occupation of my country, invited me, at the instance of Prof. Edward Heimann, to go to America and take some part in their activities. When this plan failed, the Society for the Protection of Science and Learning enabled me to come to England and continue my work in this hospitable island.

I am sincerely grateful to the Faculty of Economics and Politics in the University of Cambridge for kindly permitting me to deliver two courses of lectures. They will, I do not doubt, recognize in the following pages what might be called the Cambridge spirit of economics—the Marshallian conviction that there is an intimate link between social philosophy and economic analysis which should never be severed. My special thanks are due to Mr. Piero Sraffa and Mr. Maurice Dobb who have assisted me in many ways, and to Mrs. Joan Robinson who has read the manuscript of these essays and given me much encouragement by her sympathetic judgment and practical advice. The Rev. John F. Holt and Mr. Dennis Dobson have helped to improve the style of this book, and at the expert hands of Miss Helen Oman it has been purged of its remaining linguistic shortcomings.

I have dedicated this publication to Lord Keynes. It is meant to be a tribute, not only to his scholarly achievement, but also to the fine humanitarianism which gives colour to his every word and action. If, amid the great honours now bestowed upon him, this modest offering could hope to please him, I should be truly glad.

W. STARK.

CAMBRIDGE,
April 4, 1943.

THE PHILOSOPHICAL FOUNDATIONS OF CLASSICAL ECONOMICS

The decline and dissolution of the mediæval system of life threw mankind into the most violent crisis which had overtaken it since the dark days between the deposition of Romulus Augustulus and the accession of Charles Martel. The age of the Renaissance was a period of contradictory development : men's dominion over nature was increasing, but it was felt that men's understanding of the universe was decreasing. The old cosmology of the Schools was abandoned, but there was no modern doctrine of a similar cast to replace it. It took more than two hundred years before a comprehensive world-view corresponding to the changed realities emerged. Of this new cosmology classical economics was an integral part.

Thus the roots of the theories set forth by François Quesnay and Adam Smith lie not only in the economic and social, but also in the philosophic thought of the time that preceded them : and, indeed, they owed more to Locke and Leibniz than to Monchrétien and Mun.[1] For in Locke and Leibniz mankind regained intellectual clarity ; their ideas, curiously combined, formed the fundamental theme which, repeated in all departments of science with the appropriate variations, dominated and unified the whole system of human knowledge.

I. The Great Antithesis : Man and Nature

The fundamental idea of all Locke's philosophy, both physical and practical, is the conception that there is a deep antagonism between man and nature, self and universe. Their mutual relation, as Locke sees it, is one of action and reaction. The action of nature upon man forms the subject of his theory of

---

[1] It is neither suggested that Locke and Leibniz alone conceived the new cosmology nor that Quesnay and Smith were exclusively or even predominantly influenced by them. It would suffice to mention Descartes and Gassendi to overthrow the one, and to mention Hutcheson and Malebranche to overthrow the other assertion. Yet, in the seventeenth century, Locke and Leibniz were the greatest of the great. To discuss their relation to Quesnay and Smith is to discuss the relation of philosophy to classical economics. Locke and Leibniz were incidentally also important economists. For the former cf. Keynes, *The General Theory of Employment, Interest and Money*, 1936, Ch. xxiii ; for the latter Bortkevich (Bortkiewicz), *Wie Leibniz die Diskontierungsformel begruendete, Festgaben fuer Wilhelm Lexis*, 1907.

knowledge ; the action of man upon nature furnishes the matter
to his analysis of social life.

The task which Locke sets himself in his *Essay concerning
Human Understanding* is, according to his own words, " to
consider the discerning faculties of a man, as they are employed
about the objects, which they have to do with " (I, i, 2), and
since he intends to cover the whole extent of human knowledge,
it is plain that he does not admit of any innate ideas which the
mind might be supposed to possess before the senses come into
contact with the outer world. " Perception ", he asserts (II,
ix, 15), " is the first operation of all our intellectual faculties,
and the inlet of all knowledge in our minds." For " whatever idea is in the mind, is either an actual perception ; or
else, having been an actual perception, is so in the mind, that
by the memory it can be made an actual perception again "
(I, iv, 20).

These statements expose the foundation of Locke's epistemology, and the following simile makes it perfectly clear : " The
understanding is not much unlike a closet wholly shut from light,
with only some little opening left, to let in external visible
resemblances, or ideas of things without " (II, xi, 17). All the
higher thought proceeds from the lower sensations : " The
senses at first let in particular ideas, and furnish the yet empty
cabinet ; and the mind by degrees growing familiar with some
of them, they are lodged in the memory, and names got to them.
Afterwards the mind, proceeding farther, abstracts them, and
by degrees learns the use of general names. In this manner
the mind comes to be furnished with ideas and language "
(I, ii, 15).

Thus man, as an intellectual being, is entirely the product of
his environment : " Simple ideas . . . are only to be got by
those impressions objects themselves make on our minds, by the
proper inlets appointed to each sort. . . . Simple ideas are all
from things themselves, and of these the mind can have no more,
nor other than what are suggested to it " (III, iv, 11 ; II, xii, 2).
The origin of knowledge lies in nature's action upon man :
" The mind, in respect of its simple ideas, is wholly passive, and
receives them all from the existence and operations of things,
such as sensation or reflection offers them " (II, xxii, 2). This
active operation of things upon the passive mind of man, Locke
conceived in a narrow mechanical way : he was under the
influence of Descartes' corpuscular theory which explained the

phenomenon of light by the physical impact of minute particles of matter emitted by luminous bodies upon the retina : " I cannot (and I would be glad any one would make intelligible that he did) conceive how bodies without us can any ways affect our senses, but by the immediate contact of the sensible bodies themselves, as in tasting and feeling, or the impulse of some insensible particles coming from them, as in seeing, hearing, and smelling ; by the different impulse of which parts . . . the variety of sensations is produced in us " (IV, II, 11).

Hence Locke's theory of knowledge is the story of nature's power over man. Man cannot extend his knowledge beyond the limits set by nature : " Our faculties carry us no farther towards the knowledge and distinction of substances, than a collection of those sensible ideas which we observe in them ; which, however made with the greatest diligence and exactness we are capable of, yet is more remote from the true internal constitution, from which those qualities flow, than . . a countryman's idea is from the inward contrivance of that fame is clock at Strasburgh, whereof he only sees the outward figure and motions " (III, VI, 9).

Yet, in spite of these limits and because of these limits, our understanding of the universe is sound. It comes from nature and can therefore rely upon it : " Simple ideas . . . . since the mind can by no means make [them] to itself, must necessarily be the product of things operating on the mind in a natural way, and producing therein those perceptions which by the wisdom and will of our maker they are ordained and adapted to. From whence it follows, that simple ideas are not fictions of our fancies, but the natural and regular productions of things without us, really operating upon us, and so carry with them all the conformity which is intended, or which our state requires. . . And this conformity between our simple ideas, and the existence of things, is sufficient for real knowledge " (IV, IV, 4).

This epistemology applies not only to physical but also to moral knowledge. Neither here nor there is the mind furnished with any innate principles ; neither here nor there can the understanding draw upon any source but experience. Yet there is one important difference : physical experience comes to men almost always directly, moral experience as a rule through the medium of other men ; therefore physical experience is usually genuine, moral experience often falsified. It is the realm of prejudice : " Doctrines that have been derived from no better original than the superstition of a nurse, or the authority

of an old woman, may, by length of time, and consent of neighbours, grow up to the dignity of principles in religion or morality.
For such, who are careful (as they call it) to principle children
well . . . instil into the unwary, and as yet unprejudiced understanding (for white paper receives any characters) those doctrines they would have them retain and profess. These being
taught them as soon as they have any apprehension ; and still
as they grow up, confirmed to them, either by the open profession, or tacit consent, of all they have to do with ; or at least
by those, of whose wisdom, knowledge and piety, they have an
opinion, who never suffer these propositions to be otherwise
mentioned, but as the basis and foundation on which they build
their religion and manners ; come, by these means, to have the
reputation of unquestionable, self-evident, and innate truths "
(I, III, 22).

However, prejudice is not insurmountable : moral knowledge
is just as possible as physical knowledge. Certainly, we receive
it for the better part from tradition ; certainly, there is no moral
sense nor moral law in our breast to guide us—" but the goodness of God hath not been wanting to men without such original
impressions of knowledge, or ideas stamped on the mind : since
he hath furnished man with those faculties, which will serve for
the sufficient discovery of all things requisite to the end of such
a being " (I, IV, 12). He has furnished man with faculties
which enable him to gain genuine moral experience and to build
up reliable moral knowledge. These faculties are the susceptibility of pleasure and pain : " Nature . . . has put into
man a desire of happiness, and an aversion to misery : these
indeed are innate practical principles, which (as practical principles ought) do continue constantly to operate and influence all
our actions without ceasing : these may be observed in all
persons and all ages, steady and universal ; but these are inclinations of the appetite to good, not impressions of truth on the
understanding " (I, III, 3)—that is to say : they belong to our
sensual outfit, not to our intellectual apparatus ; they are not a
stock of knowledge, born with us, but the means for the acquisition
of a stock of knowledge, post-natal in character. Physical and
moral ideas are, therefore, of like origin. Both testify to the
power of nature over men's minds : the senses convey moral
experience to the understanding through pleasure and pain as
they do physical experience through eye and ear : that is all.
" Whiteness and coldness are no more in snow than pain is " ;

both types of ideas are in the same way " the effects of powers in things without us, ordained by our Maker to produce in us such sensations " (II, xxx, 2).

Hence, the higher and more abstract notions of morality derive in the same way from sensual experience and, in the last resort, from the world without, as do the higher and more abstract notions of science : " Things are good or evil, only in reference to pleasure or pain. That we call good, which is apt to cause or increase pleasure, or diminish pain in us ; or else to procure or preserve us the possession of any other good, or absence of any evil. And on the contrary, we name that evil, which is apt to produce or increase any pain, or diminish any pleasure in us ; or else to procure us any evil, or deprive us of any good " (II, xx, 2).

Thus man is wholly passive in the formation of his moral notions, as he is in the formation of all his simple ideas. All his thought centres around sense and sensation : " We love, desire, rejoice, and hope, only in respect of pleasure ; we hate, fear, and grieve, only in respect of pain ultimately : in fine, all these passions are moved by things, only as they appear to be the causes of pleasure and pain, or to have pleasure or pain some way or other annexed to them " (II, xx, 14). Indeed, the subjection to sense and sensation seemed to Locke the dominant trait of man : " Self ", he defined (II, xxvii, 17), " is that conscious thinking thing (whatever substance made up of, whether spiritual or material, simple or compounded, it matters not) which is sensible, or conscious of pleasure and pain, capable of happiness or misery, and so is concerned for itself, as far as that consciousness extends."

These considerations constitute at the same time a theory of moral ideas and a theory of moral actions. Yet they are purely formal in character : moral ideas spring from sensual experience, for that is called good which procures pleasure or wards off pain, and that bad which causes pain or prevents pleasure ; moral actions are directed by sensual experience, for that course is taken which procures pleasure or wards off pain, and that avoided which causes pain or prevents pleasure—but it remains to be asked what concrete things and actions do procure pleasure and ward off pain—what concrete things and actions do cause pain and prevent pleasure ?

Here Locke's sensationalism allies itself with his individualism. All men agree that happiness is the end of life, but as to what

happiness is, all men disagree ; a general canon is impossible :
" It was a right answer of the physician to his patient that had
sore eyes : If you have more pleasure in the taste of wine than
in the use of your sight, wine is good for you ; but if the pleasure
of seeing be greater to you than that of drinking, wine is naught "
(II, xxi, 54). Indeed, Locke was convinced that his sensationalist
psychology demanded an individualist ethics : if all ideas come
from personal experience, all actions must follow personal experience. If the senses gather all knowledge, the senses must control
all behaviour : " The mind has a different relish, as well as the
palate ; and you will as fruitlessly endeavour to delight all men
with riches or glory (which yet some men place their happiness
in) as you would to satisfy all men's hunger with cheese or lobsters ;
which, though very agreeable and delicious fare to some, are to
others extremely nauseous and offensive ; and many people would
with reason prefer the griping of an hungry belly, to those dishes
which are a feast to others. Hence it was, I think, that the
philosophers of old did in vain inquire, whether *summum bonum*
consisted in riches, or bodily delights, or virtue, or contemplation. And they might have as reasonably disputed, whether the
best relish were to be found in apples, plums, or nuts. . . . For
as pleasant tastes depend not on the things themselves, but their
agreeableness to this or that particular palate, wherein there is
great variety ; so the greatest happiness consists in the having
those things which produce the greatest pleasure, and in the
absence of those which cause any disturbance, any pain. . . .
Men may choose different things, and yet all choose right ", for
in this world they are " only like a company of poor insects,
whereof some are bees, delighted with flowers and their sweet-
ness ; others beetles, delighted with other kinds of viands "
(II, xxi, 55).

Precisely this individualism, precisely this egoism, appeared
to Locke the supreme guarantee of universal harmony. If all
our ideas come from nature, if all our actions are directed by
nature, what else can natural, i.e., egoistic behaviour be but a
fulfilment of the divine order of the universe ? What essential
difference can there be between real and right, between actual
and ideal action ?

" Good and evil . . . are nothing but pleasure or pain, or
that which occasions or procures pleasure or pain to us. Moral
good and evil then is only the conformity or disagreement of our
voluntary actions to some law, whereby good or evil is drawn on

us by the will and power of the law-maker ; which good and evil, pleasure or pain, attending our observance, or breach of the law, by the decree of the law-maker. is that we call reward and punishment " (II, xxviii, 5).

Pain and pleasure, or, what comes to the same, the law divine, are the guides to personal happiness : " The consideration of those objects that produce it may well persuade us, that this is the end or use of pain : our Maker . . . designing the preservation of our being, has annexed pain to the application of many things to our bodies, to warn us of the harm that they will do, and as advices to withdraw from them " (II, vii, 4).

But pain and pleasure, the institutions of the law divine, are also the guides to social ethics : " This is the only true touchstone of moral rectitude : by comparing them to this law it is, that men judge of the most considerable moral good or evil of their actions : that is, whether as duties or sins, they are like to procure them happiness or misery from the hands of the Almighty " (II, xxviii, 8). " Ethics " is indeed no more than " the seeking out those rules and measures of human actions, which lead to happiness, and the means to practise them " (IV, xxi, 3).

Hence it follows that universal harmony will be the better secured, the more freely individual egoism can operate : " The highest perfection of intellectual nature lies in a careful and constant pursuit of true and solid happiness " (II, xxi, 51).

If there is, according to Locke, any difference at all between natural and ethical action, it is only that premeditated ethical action is more likely to reach the common aim of happiness than unreflecting natural action. Ethical behaviour is refined natural behaviour—natural behaviour unchanged but perfected. Nature teaches us the pursuit of happiness ; ethics the pursuit constant and careful of happiness solid and true. God has allowed us some freedom of the will for this purpose : " This is the hinge on which turns the liberty of intellectual beings, in their constant endeavours after and a steady prosecution of true felicity, that they can suspend this prosecution in particular cases, till they have looked before them, and informed themselves whether that particular thing, which is then proposed or desired, lie in the way to their main end, and make a real part of that which is their greatest good. . . . Whatever necessity determines to the pursuit of real bliss, the same necessity with the same force establishes suspense, deliberation, and scrutiny of each successive desire, whether the satisfaction of it does not interfere with our true happiness, and mislead us from it. This, as seems to me, is the great privilege of finite intellectual beings ; and I desire it may be well considered, whether the great inlet and exercise of all the liberty men have, are capable of, or can be useful to them, . . . does not lie in this, that they can suspend their desires, and stop them from determining their wills to any action, till they have duly and fairly examined the good and evil of it, as far forth as the weight of the thing requires " (II, xxi, 52). Indeed, " the principal exercise of freedom is to stand still, open the eyes, look about, and take a view of the consequence of what we are going to do, as much as the weight of the matter requires " (II, xxi, 67).

Thus man is free to choose the best possible way to his great goal ; but he is not free to march in a different direction. So great has been the goodness of his Maker towards him that he has been given only the freedom to improve his position, not the freedom to infringe upon it. Man's liberty is only " a power to act or not to act " until the most rational behaviour be discovered (II, xxi, 71) ; not more : " A man is at liberty to lift up his hand to his head, or let it rest quiet ; he is perfectly indifferent in either ; and it would be an imperfection in him, if he wanted that power, if he were deprived of that indifference. But it would be as great an imperfection if he had the same indifferency, whether he would prefer the lifting up his hand, or its remaining in rest, when it would save his head or eyes from a blow he sees coming : it is as much a perfection, that desire, or the power of preferring, should be determined by good, as that the power of acting should be determined by the will ; and the certainer such determination is, the greater is the perfection. Nay, were we determined by any thing but the last result of our own minds, judging of the good or evil of any action, we were not free : the very end of our freedom being, that we may attain the good we choose. And therefore every man is put under a necessity by his constitution, as an intelligent being, to be determined in willing by his own thought and judgment what is best for him to do " (II, xxi, 48).

And is this necessity to choose the better not preferable to any freedom to choose the worse ? " Is it worth the name of freedom to be at liberty to play the fool, and draw shame and misery upon a man's self ? If to break loose from the conduct of reason, and to want that restraint of examination and judgment, which keeps us from choosing or doing the worse, be liberty, true liberty, madmen and fools are the only freemen : but yet, I think, nobody would choose to be mad for the sake of such liberty, but he that is mad already " (II, xxi, 50). Indeed, we cannot conceive of any higher spirits free from this necessity : on the contrary! " If we look upon those superior beings above us, who enjoy perfect happiness, we shall have reason to judge that they are more steadily determined in their choice of good than we ; and yet we have no reason to think they are less happy, or less free than we are. And if it were fit for such poor finite creatures as we are to pronounce what infinite wisdom and goodness could do, I think we might say, that God himself cannot choose what is not good ; the freedom of the Almighty hinders not his being determined by what is best " (II, xxi, 49).

On the basis of this strictly deterministic doctrine of man, Locke regarded some pleasure, be it only the pleasure of getting rid of some pain, as the end, and some pain, be it only the pain of going without some pleasure, as the motive of all human action. " The chief, if not only spur to human industry and action, is uneasiness. For whatsoever good is proposed, if its absence carries no displeasure or pain with it, if a man be easy and content without it, there is no desire of it, nor endeavour after it " (II, xx, 6). Indeed, " when a man is perfectly content with the state he is in, which is, when he is perfectly without any uneasiness, what industry, what action, what will is there left, but to continue in it? . . . And thus we see our All-wise Maker, suitably to our constitution and frame, and knowing what it is that determines the will, has put into man the uneasiness of hunger and thirst, and other natural desires, that return at their seasons, to move and determine their wills, for the preservation of themselves, and the continuation of their species " (II, xxi, 34).

It goes without saying that—if uneasiness is the spring of action—material uneasiness is the spring of economic action. Material uneasiness is constantly counterbalanced by economic action : man's subservience to nature in matters of perception is matched by man's dominion over nature in matters of production. " God ", says Locke in his *Two Treatises of Government* —and thus we pass from his theory of individual knowledge to his doctrine of social life—" God having made man, and planted in him, as in all other animals, a strong desire of self-preservation, and furnished the world with things fit for food and raiment, and other necessaries of life, subservient to his design, that man should live and abide for some time upon the face of the earth, and not that so curious and wonderful a piece of workmanship, by his own negligence, or want of necessaries, should perish again, presently after a few moments' continuance ; God, I say, having made man and the world thus . . . directed him by his senses and reason, as he did the inferior animals by their sense and instinct, which were serviceable for his subsistence, and given him as the means of his preservation ; and therefore I doubt not, but . . . man had a right to an use of the creatures, by the will and grant of God : for the desire, strong desire, of preserving his life and being, having been planted in him as a principle of action by God himself, reason, 'which was the voice of God in him,' could not but teach him and assure him that pursuing that natural inclination he had to preserve his being, he followed the will of his Maker, and therefore had a right to make use of those creatures, which by his reason or senses he could discover would be serviceable thereunto. And thus man's property in the creatures was founded upon the right he had to make use of those things that were necessary or useful to his being " (I, 86).

But the dominion of mankind over nature is not yet sufficient ; hunger and thirst and all material uneasiness are sensations of the individual : therefore the individual must be given power to appropriate the things of the earth for the satisfaction of his needs : " Though all the fruits it naturally produces, and beasts it feeds, belong to mankind in common, as they are produced by the spontaneous hand of nature ; and nobody has originally a private dominion, exclusive of the rest of mankind, in any of them, as they are thus in their natural state, yet being given for the use of men, *there must of necessity be a means to appropriate them some way or other before they can be of any use, or at all beneficial to any particular man.* The fruit, or venison, which nourishes the wild Indian, who knows no enclosure, and is still a tenant in common, must be his, and so his, i.e. a part of him, that another can no longer have any right to it, before it can do him any good for the support of his life " (II, 26).

Now, how does it happen, that the private property of individual man grows out of the common property of the human race ? Here is Locke's answer : " Though the earth, and all inferior creatures, be common to all men, yet every man has a property in his own person : this nobody has any right to but himself. The labour of his body, and the work of his hands, we may say, are properly his. Whatsoever then he removes out of the state that nature hath provided, and left it in, he hath mixed his labour with, and joined to it something that is his own, and thereby makes it his property. It being by him removed from the common state nature hath placed it in, *it hath by this labour something annexed to it that excludes the common right of other men.* For this labour being the unquestionable property of the labourer, no man but he can have a right to what that is once joined to. . . . Though the water running in the fountain be every one's, yet who can doubt but that in the pitcher is his only who drew it out ? His labour hath taken it out of the hands of nature. . . . He that is nourished by the acorns he picked up under an oak, or the apples he gathered from the trees in the wood, has certainly appropriated them to himself. Nobody can deny but the nourishment is his. I ask then, when did they begin to be his ?—when he digested ? —or when he ate ?—or when he boiled ?—or when he brought them home ?—or when he picked them up ?—and it is plain, if the first gathering made them not his, nothing else could. That labour put a distinction between them and common : that added something to them more than nature, the common mother of all, had done " (II, 27 sq.).

This investigation of the origin of private property—the centre of Locke's social analysis which organically grows out of his analysis of individual thought—contains in germ both the subjective and the objective theories of value.[1] The subjective theory which sets the value of a thing into relation to its power of satisfying human wants, is implied in Locke's individual psychology. An object is valuable if it is capable of procuring some pleasure or removing some pain, and hence the more valuable the greater the pleasure it procures or the pain it removes. The objective theory which regards the value of a thing as a function of the labour expended in its production, follows from Locke's social philosophy. An object is valuable if its possession is conditioned by undergoing some exertion, and hence the more valuable, the greater the exertion which must be undergone. Value in the subjective sense measures the contribution of

[1] The traditional terminology, here used, is not quite in agreement with Locke's way of envisaging things. Subjective value, i.e., the concept founded upon utility, he would probably have called objective—because it is a power in the object which causes in us the feeling of satisfaction ; and objective value, i.e., the concept founded upon costs, he would probably have called subjective—because it is an effort of the subject which constitutes the essence of production. But although this nomenclature would have better fitted into Locke's general language, he might have well acquiesced in the names used to-day (as we do), because subjective value—even according to his teaching—consists in and is measured by a subjective feeling of uneasiness and the corresponding satisfaction when it is overcome, while objective value consists in and is measured by the objective resistance of nature to men and the corresponding effort to overcome it.

things to men's welfare ; value in the objective sense measures the resistance of things to men's desires. Or, to put the same idea into different words : value as a subjective conception expresses men's dependence upon nature ; value as an objective conception expresses men's dominion over nature.

In Locke's thought value as a subjective, and value as an objective category demand each other and form a whole, exactly as his theory of individual knowledge and his doctrine of social life. The word value, and, indeed, the notion of value, do not occur often in his non-economic writings. Yet it is characteristic that in the *Treatises* which deal of sociology, Locke seems to favour the subjective formulation, while in the *Essay*, an inquiry into psychology, the objective conception is obviously preferred : so much did he regard the two categories as interchangeable and hence identical. In the *Treatises* we read as follows : " The earth, and all that is therein, is given to men for the support and comfort of their being " ; therefore " *the intrinsic value of things . . . depends only on their usefulness to the life of man* " (II, 26, 37). In the *Essay*, however, an interesting passage runs like this : " The removing of the pains we feel, and are at present pressed with, being the getting out of misery, and consequently the first thing to be done in order to happiness, absent good, though thought on, confessed, and appearing to be good, not making any part of this unhappiness in its absence, is justled out to make way for the removal of those uneasinesses we feel ; till due and repeated contemplation has brought it nearer to our mind, given some relish of it, and raised in us some desire : which then beginning to make a part of our present uneasiness, stands upon fair terms with the rest, to be satisfied ; and so, according to its greatness and pressure, comes in its turn, to determine the will. And thus, by a due consideration, and examining any good proposed, it is in our power *to raise our desires in a due proportion to the value of that good,* whereby in its turn and place, it may come to work upon the will, and be pursued " (II, xxi, 45 sq.). Here value describes of course the objective value of the thing, its labour-value, that is to say the exertion which we have to undergo in order to obtain it, and which we shall only undergo if our desire to possess it is equal to our aversion to toil for it, if pains and pleasures involved form an equation.

These words show how Locke conceived of the inner connection between subjective and objective value. But is this conception sound ? Is there always an equation between sub-

THE GREAT ANTITHESIS : MAN AND NATURE

jective and objective value ? Suppose a man concentrates on
the satisfaction of two wants : shelter and bread. In the subjective sense, bread is more valuable than shelter, because by
procuring bread a more pressing need is removed ; in the objective sense, shelter is more valuable than bread, because in procuring shelter a more intense exertion is undergone. This is true.
But in Locke, no self-contradiction makes its appearance. The
reason is that he always confined himself to one man and one
thing, one desire and one exertion. His individualism, which is
the basis of his individual psychology, saves here, as everywhere,
the unity of his thought : it was his deepest conviction " that
general and universal belong not to the real existence of things "
(III, III, 11) ; that only the concrete is tangible.

If we consider the real existence of things, the existence of
things in their concreteness, we discover the true interdependence
and identity of desire and action, man's dependence upon nature
and man's dominion over nature, subjective and objective value :
" We being in this world beset with sundry uneasinesses, distracted
with different desires . . . which of them has the precedency in
determining the will to the next action ? To that the answer is,
that ordinarily, which is the most pressing of those that are judged
capable of being then removed. . . . The most important
and urgent uneasiness we at that time feel, is that which ordinarily
determines the will successively, in that train of voluntary actions
which makes up our lives. The greatest present uneasiness is
the spur to action, that is constantly felt, and for the most
part determines the will in its choice of the next action "
(II, XXI, 40).

Thus the greatest present uneasiness, the pain of going without a thing in view of the pleasure that might be derived from it,
corresponds to the next action, the pain involved in the acquisition of it in view of the pleasure that its use affords. A man can
have no doubt about the agreement of subjective and objective
value, of the pleasure (or removal of pain) flowing from the
possession of an object and the pain (or sacrifice of pleasure)
caused by its production : " Things in their present enjoyment
are what they seem ; the apparent and real good are, in this case,
always the same. For the pain or pleasure being just so great,
and no greater than it is felt, the present good or evil is really so
much as it appears. And therefore, were every action of ours
concluded within itself, and drew no consequences after it, we
should undoubtedly never err in our choice of good; we should

always infallibly prefer the best. Were the pains of honest industry, and of starving with hunger and cold, set together before us, nobody would be in doubt which to choose " (II, xxi, 58). Everybody would submit to the pains of honest industry and persevere in them until the pains of starving with hunger and cold were so far decreased that an equilibrium between exertion and benefit is reached, until objective and subjective value are equalized.

Hence, at the margin want and work correspond, subjective and objective value agree. This is obviously Locke's dominant idea. Yet the last sentences suggest that he saw still another bond keeping them together : as marginal effort and marginal satisfaction correspond and agree, so do total effort and total satisfaction of any individual. Man, independent man, if he is directly confronted with nature, is just as poor and just as rich as his own industry makes him. The fulfilment of his desires goes hand in hand with the extent of his labours. This consideration gives Locke's twofold theory of value a new and higher unity—a unity not merely logical but also ethical, a unity founded not merely in a sober individual psychology, but also upon a lofty social ideal.

Although both the subjective and the objective theories of value are contained in, and may be derived from, Locke's system of thought, he and his disciples, the classical economists, only followed the one track, the track leading to the labour theory of value. It is not difficult to see why : both possible explanations are based upon an individualistic conception of man, but while the subjective view sees man with reference to his sensations, the objective view envisages him in connection with his work. Therefore the subjective theory belongs more to psychological anthropology and hence to physical science, the objective theory more to pragmatic anthropology and hence to social science.[1] The subjectivistic analysis begins and ends with isolated man, the objectivistic analysis begins with the individual and ends with society. The one leads—as far as sociology is concerned—into a blind alley, the other—however barren it may be with regard to psychology—opens up a grand view upon human relations both real and ideal, both as they are and as they ought to be.

[1] For this reason, classical economics was an economic theory which had its place within the system of the social sciences ; modern economics is an economic theory which aspires to a place within the system of the physical sciences.

In developing his objective, i.e., his social theory of value, Locke starts from man's position in and to nature, as the Maker of the Universe has ordained it to be, the Maker of the Universe, whose decree is contained in Holy Writ, in the awe-inspiring words of the Book of Genesis (i. 26–29 ; ix. 1–3) : " And God said, Let us make man in our image, after our likeness : and let them have dominion over the fish of the sea, and over the fowl of the air, and over the cattle, and over all the earth, and over every creeping thing that creepeth upon the earth. So God created man in his own image, in the image of God created he him ; male and female created he them. And God blessed them, and God said unto them, Be fruitful and multiply, and replenish the earth, and subdue it : and have dominion over the fish of the sea, and over the fowl of the air, and over every living thing that moveth upon the earth. And God said, Behold, I have given you every herb bearing seed, which is upon the face of all the earth, and every tree, in the which is the fruit of a tree yielding seed ; to you it shall be for meat." This divine donation, the material basis of man's earthly existence, was renewed after the flood ; it is part and parcel of the Sacred Covenant : " And God blessed Noah and his sons, and said unto them, Be fruitful, and multiply, and replenish the earth. And the fear of you and the dread of you shall be upon every beast of the earth, and upon every fowl of the air, upon all that moveth upon the earth, and upon all the fishes of the sea ; into your hand are they delivered. Every moving thing that liveth shall be meat for you ; even as the green herb have I given you all things."

Thus dominion over nature was bestowed upon the first men and fathers of mankind ; and all their offspring, by the will of God, were meant to partake of it : " This being the reason and foundation of Adam's property, gave the same title, on the same ground, to *all* his children . . . so that there was no privilege . . . which could exclude [any of] them from an equal right to the use of the inferior creatures, for the comfortable preservation of their beings, which is all the property man hath in them. . . . Every man had a right to the creatures by the same title Adam had, viz. by the right every one had to take care of and provide for their subsistence : and thus men had a right in common. . . ." (I, 87).

But although all humanity has a common claim to the riches of the earth, it must come into the private property of the individuals before it can serve their needs. This necessary distribution is effected by dint of labour which, under the ægis of a truly divine justice imparts to things their value and to men their income : " Nor is it so strange, as perhaps before consideration it may appear, that the *property of labour* should be able to over-balance the *community of land* : for it is labour indeed that put the difference of value on every thing ; and let any one consider what the difference is between an acre of land planted with tobacco or sugar, sown with wheat or barley, and an acre of the same land lying in common, without any husbandry upon it, and he will find, that the improvement of labour makes the far greater part of the value.   I think it will be but a very modest computation to say, that of the products of the earth useful to the life of man, nine-tenths are the effects of labour : nay, if we will rightly estimate things as they come to our use, and cast up the several expenses about them, what in them is purely owing to nature, and what to labour, we shall find, that in most of them ninety-nine hundredths are wholly to be put on the account of labour. . . .   Whatever bread is more worth than acorns, wine than water, and cloth or silk than leaves, skins, or moss, that is wholly owing to labour or industry : the one of these being the food and raiment which unassisted nature furnishes us with : the other, provisions which our industry and pains prepare for us ; which, how much they exceed the other in value, when any one hath computed, he will then see how much labour makes the far greatest part of the value of things we enjoy in this world : and the ground which produces the materials is scarce to be reckoned in as any, or, at most, but a very small part of it " (II, 40, 42).

This passage, if fully understood and rightly interpreted, reveals the true origin and solid foundation of the labour theory of value.   It contains two complementary ideas : (1) If we analyse the subjective value of things—in Locke's words : if we estimate them as they come to our use—we find that almost all their value is due to the work of men, and almost none of it to the agency of nature.   Hence it is nearly correct to say that the value of a product is created and measured by the human labour embodied in it.   Yet, this is not quite correct : however small the contribution of nature may be, there is such a contribution, and it must be taken into account, if exactness is to be achieved. However, even if we make exactness our aim, we need not take it into account, if we prefer the objective to the subjective approach.   For if we (2) analyse the objective value of **things**

—in Locke's words : if we cast up the several expenses about them—we find, that nature's co-operation in the production of commodities is gratis, because the earth and all the power it holds is a free gift of God to all men ; in modern terminology : because the productive powers of the soil (and the productive powers active in capital goods) originally were and always should be at the disposal of all men, because they originally did not and never should constitute an element of costs. There is, at least under "natural" conditions, only one such element : labour.

Locke is anxious to corroborate his thesis by applying it to the one good which seems to be exclusively the offering of nature : the soil. "An acre of land, that bears here twenty bushels of wheat, and another in America, which, with the same husbandry, would do the like, are, without doubt, of the same natural intrinsic value : but yet the benefit mankind receives from the one in a year is worth 5 _l._ and from the other possibly not worth a penny, if all the profit an Indian received from it were to be valued, and sold here ; at least, I may truly say, not one-thousandth. It is labour, then, which puts the greatest part of the value upon land, without which it would scarcely be worth any thing : it is to that we owe the greatest part of all its useful products ; for all that the straw, bran, bread, of that acre of wheat, is more worth than the product of an acre of as good land, which lies waste, is all the effect of labour : for it is not barely the ploughman's pains, the reaper's and thresher's toil, and the baker's sweat, is to be counted into the bread we eat ; the labour of those who broke the oxen, who digged and wrought the iron and stones, who felled and framed the timber employed about the plough, mill, oven, or any other utensils, which are a vast number, requisite to this corn from its being seed to be sown to its being made bread, must all be charged on the account of labour, and received as an effect of that : nature and the earth furnished only the almost worthless materials, as in themselves " (II, 43). This argument conducted in the vein of the subjective concept, holds good also if it is translated into the language of the objective theory : for the materials furnished by nature and the earth are not only " almost worthless " but at the same time " perfectly gratis "—they not only contribute very little to the happiness of man, but need not figure as an item in the costs of production. Therefore it is labour, and labour alone, which constitutes the value of all things.

This economic theory of value has obviously definite social

presuppositions and therefore wide social implications. It is
built upon the idea that the private property in the means of
consumption grows out of the free access to the means of production. But is this conception sound? Does it not imply a
self-contradiction? Can there be free access to the means of
production, if there is private property in the means of consumption? Locke did not doubt it. He thought and taught
that there is a neat line of division between individual and
common ownership—a line drawn by the purpose of appropriation, which justifies exclusive possession only within certain
limits beyond which the realm of undivided property—a no
man's land or, rather, all men's land—begins. " It will perhaps
be objected to this ", he says (II, 31 sq.), " that ' if gathering the
acorns, or other fruits of the earth, etc. makes a right to them,
then any one may engross as much as he will '. To which I
answer, Not so. The same law of nature, that does by this
means give us property, does also bound that property too. ' God
has given us all things richly,' 1 Tim. vi. 17 is the voice of
reason confirmed by inspiration. But how far has he given it
us? To enjoy. As much as any one can make use of to any
advantage of life before it spoils, so much he may by his labour
fix a property in : whatever is beyond this, is more than his
share, and belongs to others . . . The chief matter of property
being now not the fruits of the earth, and the beasts that subsist
on it, but the earth itself ; as that which takes in, and carries with
it all the rest ; I think it is plain, that property in that too is
acquired as the former. As much land as a man tills, plants,
improves, cultivates, and can use the product of, so much is his
[legitimate] property ", and no more.

As much land as a man cultivates and can use the product of :
hence the private property of individual man is limited both from
the point of view of subjective, and from the point of view of
objective, value.[1] Indeed, " the measure of property nature has

---

[1] Locke's doctrine of property is apt to be misunderstood because he used a terminology at variance with the common usage. He indeed proclaimed that " government has no other end but the preservation of property " (II, 94) but property, as he
defines it, does not describe riches or even pre-eminently signify wealth but " life,
liberty, and estate " (II, 87, 123, 173)—that is to say all man's goods both personal
and real, both spiritual and material. His definition of what we call property runs
as follows : " Property, whose original is from the right a man has to use any of the
inferior creatures, for the subsistence and comfort of his life, is for the benefit and sole
advantage of the proprietor, so that he may even destroy the thing, that he has
property in ", but, he adds, only " by his use of it, where need requires " (I, 92).
This modification and limitation distinguishes Locke's view from that of the Roman
lawyers : like them he included the *jus utendi* and *fruendi*, but unlike them he excluded

well set by the extent of men's labour, and the conveniencies of life : no man's labour could subdue, or appropriate all ; nor could his enjoyment consume more than a small part ; so that [—wherever things could take their natural course—] it was impossible for any man, this way, to intrench upon the right of another, or acquire to himself a property, to the prejudice of his neighbour, who would still have room for as good, and as large a possession (after the other had taken out his) as before it was appropriated. This measure did confine every man's possession to a very moderate proportion, and such as he might appropriate to himself, without injury to any body, in the first ages of the world, when men were more in danger to be lost, by wandering from their company, in the then vast wilderness of the earth, than to be straitened for want of room to plant in " (II, 36).

That golden age of the distant past may well teach us what is the law of nature with regard to the relation of individual and society, private property and common ownership : " Before the appropriation of land, he who gathered as much of the wild fruit, killed, caught, or tamed, as many of the beasts as he could ; he that so employed his pains about any of the spontaneous products of nature, as any way to alter them from the state which nature put them in, by placing any of his labour on them, did thereby acquire a propriety in them : but if they perished, in his possession, without their due use ; if the fruits rotted, or the venison putrified, before he could spend it ; he offended against the common law of nature, and was liable to be punished ; he invaded his neighbour's share, for he had no right, farther than his use called for any of them, and they might serve to afford him conveniencies of life. The same measures governed the possession of land too : whatsoever he tilled and reaped, laid up and made use of, before it spoiled, that was his peculiar right ; whatsoever he enclosed, and could feed, and make use of, the cattle and product was also his. But if either the grass of his enclosure rotted on the ground, or the fruit of his planting perished without gathering and laying up ; this part of the earth, notwithstanding his enclosure, was still to be looked on as waste, and might be the possession of any other " (II, 37 sq.).

the *jus abutendi* from his definition (cf. also e.g. *Code Civil*, Art. 544). Indeed, from a higher point of view, Locke held, property could not be regarded as an absolute right. For " however, in respect of one another, men may be allowed to have propriety in their distinct portions of the creatures ; yet in respect of God . . . man's propriety in the creatures is nothing but that liberty to use them, which God has permitted " (I, 39).

Much may have changed since then ; but the law of nature had no need to change : " This I dare boldly affirm, that the same rule of propriety, viz. that every man should have as much as he could make use of, would hold still in the world, without straitening any body ; since there is land enough in the world to suffice double the inhabitants ". If there should be some one now as poor as Adam was after the fall " let him plant in some inland, vacant places of America ; we shall find that the posses-sions he could make himself, upon the measures we have given, would not . . . even to this day, prejudice the rest of mankind, or give them reason to complain, or think themselves injured by this man's encroachment ; though the race of men have now spread themselves to all the corners of the world, and do infinitely exceed the small number was at the beginning " (II, 36).

Thus Locke held that there is still free access to the good things of the earth. But he acknowledged that this access had become difficult. He did not deny that there was a social problem. He realized that the expedient of emigration and colonization, how-ever effective it might be, did not suffice because it demanded higher courage and greater endurance than could be expected of average men. Therefore he searched for other means of equaliz-ing opportunities, and it is not surprising that he first of all hit upon the idea to confine private property to the life of the indi-vidual that had created it by his labours and thus to confront all new citizens of the world with the undivided fund of nature, con-tinually re-establishing itself by the regular return of the riches that had been taken out of it. Yet he started this question only in order to answer it in the negative. " It might reasonably be asked here ", we read, " how come children by this right of possessing before any other, the properties of their parents upon their decease ? for it being personally the parents', when they die, without actually transferring their right to another, why does it not return again to the common stock of mankind ? It will per-haps be answered, that common consent hath disposed of it to their children." Such an explanation, however, would not be very strong. " If common tacit consent hath established it, it would make but a positive, not a natural right of children to inherit the goods of their parents." Locke thought there must be a better answer : he conceived the right of inheritance as a natural right. But a natural right must have its foundation in nature. Locke thought he knew this foundation : " The ground . . . I think to be this : the first and strongest desire God

planted in men, and wrought into the very principles of their
nature, being that of self-preservation, that is the foundation of
a right to the creatures, for the particular support and use of each
individual person himself. But, next to this, God planted in men
a strong desire also of propagating their kind, and continuing
themselves in their posterity ; and this gives children a title to
share in the property of their parents, and a right to inherit their
possessions. . . . Children being by the course of nature born
weak, and unable to provide for themselves, they have by the
appointment of God himself, who hath thus ordered the course of
nature, a right to be nourished and maintained by their parents ;
nay, a right not only to a bare subsistence, but to the conveniencies
and comforts of life, as far as the conditions of their parents can
afford it. Hence it comes, that when their parents leave the
world, and so the care due to their children ceases, the effects of
it are to extend as far as possibly they can, and . . . nature
appoints the descent of their property to their children, who thus
come to have a title, and natural right of inheritance to their
fathers' goods, which the rest of mankind cannot pretend to "
(I, 88, 89).

However, as the right of property is justified and at the same
time limited by its great purpose, so is the right of inheritance :
as the right of property gives only a claim to an equal share in the
heritage of mankind, so the right of inheritance gives only a claim
to an equal share in the heritage of men. Neither the one nor
the other must or need infringe upon the principle of equality :
" If Adam had a property in the whole earth and its product ;
yet all his children coming to have, by the law of nature, a right
of inheritance, a joint title, and a right of property in it after his
death, it could convey no right of sovereignty to any one of his
posterity over the rest ; since every one having a right of inheritance to his portion, they might enjoy their inheritance, or any
part of it, in common, or share it or some parts of it, by division,
as it best liked them. But no one could pretend to the whole
inheritance, or any sovereignty supposed to accompany it ; since
a right of inheritance gave every one of the rest, as well as any
one, a title to share in the goods of his father " (I, 91). So much
is sure : " The first-born has not a sole or peculiar right by any
law of God and nature, the younger children having an equal title
with him, founded on that right they all have to maintenance,
support, and comfort from their parents, and on nothing else "
(I, 93). Thus the right of inheritance, as the right of property,

conforms to the great commandment of justice : " All that share
in the same common nature, faculties, and powers, are in nature
equal, and ought to partake in the same common rights and
privileges " (I, 67).

But if the right of property was originally so limited, and the
right of inheritance so qualified, as continually to make for
equality, how can the inequality in the world be explained ?
How could the difference between rich and poor arise ? [1]   It
arose from the moment and by the fact that men found a means
for the storing-up of value and hence for the accumulation of
wealth : " Supposing an island, separate from all possible commerce with the rest of the world, wherein there were but an
hundred families, but there were sheep, horses, and cows, with
other useful animals, wholesome fruits, and land enough for corn
for a hundred thousand times as many, but nothing in the island,
either because of its commonness, or perishableness, fit to supply
the place of money ; what reason could any one have there to
enlarge his possessions beyond the use of his family and a plentiful
supply to its consumption, either in what their own industry produced, or they could barter for like perishable, useful commodities
with others ? . . .   Find out something that hath the use and
value of money amongst his neighbours, you shall see the same
man will begin presently to enlarge his possessions " (II, 48 sq.).

Thus it was the invention of money which led mankind from
a state of equality into the state of inequality. But was the
invention of money therefore the second fall of man ?   Was it the
second original sin which must be regarded as the arch-source of

---

[1] There was, of course, a class contrast in the seventeenth century, but it was far
less sharp than it is to-day.   " It is important . . . to remember ", says P. Larkin in
his book *Property in the Eighteenth Century* (1930, 56 sq.), " that the England into which
Locke was born was one in which property was widely distributed."   Very true !
Unfortunately, Larkin himself forgets this fact which is the key to the understanding
of classical economics, just when it is most essential to bear it in mind : in the discussion of Locke.   " His main object was to insist on the individual's right to his
property as against the arbitrary interference of the State, and possibly that prevented
him from recognizing more explicitly than he does that private property is a social
function as well as an individual right ", he says (*l.c.*, 65 sq.).   " He nowhere puts
the responsibility which should accompany ownership on the same plane as the right
to private property itself. . . .   One might almost say that he tends to confuse the
fact of private property with the right to private property.   This weakness in his
theory of property appears to be directly due to the subjective character of his ethical
philosophy, or to his lack of faith in social ideals [!].   What Taine said of Locke's
intellectual indecisiveness " applies here.   This criticism of Locke is quite unjustified.
In an egalitarian society as the age envisaged it, the social function of and individual
interest in private property coincide, and so do the fact of and the right to private
property : when the wealth of the community is equally divided among its members,
the greatest happiness of all is best secured by the greatest selfishness of each.   There
is no " intellectual indecisiveness " in Locke—neither here nor anywhere else.

all social evils ? Locke does not think so.   His description of the
development of money as a hoard of value is at the same time a
justification : " The greatest part of things really useful to the
life of man, and such as the necessity of subsisting made the first
commoners of the world look after, as it doth the Americans now,
are generally things of short duration ; such as, if they are not
consumed by use, will decay and perish of themselves : gold,
silver, and diamonds, are things that fancy or agreement hath put
the value on, more than real use, and the necessary support of life.
Now of those good things which nature hath provided in common,
every one had a right (as hath been said) to as much as he could
use, and property in all that he could effect with his labour ; all
that his industry could extend to, to alter from the state nature
had put it in, was his.   He that gathered a hundred bushels of
acorns or apples, had thereby a property in them, they were his
goods, as soon as gathered.   He was only to look, that he used
them before they spoiled, else he took more than his share, and
robbed others.   And indeed it was a foolish thing, as well as dis-
honest, to hoard up more than he could make use of. . . And if he
also bartered away plums, that would have rotted in a week, for
nuts that would last good for his eating a whole year, he did no
injury ; he wasted not the common stock ; destroyed no part of
the portion of the goods that belonged to others, so long as nothing
perished uselessly in his hands.   Again, if he would give his nuts
for a piece of metal, pleased with its colour ; or exchange his sheep
for shells, or wool for a sparkling pebble or a diamond, and keep
those by him all his life, he invaded not the right of others; he
might heap as much of these durable things as he pleased ; the
exceeding of the bounds of his just property not lying in the large-
ness of his possession, but the perishing of any thing uselessly in
it " (II, 46).
    In this way the differences of wealth due to the accumulation of
monetary means are not at variance with the limitations of private property set by the law of nature.   And, indeed, they were
confirmed by the law of society, by the resolution of the free and
equal individuals themselves : " Since gold and silver, being little
useful to the life of man in proportion to food, raiment, and
carriage, has its value only from the consent of men . . . it is
plain, that men have agreed to a disproportionate and unequal
possession of the earth ; they having, by a tacit and voluntary
consent, found out a way how a man may fairly possess more land
than he himself can use the product of, by receiving, in exchange

for the overplus, gold and silver, which may be hoarded up without injury to any one " (II, 50).

Does all this mean that John Locke had no objection to any class contrast ? Does it mean that he bowed to the altar of equality only to turn his back on it irreverently ? Does it mean that he spoke of the natural limitations to private property only for the sake of theory, in order to forget them as soon as he was confronted with the facts of practice ? Indeed not. He was a master of consistency,[1] and nowhere is his consistency more apparent than here—if we know how to understand him !

The inequality of wealth which Locke accepted is not at variance but in keeping with the equality of opportunities which he cherished. This sounds odd, but it is true. His plain words leave no room for misunderstandings : the riches whose possession he condoned are described as a stock of things " little useful to the life of man ". Surely, these things are gold and silver, the monetary metals, and, indeed, money ; but it is significant that Locke makes no difference between them and " sparkling pebbles " which men gather because they are " pleased with their colour " and do not part with, but " keep by them all their life ". Obviously he regarded a stock of money as a dead treasure, not as living capital. " Money, and such riches and treasure ", he says (II, 184), " are none of nature's goods, they have but a fantastical imaginary value ; nature has put no such upon them : they are of no more account by her standard, than the wampompeke of the Americans to an European prince, or the silver money of Europe would have been formerly to an American."

Hence it is clear that Locke regarded the individual wealth which he considered as justified, only as a collection of things the possession of which gives no advantage in the struggle for existence. He thought, and was right in thinking, that it was of little consequence if a man possessed a heavier watch-chain, a more costly diamond-ring, or, for that matter, a richer collection of coins, than another. He held, and was right in holding, that an unequal distribution of the means of enjoyment was not prejudicial to social harmony—provided that there is an equal and equally free access to the means of production. It is this that matters : happiness may dwell in a country where the riches of society are disproportionately distributed ; but happiness will flee a state

---

[1] Bonar (*Philosophy and Political Economy*, ed. 1922, 91 sq.) says of Locke : " He takes no pains to be consistent." Ritchie (" Locke's Theory of Property ", *The Economic Review*, 1891, 29 sq.) even suggests that there is " an endless series of difficulties ". The present essay may be taken as an attempt to prove the opposite.

where the riches of nature are monopolized : for " he that is proprietor of the whole world, may deny all the rest of mankind food, and so at his pleasure starve them, if they will not acknowledge his sovereignty, and obey his will ". And as exclusive possession of the soil gives men power over men, so does exclusive control over the other means of production, derived from nature and embodied in capital : " Upon this ground a man's . . . having money in his pocket . . . may as well be the foundation of rule and dominion, as being possessor of all the land in the world : and any thing . . . that may be an occasion of working upon another's necessity to save his life . . . at the rate of his freedom, may be made a foundation of sovereignty " (I, 41, 43).

For this sort of inequality, for an inequality in the access to nature, there is no basis in nature and no justification in the law of nature. On the contrary ! " We know God hath not left one man so to the mercy of another, that he may starve him, if he please. . . . God never gave any such private dominion." That is to say, God never gave exclusive property in the means of production that are the sources of life to a chosen few only. " It is more reasonable to think, that God, who bid mankind increase and multiply, should rather himself give them all a right to make use of the food and raiment, and other conveniencies of life, the materials whereof he had so plentifully provided for them, than to make them depend upon the will of a man for their subsistence, who should have power to destroy them all when he pleased, and who, being no better than other men, was in succession likelier, by want and the dependence of a scanty fortune, to tie them to hard service, than by liberal allowance of the conveniencies of life to promote the great design of God " (I, 42, 41). Indeed, " a man can no more justly make use of another's necessity to force him to become his vassal, by withholding that relief God requires him to afford to the wants of his brother, than he that has more strength can seize upon a weaker, master him to his obedience, and with a dagger at his throat offer him death or slavery " (I, 42).

Hence the commandment of the law of nature whose " obligations . . . cease not in society " but " stand as an eternal rule to all men " (II, 135), with reference to the property in the material conditions of production, runs as follows : " He that is master of himself, and his own life, has a right too to the means of preserving it " (172). The " state all men are naturally in " is " *a state of perfect freedom* to order their actions and dispose of their possessions and persons, as they think fit, within the bounds of the law of nature ; without asking leave, or depending upon the will of any other man. *A state also of equality*, wherein all the power and jurisdiction is reciprocal, no one having more than another ; there being nothing more evident, than that creatures of the same species and rank, *promiscuously born to all the same advantages of nature*, and the use of the same faculties, should also be equal one amongst another without subordination or subjection " (II, 4).

Thus all avenues in Locke's thought lead up to one principle : to the concept and postulate that men should be directly confronted with, and have free access to, nature, for only so can subjective and objective value agree, individual happiness and individual effort correspond. This agreement, however, and this correspondence, form the pivot of social harmony, the theory of which, implied in Locke's philosophy, is developed in the philosophy of Gottfried Wilhelm Leibniz.

II. THE GREAT SYNTHESIS : THE ORDER DIVINE

In the preface to his *Théodicée* Leibniz describes " the discussion of continuity and of the indivisible points which appear to be its elements " as the last and greatest *problema philosophorum*. Latta, the best among Leibniz's English interpreters, states the difficult question implied in these words in the following terms : " How are we to interpret the relation of whole and parts so that the continuity or complete unity of the whole shall not be in conflict with the definiteness or real diversity of the parts ? To say that the whole is continuous or really one seems to mean that, if it is divisible at all, it is infinitely divisible. If it were not infinitely divisible, it would consist of insoluble ultimate elements, and would thus be discontinuous. Accordingly, if the whole be really continuous there seem to be no fixed boundaries or lines of division within it, that is to say, no real, but only arbitrary parts. On the other hand, if the whole consists of real parts and not merely possible subdivisions, these parts must be definite, bounded, separate from one another, and consequently the whole which they constitute must be, not a real continuous unity, but a mere collection or arbitrary unity. Nevertheless, we cannot hold either that the whole is real and the parts unreal, or that the parts are real and the whole unreal " (*The Monadology* [1], ed. 1925, Introduction, 22).

---

[1] The quotations which follow are mostly taken from Latta's text. The *Théodicée* is the principal exception ; it is not translated into English. Here Erdmann's edition (*God. Guil. Leibnitii opera philosophica quæ extant latina gallica, germanica omnia*, 1840) served as a basis.

This technical and therefore esoteric language does more to conceal than to reveal the true character and importance of Leibniz's thought. For behind the formal problem of the relation between the continuum and its points, between whole and parts, lies hidden the material problem of the relation between the universe and its elements, between society and individuals. His sober mathematics contains a deep cosmology and sociology. How does it come about that the independent units of physical and social reality combine to form an ordered system, if the units are really independent, i.e., more than unfree organs of the whole, and the system is really ordered, i.e., more than a mere sum of the parts ? This is the question to which Leibniz sought an answer. In other words : he endeavoured to find the organizing principle underlying the order in nature and the human world ; he tried to discover the secret of the harmony which, as he was convinced, is visible in the creation. Thus his abstract investigation is full of meaning for concrete life : " The unity in diversity is nothing but concord ", and from concord comes order, from order beauty, and from beauty love (Gerhardt, *Die philosophischen Schriften von Gottfried Wilhelm Leibniz*, 1875 sq., VII, 87).

The first difficulty with which Leibniz was confronted when he set about his task was the difficulty of defining the true meaning of the concepts whole and part, i.e., of stating the realities for which they stand. In the deepest and widest sense, in the sense of cosmology, both concepts, the comprehensive whole as well as the ultimate part, necessarily lie beyond full human comprehension, exactly as the infinitely small and the infinitely great number " of which no one could say whether it is even or uneven " (*Théodicée*, II, 195). Yet, metaphysically speaking, the idea of the whole is clear from the very outset : the macrocosm is simply the universe ; what exactly the universe is, we cannot say since we cannot conceive of anything without limits in space and time, but for the purpose in hand, it suffices to know that there is nothing which the universe would not hold. Unfortunately, the idea of the ultimate part is much more problematic than the idea of the comprehensive whole. The concept of the atom does not help. For atom, by definition, is a body so small that it cannot be further divided. But this is a contradiction in terms : if it is a body, i.e., if it has bulk, if it has extension, it must be further divisible, at least ideally. Even the smallest particle of matter can—because it is matter—be envisaged as cut into parts : in this way we shall never reach a truly elementary unit. Therefore, Leibniz judged, the conception of an atom in the physical sense is but " the effect of the weakness of our imagination, which likes to rest and to hasten to an end in subdividing or analysing [while] it is not so in nature, which comes from infinity and goes to infinity " (Letter to Hartsoeker, cit. Latta, 30). We must not meekly submit to this weakness ; we must boldly face the facts : " I hold it as true that matter (and even each part of matter) is divided into a greater number of parts than it is possible to imagine. And accordingly I often say that each body, however small it may be, is a world of creatures infinite in number. Thus I do not believe that there are atoms, that is to say, parts of matter which are perfectly hard or of invincible solidity " (Third Explanation, etc., Latta, 335).

But if we cannot conceive of atoms in the physical sense, we can well conceive of atoms in the metaphysical sense ; if we cannot conceive of indivisible units of matter, we can well conceive of indivisible units of life : the soul of man is the prototype of such a unit which has no extension and is therefore without parts. This is the way out which Leibniz chose : " I regard souls ", he says (*Réplique aux Réflexions de Bayle*, cit. Latta, 33), " as atoms of substance, since, in my opinion, there are no atoms of matter in nature and the smallest portion of matter has still parts." Thus he arrives at an extremely spiritualistic view of the world : " Mere soulless body has no real existence : it is an abstraction. The world is active, living through and through, even in its infinitesimal parts. It is compact of souls " (Latta, 105). This doctrine sounds strange in an age which seems to have forgotten that men have souls ;[1] it did not sound strange at a time which believed that God's spirit is all in all

The soul-units which Leibniz thus assumed to be the ultimate parts of the whole of the universe, he called, with an expression handed down from the Greeks, monads : " The Monad . . . is nothing but a simple substance [i.e., a substance without parts] which enters into compounds. . . . These Monads are the real

---

[1] Yet, even the coldest rationalist (and, indeed, precisely the coldest rationalist) will have to acknowledge that the idea of purely qualitative, i.e., intensive units is prima facie not more difficult than the idea of quantitative, i.e., extensive units : " I would fain have instanced any thing in our notion of spirit more perplexed, or nearer a contradiction than the very notion of body includes in it," Locke writes in his *Essay* (II, xxiii, 31), and he was anything but friendly to Leibniz's way of philosophizing. " The divisibility *in infinitum* of any finite extension involving us whether we grant or deny it, in consequences impossible to be explicated or made in our apprehensions consistent ; consequences that carry greater difficulty, and more apparent absurdity, than any thing can follow from the notion of an immaterial knowing substance."

atoms of nature and, in a word, the elements of things " (*Mon.*, 1, 3). Matter, he thought, is their garb : " All souls, all created simple substances, are always combined with a body " (*New Essays*, Latta, 380). The things with which we meet in the world of reality are aggregates of these simple substances.[1] The apparent unity of the aggregates consists only in the fact that each of them has a central and dominant monad : " Each living body has a dominant entelechy, which in an animal is the soul ; but the members of this living body are full of other living beings, plants, animals, each of which has also its dominant entelechy or soul " (*Mon.*, 70).

Thus universe and monad are the terms of the theory of the divine order which Leibniz sought to establish. How can it be, he asked, that the independent monads form together a harmonious universe ? The key-thought of his answer is this : the universe is not a sum of homogeneous monads but rather a series of monads differing from each other in quality ; indeed a continuous series, for the monads which are its members all differ by an infinitely small degree and thus find each their pre-ordained place in it as a necessary link without which the continuity of the chain would be broken. The essence of continuity, however, is order, and the essence of order—harmony.

This idea is not quite alien to Locke's thought. It makes an isolated and somewhat unmotivated appearance in an interesting passage of the *Essay* : " In all the visible corporeal world ", we read there, " we see no chasms or gaps. All quite down from us the descent is by easy steps, and a continued series of things, that in each remove differ very little one from the other. There are fishes that have wings, and are not strangers to the airy region ; and there are some birds that are inhabitants of the water, whose blood is cold as fishes, and their flesh so like in taste, that the scrupulous are allowed them on fish-days. There are animals so near of kin both to birds and beasts, that they are in the middle between both : amphibious animals link the terrestrial and aquatic together ; seals live at land and sea, and porpoises have the warm blood and entrails of a hog, not to mention what is confidently reported of mermaids or sea-men. There are some brutes, that seem to have as much knowledge and reason, as some that are called men ; and the animal and vegetable kingdoms are so nearly joined, that if you will take the lowest of one, and the high-

---

[1] On the logical difficulties of this position, cf. Kant, *Kritik der reinen Vernunft*, 2. Theil, 2. Abtheilung, 2. Buch, 2. Hauptstueck, 2. Antinomie.

est of the other, there will scarce be perceived any great difference between them ; and so on, till we come to the lowest and most inorganical parts of matter, we shall find everywhere, that the several species are linked together, and differ but in almost insensible degrees. And when we consider the infinite power and wisdom of the Maker, we have reason to think, that it is suitable to the magnificent harmony of the universe, and the great design and infinite goodness of the architect, that the species of creatures should also, by gentle degrees, ascend upwards from us toward his infinite perfection . . ." (III, vi, 12).

Yet Locke conceived these innumerable species as " separated and diversified one from another by distinct properties ", i.e., divided by essential differences [1] so that there is no real continuum, in spite of all the intermediary links. There is an essential difference between man and animal : " The understanding . . . sets man above the rest of sensible beings " (I, i, i). There is an essential difference between animal and plant : " It is perception [in Leibniz's terminology : apperception, i.e., conscious perception] . . . which puts the boundaries between animals and the inferior ranks of creatures " (II, ix, 15). There is an essential difference between plant and the inorganic : " An oak differs from a mass of matter . . . in this, that the one is only the cohesion of particles of matter any how united, the other such a disposition of them as constitutes the parts of an oak ; and such an organization of those parts as is fit to receive and distribute nourishment, so as to continue and frame the wood, bark, and leaves, etc., of an oak, in which consists the vegetable life " (II, xxvii, 4).

It is true that Leibniz made similar divisions : " When the Monad has organs so arranged that they give prominence and sharpness to the impressions they receive . . . this may lead to *feeling.* . . . Such a living being is called an animal, as its Monad is called a soul. And when this soul is raised to *reason,* it is something more sublime and is reckoned among spirits . . ." (*Nature and Grace,* 4). In this sense Leibniz distinguished *monades nudæ sive*

---

[1] Locke was indeed a nominalist. He held that we must be " content with knowing things one from another by their sensible qualities " and that " it is not . . . [their] real essence that distinguishes them into species " since " the real essence of . . . substances it is evident we know not ". But although it is " true that the boundaries of the species whereby men sort them, are made by men " he assumed that " things which do agree one with another, in many sensible qualities " agree " probably too in their internal frame and constitution " so that the boundaries of the species distinguished by different names correspond more or less to the real boundaries set by nature (III, vi, 24 sq.).

dormientes or unconscious monads ; *monades sensitivæ* or conscious monads ; and *monades reflectentes sive rationales* or self-conscious monads—the elements of nature, the souls of the animals, and the spirits of men.

But in spite of this apparent agreement, there is a deep and decisive opposition between Locke and Leibniz. To Locke, the differences between the several realms are differences in essence ; to Leibniz, they are but differences of degree. The contrast is obvious. There are, according to Locke, in any case " two sorts of beings in the world, that man knows or conceives : First, such as are purely material, without sense, perception or thought, as the clippings of our beards, and parings of our nails. Secondly, sensible, thinking, perceiving beings, such as we find ourselves to be " (IV, x, 9). It is precisely this distinction which Leibniz is not willing to accept and admit : " In all bodies including the [so-called] inorganic, organic bodies lie hid ", he says, " so that every mass which to outward appearance is formless and quite undifferentiated is inwardly not undifferentiated but diversified, and yet its variety is not confused but orderly. Thus there is everywhere organism . . ." (*Antibarbarus Physicus*, cit. Latta, 112). Indeed, he asserts, " it may be, nay it must be, that in the very smallest grains of dust . . . there are worlds not inferior to our own in beauty and variety " (*Epistola ad Bernoullium, ib.*, 116). If Locke maintains that " matter . . . is evidently in its own nature void of sense and thought " (IV, 3, 6), Leibniz sets against this statement the main article of his creed : " All nature is full of life " (*Nature and Grace*, 1).

Thus the idea of a continuum has a much deeper sense in the mouth of Leibniz than in the mouth of Locke ; to Locke it is only a rough simile, to Leibniz, however, an exact conception : " I think . . . that all the different classes of beings, the totality of which forms the universe, are, in the ideas of God, who knows distinctly their essential gradations, merely like so many ordinates of one and the same curve, the relations of which do not allow of others being put between any two of them, because that would indicate disorder and imperfection. Accordingly men are linked with animals, these with plants, and these again with fossils, which in their turn are connected with those bodies which sense and imagination represent to us as completely dead and inorganic. But the law of continuity requires that, *when the essential determinations of any being approximate to those of another, all the properties of the former must gradually approximate to those of the latter.* Therefore all the orders of natural beings must necessarily form only one chain, in which the different classes, like so many links, are so closely connected with one another that it is impossible for sense or imagination to determine exactly the point where any one of them begins or ends ; all the species which border upon or which occupy, so to speak, disputable territory, being necessarily ambiguous and endowed with characteristics which may equally be ascribed to neighbouring species. Thus, for instance, the existence of zoophytes or . . . plant-animals does not imply monstrosity, but it is indeed agreeable to the order of nature that they should exist. And so strongly do I hold to the principle of continuity that not only should I not be astonished to learn that there had been found beings which, as regards several properties—for instance, those of feeding or multiplying themselves—might pass for vegetables as well as for animals, and which upset the common rules, founded upon the supposition of a complete and absolute separation of the different orders of beings which together fill the universe : I say, I should be so little astonished at it that I am even convinced that there must be such beings, and that natural history will perhaps some day come to know them, when it has further studied that infinity of living beings whose smallness conceals them from ordinary observation, and which lie hid in the bowels of the earth and in the depths of the waters '' (Letter to an unknown correspondent, cit. Latta, 37 sq.).

However, if the universe is to be a true continuum ; if there are no essential differences between the things, and, since the things are not ultimate realities, between the monads which compose them, because all partake of life, this common nature must find expression in common properties, properties common to all things and monads. There are such properties, Leibniz taught, and perception is the most important of them. Now, what exactly is perception ? '' Perception is nothing else than the expression of many things in one '' (*Epistola ad Des Bosses*, cit. Latta, 224). The best illustration is again the human mind : there are a great many ideas in me and yet I am and remain one. '' We have in ourselves experience of a multiplicity in simple substance, when we find that the least thought of which we are conscious involves variety in its object. Thus all those who admit that the soul is a simple substance should admit this multiplicity in the Monad '' (*Mon.*, 16). Perception must not be confused with apperception ; apperception is a higher form of perception, it is conscious perception and as such characteristic only of the higher monads ; but even the lower monads have perception though it be a lower form of perception, that is to say, unconscious perception. The mistake made by Locke and all those who try sharply to divide dead matter and living beings consists in regarding the unconscious as unreal. This is unjustifiable : " The Cartesian view is extremely defective, for it treats as non-existent those perceptions of which we are not consciously aware " (ib., 14). Even where there is no consciousness there may be " expression of many things in one " or " multiplicity in the unit " ; what remains is the objective connection : " One thing expresses another (in my sense)," Leibniz once defines perception, mainly with regard to the bare monads, as it seems (Letter to Arnauld, cit. Latta, 136), " when there is a constant and regular relation between what can be said of the one and what can be said of the other. It is thus that a projection in perspective expresses the original figure." Hence all monads have this one essential property : " Expression is common to all soul-principles. It is a genus, of which natural perception, animal feeling, and intellectual knowledge are species " (Letter to Arnauld, cit. Latta, 136).

But while all monads have perception, they have it in very various degrees, and that constitutes the differences between them. " Each soul knows the infinite, knows all, but confusedly ; as when I walk on the sea-shore and hear the great noise the sea makes, I hear the particular sounds which come from the particular waves and which make up the total sound, but I do not discriminate them from one another. Our confused perceptions are the result of the impressions which the whole universe makes upon us. It is the same with each Monad " (Nature and Grace, 13). Yet the degree of confusion and distinctness is very different : the lower a monad the greater the confusion, the higher it is, the greater the distinctness : " It has perfection in proportion to its distinct perceptions. . . . The Angels and the Blessed are creatures precisely like us, in whom there is always some confused perception mixed with distinct knowledge . . . God alone has a distinct knowledge of all " (ib., Théodicée, II, 310). Therefore, God is perfect ; but even between him and us, and, indeed, even between him, the highest, and the most humble monad, obtains only a difference of degree : " The perfections of God are those of our souls, but he possesses them without limits : he is an ocean of which we have received drops. . . . Our light is a ray of the light of God. . . . His goodness and his justice and also his wisdom differ from ours only because they are infinitely more perfect " (*Théodicée*, Preface ; Remarques, etc. 6 ; 4).

While the fact that all monads, from the most sublime to the most modest, are endowed with perception proves that there are no essential differences between them which could break the continuity and thus disturb the harmony of the universe, the tensions between the clear and the confused—indeed, we should rather say, between the clearer and the more confused—ways of envisaging and representing the world are overcome by the circumstance that all species and, what is more, all individuals, nay, in the last analysis, all monads, form an unbroken series according to the measure of clearness or confusion they attain, in which even the differences of degree disappear—disappear because they are between any two links quite imperceptible and therefore practically negligible, because they are—to use the technical term which Leibniz the mathematician introduced--truly infinitesimal.[1] " There is an infinity of degrees in the Monads ", and this infinity expresses, as Leibniz himself once put it, " the continuity of all souls, from the soul of the pebble to the soul of the angel " (*Nature and Grace*, 4 ; Letter to Joh. Bernouilli, cf. Latta, 131 sq.).

In this way the differences between things are not only not prejudicial but even necessary to the harmony of the whole : " If simple substances did not differ in quality, there would be absolutely no means of perceiving any change in things. . . . The Monads, if they had no qualities, would be indistinguishable from one another, since they do not differ in quantity. Consequently, space being a *plenum*, each part of space would always receive, in any motion, exactly the equivalent of what it already had, and no one state of things would be discernible from another. Indeed, each Monad must be different from every other. For in nature there are never two beings which are perfectly alike and in which it is not possible to find an internal difference, or at least a difference founded upon an intrinsic quality " (*Mon.*, 8 sq.). Here again, we must not rely on our senses which are weak : " There are no two indiscernible individuals. . . . Two drops of water or of milk, looked at through a microscope, will be found discernible.

---

[1] May those who endeavour to make a science of concrete life as economics should be into a science of abstract conceptions as is mathematics, find food for thought in the fact that the idea underlying the differential calculus and hence all modern mathematics has sprung from a contemplation of reality : " *Quodam modo Deum imitantur Geometrae per novam infinitesimorum analysin,*" says Leibniz, the inventor (or at least co-inventor) of the infinitesimal calculus (*Théodicée*, Causa Dei asserta, 122) : " By the new infinitesimal analysis the geometers do only somehow imitate God " and his creation.

. . . To suppose two indiscernible things is to suppose the same thing under two names " (4th letter to Clarke, cit. Latta, 37).

Thus the infinity of degrees of perception is an infinity of individuals in the universe. And this infinity of individuals in its turn implies an infinity of view-points from which the universe is perceived : " Any one Monad in itself and at a particular moment can be distinguished from any other only by internal qualities . . . which cannot be other than its perceptions (that is to say, the representation of the compound, or of that which is outside, in the simple). . . . For the simplicity of substance is by no means inconsistent with the multiplicity of the modifications which are to be found together in that same simple substance, and these modifications must consist in variety of relations to the things which are outside. It is as in the case of a centre or point, in which, although it is perfectly simple, there is an infinite number of angles formed by the lines which meet in it " (*Nature and Grace*, 2).

But this infinity of view-points no more infringes upon the continuity and harmony of the whole than the infinity in the degrees of perception ; both are in fact conditions of the divine order : " Each simple substance has relations which express all the others, and, consequently, . . . it is a perpetual living mirror of the universe [representing it, so we may add, to give Leibniz's whole doctrine, with more or less distinctness]. As the same town, looked at from various sides, appears quite different and becomes as it were numerous in aspects ; even so, as a result of the infinite number of simple substances, it is as if there were so many different universes, which, nevertheless, are nothing but aspects of a single universe, according to the special point of view of each Monad. And by this means there is obtained as great a variety as possible, along with the greatest possible order " (*Mon.*, 56–8). This order is " the pre-established harmony between all substances [which exists] since they are all representations of one and the same universe " (78).

Yet the conception that " the pre-established harmony between all substances " rests upon the fact that " they are all representations of one and the same universe " is, as it stands, purely static in character. Therefore it must be further developed, if it is fully to explain the order divine which persists though reality is dynamic, though " every created being, and consequently the created Monad, is subject to change " (*Mon.*, 10). Only if the continuation of harmony through all changes is explained, can

the theory claim to be truly realistic : " Not only is the variety
of the object represented in that which has perception ; but there
is also variation in the representation itself, since that which is to
be represented varies " (*De anima brutorum*, cit. Latta, 33).

Now, the monads are units of life, and life consists not only in
perception but also in " a tendency to new perceptions " (Letter
to Bourguet, *l.c.*, 35)—not only in perception but also in appetition. Appetitions can be defined as " tendencies to pass from
one perception to another ", and they are " the principles of
change " (*Nature and Grace*, 2). Only both properties together
constitute the essence of the monad : " The soul has perceptions
and appetitions, and its nature consists in these " (*Epistola ad
Bierlingium*, cit. Latta, 35).

Naturally there is a thorough-going parallelism between perception and appetition ; the degrees of the one are also the degrees
of the other : " There are unfelt inclinations, of which we have
no consciousness ; there are felt inclinations, whose existence and
object we know, but which are formed without our being aware of
it, and these are confused inclinations, which we attribute to the
body . . . ; and finally, there are distinct inclinations which
reason gives us, and of whose force and formation we are aware "
(*New Essays, etc.*, cit. Latta, 138). Hence Leibniz distinguishes
—if we may speak of distinction—(1) mere impulse (like that of a
watch-spring wound up) ; (2) blind desire (such as animal
instincts and the urges of human passions) ; and (3) rational will.
Mere impulse is characteristic of the bare monad and corresponds
to natural or unconscious representation ; blind desire is characteristic of the conscious monad and corresponds to animal perception ; lastly rational will is characteristic of the self-conscious
monad and corresponds to intellectual knowledge.

Appetition, like perception, is strictly individual ; each monad
has a principle of change which is exclusively its own, as it has
a view-point which it occupies alone : " There is no way of
explaining how a Monad can be altered in quality or internally
changed by any other created thing ; since it is impossible to
change the place of anything in it or to conceive in it any internal
motion which could be produced, directed, increased or diminished therein, although all this is possible in the case of compounds,
in which there are changes among the parts. The Monads have
no windows, through which anything could come in or go out "
(*Mon.*, 7).

Every " Ego " depends upon itself and is independent of all

others.   If there is alteration, its source can only be the proper force of the life-unit which experiences it : " It follows from what has . . . been said, that the natural changes of the Monads come from an internal principle, since an external cause can have no influence upon their inner being " (*Mon.*, 11).   Hence, here too, Leibniz develops his principle of individuation to its utmost limits : " Each simple substance (that is to say, each real substance) is the true immediate cause of all its internal actions and passions ; and, to speak with metaphysical exactness, it has no other than those which it produces " (*Théodicée*, II, 400).

But if all beings follow exclusively their own bent, how can it be that they are constantly in agreement ?   If the musicians composing an orchestra play only the tunes which their individual fancy suggests to them, will not a cacophony rather than a symphony be the result ?   The result will be a symphony if individual fancy suggests to every musician a tune which corresponds to all the others and spontaneously combines with them to form a harmonious whole.   This is the great secret of the divine order : " God in the beginning regulated one substance according to the other . . . God instituted in advance the harmony that should exist among them " (*Théodicée*, II, 66).   The monads are independent in their impulses and instincts and wills : but all these free tendencies are so constituted in their very core as to produce perfect agreement :   " Each of these substances contains in its own nature the principle of succession of the series of its own operations and all that has happened and shall happen to it.   All its notions come from its own inner being. . . .   The operation of one substance upon another consists only in the perfect mutual accord of substances, definitely established through the order of their first creation, in virtue of which each substance, following its own laws, agrees with the rest, meeting their demands ; and the operations of the one thus follow or accompany the operations or change of the other " (Letter to Arnould, cit. Latta 106).

Hence not only is the universe harmonious because the monads which compose it form a continuous series ; it is also harmonious because the motions which change it take place in spontaneous correspondence.   The divine order is not only real but also lasting : it is not only static but also dynamic.

The dogma of the pre-established harmony in its highest form, the dogma of the harmony of the universe not only in space but also through time, gives the ultimate answer to the question of how independent parts can combine into an ordered whole without the parts losing their independence in the combination or the whole losing its order by the division.   Its fundamental idea is splendidly expressed in the classical simile which Leibniz used to explain it : " Suppose two clocks or two watches which perfectly keep time together.   Now that may happen in three ways. . . . The first way . . . was ascertained on trial by the late M. Huygens, to his great astonishment.   He attached two large pendulums to the same piece of wood.   The continual swinging of these pendulums imparted similar vibrations to the particles of the wood ; but as these different vibrations could not continue in their proper order, without interfering with one another, unless the pendulums kept time together, it happened . . . that even when their swinging was deliberately disturbed, they soon came to swing together again, somewhat like two stretched strings that are in unison " (Third Explanation, etc., Latta, 331 sq.).   In this case we can hardly speak of independent parts : the harmony of the whole is secured by the very act which deprives the parts of their independence.   Order indeed there is, but the pendulums are forced into it.   " The second way of making two clocks (even though they be bad ones) constantly keep time together would be to put them in charge of a skilled workman who should keep them together from moment to moment."   In this case again we can hardly speak of a harmonious whole.   The very fact that the parts are independent deprives the whole of its harmony.   Order indeed there is, but it is incessantly destroyed and must be incessantly re-established.   Yet, there is one more possibility, avoiding the Scylla of monism and the Charybdis of atomism : the *harmonia præstabilita*.   " Finally, the third way will be to make the two clocks at first with such skill and accuracy that we can be sure that they will always afterwards keep time together."

The great order of the universe was explained by the Schoolmen in the first way, the way of influence ; by the Cartesians in the second way, the way of assistance ; by Leibniz in the third way which alone he regarded as corresponding to the facts : " The way of influence is that of the common philosophy ; but as we cannot conceive material particles or immaterial species or qualities which can pass from one of these substances into the other, we are obliged to give up this opinion.   The way of assistance is that of the system of occasional causes ; but I hold that this is to introduce *Deus ex machina* in a natural and ordinary matter.

. . . Thus there remains only my hypothesis, that is to say, the way of the harmony pre-established by a contrivance of the Divine foresight, which has from the beginning formed each of these substances in so perfect, so regular and accurate a manner that by merely following its own laws which were given to it when it came into being, each substance is yet in harmony with the other, just as if there were a mutual influence between them, or as if God were continually putting His hand upon them. . . . It is very evident that this is the best way and the most worthy of Him." The order of the universe has sprung from God's infinite perfection ; God's infinite perfection is reflected in the order of the universe. Thus contemplation and study of reality led Leibniz from mathematics to religion, and from science to faith.

The Leibnitian creed implies the conviction " that there is a perfect harmony . . . between the physical realm of nature and the moral realm of grace " (*Mon.*, 87) ; as a matter of course it also implies the conviction that there is a perfect harmony within each of these realms. " His providence shines forth as strikingly . . . in the laws to which He has subjected men's interests and men's wills, as in the laws which He has imposed upon weight and velocity ", Bastiat wrote at a later date, but in the same vein (*A la Jeunesse Française*, Œuvres Complètes, 1854, VI, 19, 11) : " He has combined, and caused to move in harmony, free agents as well as inert molecules. . . . Celestial and social mechanism alike reveal the wisdom of God and proclaim His glory." Yet, according to Leibniz, the free agents stand above the inert molecules in the order of the universe because they are endowed with reason ; and therefore the harmony among them as self-conscious monads must be higher and deeper than the harmony among the monads which are but conscious or unconscious : " Among other differences which exist between ordinary souls and [human or super-human] minds . . . there is also this : that souls in general are living mirrors or images of the universe of created things, but that minds are also images of the Deity or Author of Nature Himself. . . . It is this that enables [human] spirits to enter into a kind of fellowship with God, and brings it about that in relation to them He is not only what an inventor is to his machine (which is the relation of God to other created things), but also what a prince is to his subjects, and, indeed, what a father is to his children. Whence it is easy to conclude that the totality of all spirits must compose the City of God, that is to say, the most perfect

State that is possible, under the most perfect of Monarchs " (*Mon.*, 83–5).

Thus God " formed of the spirits the most beautiful of all conceivable societies " as he " made of matter the most beautiful of all possible mechanisms " (*Théodicée*, II, 140). If we try to fathom the mystery of creation, we see why it is so : " As in the ideas of God there is an infinite number of possible universes, and as only one of them can be actual, there must be a sufficient reason for the choice of God, which leads Him to decide upon one rather than another. And this reason can be found only in the fitness,[1] or in the degrees of perfection, that these worlds possess, since each possible thing has the right to aspire to existence in proportion to the amount of perfection it contains in germ. Thus the actual existence of the best that wisdom makes known to God is due to this, that His goodness makes Him choose it, and His power makes Him produce it " (*Mon.*, 53–5).

This is the glorious doctrine of optimism so fervently believed by Jean-Jacques Rousseau, so acidly ridiculed by Voltaire : " If all the time and all the space were filled, it remains always true that they could have been filled in an infinity of ways, and that there is an infinity of possible worlds, of which God has necessarily chosen the best, because He does nothing without acting according to the highest Reason " (*Théodicée*, II, 8).

As always in Leibniz, this act of faith contains also a principle of science ; the perfection of the Creator is the key to the understanding of the Creation : " It follows from the supreme perfection of God that in producing the universe He has chosen the best possible plan, in which there is the greatest variety along with the greatest order ; the greatest effect produced by the simplest ways ; the most power, knowledge, happiness, and goodness in created things that the universe allowed " (*Nature and Grace*, 10). Indeed, a short formula is sufficient to reveal the fundamental law of the universe, impressed upon it when it came into existence : this law is " a principle of determination according to maximum and minimum, so that . . . the maximum effect is produced with the minimum outlay " (*Ultimate Origination*, Latta, 340 sq.). If we look around us in nature and society, we see it at work everywhere : " It is wonderfully made known to us how in the very origination of things a certain Divine mathematics or metaphysical mechanics is employed and the greatest quantity is

---

[1] The word used in the original French is " convenance "—a term very near to the meaning of the English expression " utility ".

brought into existence." In the physical world this quantity is quantity of essence, since being is superior to not being ; in the moral world it is quantity of happiness, since pleasure is better than pain. Therefore " the world is not only the most admirable mechanism, but it is also, in so far as it is made up of minds, the best commonwealth, through which there is bestowed upon minds the greatest possible happiness or joy, in which their physical perfection consists " (*ib.*, 342, 345).

But is the world, as it is, really the best commonwealth ? Does it in fact bestow upon men the greatest possible happiness and joy ? Leibniz did not hesitate to answer this question in the affirmative : " If the least evil which takes place in the world, would be missing, this would no longer be the same world, which, all taken into account, all considered, has been found the best by the Maker who has chosen it " (*Théodicée*, II, 9).

This statement sounds self-contradictory. How can the actual world be the best possible, if it implies evil ? Does not the very idea of perfection demand that all blemish should be excluded ? Indeed not ; for the evil in the world serves to enhance the good : " Do we enough enjoy our health, and do we thank our God enough for it, without having ever been ill ? And is it not very often necessary that a little pain should make the pleasure more sensible, that is to say, more intense? . . . The shadows accentu- ate the colours ; and even a dissonance placed in the right way, makes the harmony the more prominent " (12). Thus the evils in the world are " as useful for the enhancement of the beauty of the rest as the beauty-spots which, although they have nothing attractive in themselves, are found proper by the fair sex for the embellishment of the whole face, though they spoil the part which they cover " (*ib.*, Remarques, etc., 27).

Hence this world is the best not in spite of the evils that infest it, but because of them. In making it, the Highest Monad con- sistently followed the principles of a sublime and enlightened utilitarianism ; his thought before he decided upon the creation passed through three stages, from a good to a better and from the better to the best order of things : " The antecedent and initial will has for its object each good and each evil in itself, detached from all combination, and tends to enhance the good and to check the evil : the intermediate will is directed to combinations, as in the case when one particular good is connected with one particular evil ; and then the will will have some inclination for the com- bination if the good in it surpasses the evil : but the final and decisive will results from the consideration of all the goods and all the evils which enter into deliberation, it results from a total combination . . . Thus the good which God does can only be sufficiently appreciated if its whole extent is considered with regard to the entire universe " (*Théodicée*, II, 119). So understood, all pain is justified : " God has a very . . . strong reason, and a reason very . . . worthy of Him, to tolerate the evils. He not only draws from them greater goods, but he finds them even connected with the greatest good possible : so that it would be a fault not to permit them " (*ib.*, 127). Indeed : " To permit the evil as God permits it, is the greatest goodness " (*ib.*, 121).

Yet, to prove the 'goodness of God from the harmony of the creation, or to derive the harmony of the creation from the goodness of God, it is not sufficient to show, that some evil is justified because it engenders some good. It is necessary also clearly to demonstrate that there is a tendency towards self-annihilation in evil and a tendency towards self-multiplication in good ; that the world is so ordered as to lead to a maximization of happiness and to a minimization of misery ; that all is truly for the best. Leibniz was firmly convinced that even this could be done. " It may also be said ", he claims, " that . . . sins . . . bear their penalty with them, through the order of nature, and even in virtue of the mechanical structure of things ; and similarly that noble actions will attain their rewards by ways which, on the bodily side, are mechanical. . . . Under this perfect government [of God] no good action would be unrewarded and no bad one unpunished, and all should issue in the well-being of the good " (*Mon.*, 89 sq.). Indeed, in the City of God, he asserts, which is a moral world in the natural world, " there is no crime without punishment, no good action without a proportionate reward, and in short as much virtue and happiness as is possible ; and this, not by any interference with the course of nature, as if what God prepares for souls were to disturb the laws of bodies, but by the very order of natural things, in virtue of the harmony pre-established from all time between the realms of nature and of grace, between God as Architect and God as Monarch, so that nature itself leads to grace, and grace, by the use it makes of nature, brings it to perfection " (*Nature and Grace*, 15).

In order to prove this thesis ; in order to demonstrate the perfection and harmony of the social world ; in order to establish that not only is in the whole of society the greatest possible happiness realized (economically speaking : the maximum of pro-

duction achieved) but also that every member of it receives a
share in proportion to his merit (in economic language : in proportion to his labour), Leibniz developed a theory of individual
action and social ethics closely akin to that propounded at the
same time by John Locke. Sociology is the field where the great
antagonists meet : the one started from a materialistic doctrine of
psychology, the other from an idealistic doctrine of cosmology, but
about the social aspect of man and mankind they thought almost
alike. This is the deeper reason for the union of their ideas which
is visible in classical economics from Adam Smith to Frédéric
Bastiat.

Leibniz's theory of individual action and social ethics is, like
that of Locke, entirely hedonistic and utilitarian : " The will is
never led to an action if it is not by the representation of some
good which prevails over the contrary representations. . . .
There is always a prevalent reason which leads the will to its
choice, and it suffices for the preservation of its liberty if this
reason inclines without necessitating. . . . The same is true
even with regard to God, the good Angels, and the blessed Souls :
and it must be recognized that they are not less free for it. God
does not fail to choose the best, but he is by no means forced to do
so. . . . It is for this reason that the choice is free and independent of necessity because it takes place between several possibilities, and because the will is determined only by the prevalent
goodness of the object. This is certainly not a fault with regard to
God and the Saints ; on the contrary, it would be a great fault, or
rather a manifest absurdity, if it would be otherwise, even in men
down here, and if they were capable of acting without an inclining
reason. Of this we shall never find any example, and if some-one
takes a certain course through caprice, to show his liberty, the
pleasure or the advantage which he believes to find in this affect-
ation, is one of the reasons which leads him to it " (*Théodicée*, II,
45). The feeling of indifference experienced by us is misleading
because it takes no account of subconscious urges : " The will is
proportioned to the sentiment which we have of the good and
follows its pre-eminence. . . . Although I do not always see the
reason of an inclination which makes me choose between two
possibilities that appear equal, there is always some impression, be
it only an imperceptible one, which determines us " (*ib.*, 287, 305).

Certainly, there are now and then conflicting tendencies within us, but the stronger one will ultimately prevail : " We oppose
ourselves to natural appetites by help of other natural appetites.

We support sometimes incommodities and do it with joy ; but this is because of some hope or some satisfaction which is connected with the evil, and which surpasses it : we expect some good from it or find some good in it " (*Théodicée*, Remarques etc., 23).

Now, this action according to our inborn desires is—by dint of the harmony pre-established between the physical realm of nature and the moral realm of grace—in no way at variance with the dictates of our external duties : " We must judge that it is not permitted to act otherwise because it is not possible to do better. This is . . . a moral necessity which far from being contrary to liberty, is the effect of its choice " (*ib.*, 124).[1]   Here it is manifest " that God as Architect satisfies in all respects God as Lawgiver " for " the necessary and the due are equivalent things " (*Mon.*, 89 ; *Théodicée*, Abrégé, etc.).   Here we can see that the order of the whole is consistent with the independence of the parts : " These laws [of ethics] . . . do not constrain : they are stronger still because they persuade " (*ib.*, 121).   For what is it that these laws demand ?   What is it that constitutes the essence of ethics ? Nothing but the pursuit of our spontaneous end : " The love of virtue and the hatred of vice which tend indefinitely to secure the ascendancy of virtue and to prevent that of vice, are but the will to secure the felicity of all men [2] and to prevent their misery " (*ib.*, 222).

Here again we must ask : is there no difference at all between action and right action, between the Is and the Ought ?   And here again we must answer : there is no difference in essence.   To Leibniz, as to Locke, moral conduct is actual conduct unchanged

---

[1] On the problem of free will Locke's and Leibniz's opinions do not wholly coincide.   The difference is, however, one of emphasis rather than of essence.   Leibniz, it is true, paid lip-service to men's liberty of action, but not more than lip-service : " One can say in a certain sense that it is necessary . . . that man should follow the course which in the end appeals to him most ", he admits (*Théodicée*, 282).   " But this necessity is by no means opposed to contingency . . .   We judge it to be impossible that a wise and worthy judge who has not lost his sense, should publicly commit some great extravagance as it would be, for example, to run through the streets without clothes."   Hence, although the soul is not determined with necessity, it is determined with certainty (*ib.*, 371) : " Let us distinguish between the necessary and the certain.   It is not impossible that what is expected does not arrive ; but it is infallible that it will arrive " (408).   The psychologist may find some difference between the two points of view ; for the sociologist it is hardly important.

[2] " We demand that one should be virtuous, thankful, just, *not only* for reasons of interest, calculation, or fear ; but *also* because of the pleasure which one should find in good actions " (*ib.*, Remarques, etc., 17).   This passage exposes all Leibniz's utilitarianism ; there are, according to him, two incentives to moral conduct : first, the positive reward, to which a good action leads up ; and secondly, the agreeable sensation (in Bentham's terminology : the pleasure of sympathy) with which it is spontaneously connected.   Hence egotism is the root of all altruism.

but perfected : " The free will tends towards the good, and if it encounters the evil, it is only by accident, it is because the evil is hidden under the good and so to speak masked. The words which Ovid ascribes to Medea, I see the better and approve of it, but I follow the worse, mean that the good of real worth is surmounted by the good of agreeable appearance which makes more impression on the souls if they find themselves agitated by the passions " (*ib.*, 154).

Hence as Locke covers actual and ethical action by one definition, describing the one as the pursuit of happiness, the other as the careful and constant pursuit of true and solid happiness, so does Leibniz : " I hold ", he says (*ib.*, Remarques etc., 13) " that the will follows always the most advantageous representation, distinct or confused, of good and evil, which results from reasons, passions, and inclinations." Natural action consists in the pursuit of some confused object suggested by the passions ; ethical action is the pursuit of some distinct object born of reason. This is their only difference.

This is their only difference, and it is a difference intellectual in character : the higher a being stands in the continuous series of monads—that is to say : the clearer the perception is that it has of the universe—the better it will serve both the subjective aim of individual happiness and the objective command of social morality : " God determines himself by himself [as we do] . . . [but] as his understanding is perfect . . . he never fails to do the best : while we can be deceived by the false appearances of the true and the good " (*ib.*, 21). The true and the good : they are not superficially similar but ultimately identical. " As wisdom, or the cognition of the true, is the perfection of the intellect, so goodness, or the pursuit of the good, is the perfection of the will. And although all voluntary action has some good for its object, be it also an apparent good only, the divine will [alone follows] nothing but what is good and true at the same time " (*ib.*, Causa Dei asserta, 18).

Yet, what can man do, imperfect as he is, to avoid all deception ? Not much, to be sure, but still something. He can ponder his actions well, and in doing so he will approach moral perfection as much as it is possible. " There is only ignorance or passion which might keep us in suspense, and . . . this is the reason why God is never undecided " (*ib.*, II, 318). It is the same rationalistic imperative at which Locke and Leibniz arrive : " God and the wise man decide upon nothing without considering

the consequences. . . . The empire of God, the empire of the
wise man, is that of reason " (*ib.*, Preface ; II, 327).

The more rational therefore a being is, the clearer will it perceive wherein true happiness consists and how it may be secured :
" The will tends towards the good in general ; it should follow
the perfection which is proper to us. . . . All pleasures have in
themselves some sentiment of perfection ; but if a man "—we
may interpose : foolishly—" confines himself to the [petty]
pleasures of the senses or others [of so low a character], to the
prejudice of greater goods as those of health, virtue, union with
God, felicity, it is in this privation of wider pursuits "—of pursuits
which, by their very nature, engender more intense and more lasting delights—" that the fault consists " (*ib.*, II, 33). In other
words : everybody is as happy as he deserves to be. If he runs
after the mean gratifications of the senses, his happiness will be
small ; if he follows the sublime enjoyments of reason, his happiness will be great. Subjectively speaking, each realizes the
maximum of pleasure according to his desires ; objectively speaking, each realizes the maximum of pleasure according to his
merits. Thus Leibniz's cosmology and Locke's psychology lead
through a similar sociology to an identical result.

Surveying his argument, Leibniz is well satisfied. *Demons-
travit quod erat demonstrandum :* " All that God created is harmonious in perfection . . . God established . . . such a connection between . . . bad and good action that . . . virtue and
vice themselves bring about their recompense and chastisement
by dint of the natural concatenation of things " (*ib.*, II, 74).

However, is this demonstration perfect ? From the fact that
the individual of higher morality and rationality better knows the
means of, and the ways to, true felicity it does not necessarily
follow that it will in reality safely reach its goal. Leibniz
described an admirable order, but he failed to show that it is
actually at work. And, in fact, the appearance is against it.
Leibniz knew this objection and anticipated it : " You will say ",
he speaks to his readers, " we find that the opposite of this takes
place in the world, for very often the best people suffer the worst
things . . . and indeed the world, especially if we consider the
government of the human race, seems rather a confused chaos
than anything directed by a supreme wisdom. So, I confess, it
seems at a first glance, but when we look at it more closely the
opposite conclusion manifestly follows . . . namely, that the
highest possible perfection of all things, and therefore of all minds,

is brought about " (*Ultimate Origination*, Latta, 346). We must not take the narrow view of things, for it is certain that " God wishes the order and the good ; but it sometimes happens that what is disorder in a part, is order in the whole " (*Théodicée*, II,. 128). Therefore it is indispensable to comprehend reality in all its depth and breadth to understand the working of the mechanism of which we can only discern the form : " One must not be astonished that I attempt to explain these things by comparisons taken from pure mathematics where all takes place in order and where there are means of penetrating them by an exact meditation which, so to speak, allows us to enjoy a view of the ideas of God. We can envisage a set or series of numbers totally irregular in appearance where the numbers increase and diminish unsteadily · without there seeming to be any order ; and yet he who possesses the key of the chiffre and understands the origin and construction of that set of numbers will be able to give a rule which . . . will make us perceive that the series is entirely regular and that it has even beautiful proportions " (*ib.*, 242).

All we can say then is that he who knows the secret, he who understands the origin and construction of the social (and natural) world, will not doubt its perfection and harmony : " If we could sufficiently understand the order of the universe, we should find that it exceeds all the desires of the wisest men, and that it is impossible to make it better than it is, not only as a whole and in general, but also for ourselves in particular " (*Mon.*, 90). But we must not forget that we are only men. A finite spirit cannot fathom the infinite, a limited understanding cannot penetrate an all-embracing system. Here, Leibniz thought, is the boundary-line between intellect and faith : " If the soul follows reason and the orders God has given to it, it is certain of its happiness, even if it cannot find enough happiness in this life " (*Théodicée*, Remarques, 18). That there is ·a life hereafter, and that it will bring just retribution, seemed to Leibniz propositions which neither need rational demonstration nor admit of it. Indeed, he wholeheartedly agreed with the Bishop of Derry (William King), who held " that the greatest felicity down here consists in the hope of the happiness to come,[1] and that it can

---

[1] In view of this attitude it is not surprising to find that Leibniz took the social problem very lightly. " The inequality of stations cannot be reckoned among the disorders ", he asserts in one place (*Théodicée*, II, 246), and in another connection he goes so far as to suggest that the greatest-happiness-principle is satisfied if " the excellence of the total good in the smaller number prevails over the total evil in the greater " (*ib.*, Abrégé, etc.). Yet he was aware of the fact that the idea of class

therefore be stated that nothing happens to the evildoers which would not serve to better or chastise them; and that nothing happens to the good that would not lead to their greatest welfare " (*ib.*, Remarques, 27). This then is Leibniz's ultimate argument : " God warrants that in order to be happy, it is sufficient to be virtuous " (*ib.*, 18).

Thus a deep trust in God is the closing link in Leibniz's chain of thought as it is the first. Therefore it was accepted by theists like Rousseau and rejected by atheists like Voltaire. The eighteenth century as a whole stood half-way between theism and atheism. On the one hand, it was not yet willing to abandon the faith in a beneficent divine order, but on the other it was no longer satisfied with proofs which ended in the transcendent. Tangible arguments were demanded, and tangible arguments were supplied. It was Locke's philosophy which took up the task of rational demonstration at the point where Leibniz's philosophy had left it off, and so Locke's theory of the individual and Leibniz's theory of the universe, identical from the outset in the social doctrine with which they were connected, became in the end one system of thought.

To be sure, Locke did not hold that the world as it is, is the best that is possible. Reality will fall short of the ideal, he taught, as long as one condition is not realized : this condition is the equality of opportunities, embodied in free access for all members of society to the treasures of nature. Only where the means of production are not monopolized, will the glorious harmony envisaged by Leibniz become true. For it is the great principle of the divine order that every individual should take his place in accordance with his abilities and achievements ; and this is impossible if privileges bar the way.

So it happened that by its union with Locke's individualism, Leibniz's theory of concord acquired a new meaning and importance. It had been a doctrine of theology ; it was now a programme of politics. It had been conservative ; it was now revolutionary. The principle which the age of faith had regarded as the fundamental law of the *civitas divina*, the age of reason endeavoured to make the fundamental law of the *civitas terrena* : " As in a thoroughly well-constituted commonwealth care is taken, as far as may be, for the good of individuals, so the universe

society is at variance with the ideal of utilitarianism : " What is an evil for me will not cease to be one because it is a good for my master " (II, 217). God is an egalitarian : " The all-highest wisdom that there is in Him connected with the greatest goodness cause Him . . . to take care of all " (*ib.*, Causa Dei asserta, 120).

will not be sufficiently perfect unless the interests of individuals are attended to, while the universal harmony is preserved. And for this no better standard could be set up than the very law of justice which declares that each should participate in the perfection of the universe and in a happiness of his own in proportion to his virtue " and to the degree in which his actions contribute to the common good [1] (*Ultimate Origination of Things*, Latta, 348 sq.). Throughout the eighteenth century, all forces of progress were bent upon the realization of a society whose members would be able to say, and say with assurance and conviction : " In following [our individual] reason we fulfil the commands of Supreme Reason. . . . In doing so we find that nothing is more in the proper interest of private men than to embrace the general interest of the public, and that we gratify ourselves if we delight in promoting the true advantages of mankind " (*Théodicée*, Preface). To this sublime ideal of Gottfried Wilhelm Leibniz, John Locke's clear and sober ideas showed the way. Their synthesis has come to be known as classical economics.

The great current of life which led mankind towards liberty and equality, seemed after 1750 to be near its goal. Classical economics, arising by this time, was therefore at once realistic and idealistic : realistic because it described and analysed a society of independent individuals with similar chances of success whose interests, antagonistic in appearance, are in fact perfectly harmonized by an admirable mechanism—a society as it then seemed in the making ; and idealistic because it asserted and sought to prove that an order of this kind, an order built on the free play of equal forces, was the best form of social life that pure reason could possibly conceive. But—alas !—realism and idealism cannot for long go hand in hand. The industrial revolution changed the outlook : the trend of development no longer pointed towards a social organization of small-scale production, based on the concord of peasants and artisans ; under its influence an economic system of large-scale industry sprang up, carrying with it the discord of possessing and dispossessed. The same year that

---

[1] These words are a free rendering of Leibniz's idea. Latta's translation (" to the degree in which his will has regard to the common good ") is very problematical : it interprets the passage in the vein of altruistic ethics, and this is at variance with Leibniz's general utilitarianism. Unfortunately, the original Latin text given by Gerhardt (*l.c.*, VII, 307) differs from that in Erdmann's edition (*God. Guil. Leibnitii Opera Philosophica*, 1840, 149). Kirchmann (*Die kleineren philosophisch wichtigeren Schriften von G. W. Leibniz*, 1879, 101) translates : " nach Verhaeltnis der eigenen Tugend und seiner Fuersorglichkeit fuer das gemeine Beste ".

brought Smith's *Wealth of Nations* brought also Watt's steam-engine : a dismal and significant coincidence ! While men-of-letters admired the one, men-of-action spread the other. When the new century dawned, capitalism had won the field. The market, far from being the meeting-place of harmonizing individuals, had become the battle-ground of hostile classes. The glorious vision of François Quesnay and Adam Smith was now a contrast to, rather than a picture of, reality. For a short while, men continued to dream of a happy commonwealth of peaceful cottages ; but soon they awoke, and, terror-stricken, their eyes beheld the hideous workshops of Manchester and Sheffield.

THE END OF CLASSICAL ECONOMICS
OR
LIBERALISM AND SOCIALISM AT THE CROSSROADS

In the first quarter of the nineteenth century there was still but one social ideal which all men of good will strove to establish and secure : a society of liberty and equality as it had been conceived by John Locke and propagated by Adam Smith. No open conflict had yet ensued between liberalism and socialism. Both were bent upon the realization of social equality : and if the liberals proposed to bring it about by a wide distribution of national wealth, while the socialists preferred the general abolition of private property, the end was still the same and only the means different. In fact, the decision between individualism and collectivism was as yet a matter of expediency rather than a question of principle.

In and through the industrial revolution, the principles of liberty and equality became irreconcilable. Large-scale production proved its technical superiority. It became increasingly clear that full liberty would split society into a minority of possessing capitalists and a majority of dispossessed proletarians, while full equality would arrest all progress and ossify economic life. Thus mankind was faced with an awful alternative : should liberty take precedence of equality, or equality of liberty ?

In the realm of facts the materially superior system easily carried the day. Yet, in the realm of thought, the intellectual problem remained undecided : both possibilities, in fact, appeared equally forlorn. Without social equality, freedom becomes a mere mockery : " The law ", says Anatole France, " forbids the rich as well as the poor to sleep under bridges, to beg in the streets, and to steal bread." Without economic freedom, equality would hardly be worth having : the state, it could be said, would allow all men alike to toil in the public workshops and to eat at the common soup-kitchens.

The economists of 1825 were, in spite of themselves, forced to choose between economic liberty without social equality, and social equality without economic liberty. The old ideal, reconciling the two hostile principles on the basis of an equal distribution of social wealth by giving each citizen enough productive property to gain his living independent of masters and men, had for the last time been stated and re-stated by Jeremy Bentham. Of his two immediate disciples, the one, Thomas Hodgskin, looked to the right, the other, William Thompson, turned to the left. Liberalism and socialism had arrived at the crossroads. The end of classical economics had come.

I. THE LIBERTARIAN ALTERNATIVE : THOMAS HODGSKIN

The fundamental idea from which Thomas Hodgskin starts is essentially the same as the one from which François Quesnay and Adam Smith had started : the conviction that there is a great and beneficent order of the universe which comprises the human and physical worlds alike. " Society is a natural phenomenon ", he says (*The Natural and Artificial Right of Property Contrasted*, 1832, 160), " and I inquire into the laws which regulate it, as I would inquire into the laws which regulate the course of the seasons." Like the physical macrocosm, the economic microcosm is governed by the principle of spontaneity, and the discipline which studies it must necessarily assume the character of a natural science : " The division of labour among individuals, and the wonderful co-operation of different classes of labourers to produce a common result, by which the productive power of the whole is amazingly increased, are not the result of human or legislative wisdom . . . but of an instinct in man, by which he takes to this peculiar practice, as a duck takes to the water and a fox to his cave. It is with these natural interests, passions, instincts, and affections, and with their consequences— they not being suspended at any moment, and continuing to operate as powerfully when society is in its most advanced state as at its commencement—that political economy principally deals. . . . On them, and on their permanency, together with the permanency of those laws by which the material world excites similar sensations in us, at all times and places, is founded the natural science of national wealth " (*Popular Political Economy*, 1827, 25).

Yet, closely akin though the physical and social sciences may be, there is this difference between them that the physical sciences lead only to theoretical, the social sciences also to practical results : " As a part of the great system of the universe . . . the natural laws which regulate the progress of population and wealth ought to be, like the instincts of bees and ants, or like the motions of the planets, objects of rational curiosity ; but . . . we know, in addition, that on them the welfare of mankind depends." Certainly, " political economy is a natural, not a political science " ; yet " it does not end in barren speculation ". On the contrary : " An inquiry into the laws which regulate the production of wealth, is, in fact, an inquiry into the laws which regulate national prosperity and national decay " (*ib.*, 262 sq., 32).

This fact not only proves the importance, but also determines the task, of economic science : " We want to know all the circumstances which influence the productive power of labour . . . and, in a general sense, the opulence and poverty of individuals ; and to ascertain all these circumstances is the great object of political economy." Indeed, this fact not only determines the intellectual task, but even suggests the systematic scope and methodical procedure, of scientific economics : " There are two distinct classes of circumstances—or natural circumstances, independent of all governments, and social circumstances, derived from governments—which influence both the production and the distribution of wealth. The science of political economy, when complete, embraces both these classes of circumstances, and has no other limit than the whole of them. But . . . each of these two classes of circumstances must be treated in a perfectly distinct manner. . . . We have first to discover all the natural circumstances which influence production and distribution at all times and places ; and by them, as a test, we examine the effects of social regulations " (*ib.*, 15, 34 sq.). In this way, scientific rigour is combined with practical utility ; the rule of political action grows out of the findings of theoretical contemplation ; economic analysis becomes the solid foundation of social reform : in short, a method is given which allows us to judge the real by the ideal and to develop the ideal from the real.

Now, what is the ultimate truth, unassailable and unchanging, on which the pure science of economic reality must base its doctrinal system ? It is the truth which had been at the root of Locke's physical and practical philosophy, the fact that man is dependent upon nature and nature is subjected to man : " It is a law of our being, that we must eat bread by the sweat of our brow ; but it is reciprocally a law of the external world, that it shall give bread for our labour, and give it only for labour. Thus we see that the world, every part of which is regulated by unalterable laws, is adapted to man, and man to the world." It is the hard necessity to toil, which constitutes the eternal fate of human kind, that enables us to say : " the principles of the science of the production of wealth are expressions of natural facts. They are true at all times and places. At every period of the world labour has been the parent of wealth—the foundation of all property " (*ib.*, 28 ; *Economist*, 1852, 1327).

From this statement, which is above all difficulty and doubt, there follow at once two further truths, both equally basic to the natural science of social economy. One is positive, the other negative : " All wealth is created by labour, and there is no wealth which is not the produce of labour ", runs the first ; and the second says : " We may . . . reject from our inquiries all the physical circumstances, and all material things not inherent in man himself, and not created by labour, which are supposed in general to influence most strongly the prosperity of our race. Climate and situation, however apparently influential, have in reality so slight a degree of power, and their peculiar. effects depend on causes so little known to us, that at present they are inappreciable. . . . The land falls not within the limits of the science any more than the sea or the air. It was as extensive for the Indians in America as for the Europeans. . . . Little as the continent of America yielded to the savage, it yielded even that little only to his labour ; and excluding from our view the different kind and degree of labour exercised by the two races, it now yields as much to him as to the civilized European. In fact, the spontaneous productions of the most fertile districts, do not amount to the ten thousandth part of what civilized man can obtain from the soil. Labour, enlightened, well-directed labour, converts the sterile rock into a fertile field ; and it is no exaggeration to say that it gathers bread from the salt wave. . . . Land, therefore, however fertile, does not create wealth, any more than sunshine and rain ; and as well as these, it may, both as to dimensions and fertility, be entirely overlooked without the chance of falling into an error " (*Pol. Ec.*, 19, 15 sq.).

Yet, while the first assertion will hardly be contested, is not the second open to grave objections? It is obvious and undeniable that all social wealth is the outcome of human exertion, but is human exertion alone sufficient to create social wealth? Two things, Hodgskin seems to answer to this argument, must necessarily be kept apart : the technical, and the social, production of wealth. Technically speaking, the soil is, of course, a factor of production—but so are all the things which economists are wont to disregard because they are free : technically speaking, land is " like atmospheric air and sunshine . . . one of the material elements indispensable to the production of food.

With them, it gives us food as labour directs the fructifying power that is the result of their combined operation " (*ib.*, 20). But from the social point of view, land is, in the state of nature, which must form the basis of the natural science of economic life, as little an element of costs as wind and light. Before the intervention of human—that is to say : artificial and therefore unnatural—institutions, the powers fixed in the ground were as accessible to everyone as the powers floating in the air. God has given them to men for their use, and only labour is required to make them useful.

What is true of the productive capacity of the soil, is true also of the productive capacities of capital. Its technical contribution to production is undoubted : " Fixed capital consists of the tools and instruments the labourer works with, the machinery he makes and guides, and the buildings he uses either to facilitate his exertions or to protect their produce. Unquestionably by using these instruments man adds wonderfully to his power. Without a hand-saw, a portion of fixed capital, he could not cut a tree into planks ; with such an instrument he could, though it would cost him many hours or days ; but with a saw-mill he could do it in a few minutes. Every man must admit that by means of instruments and machines the labourer can execute tasks he could not possibly perform without them : that he can perform a greater quantity of work in a given time, and that he can perform the work with greater nicety and accuracy than he could possibly do had he no instruments and machines " (*Labour Defended against the Claims of Capital*, 1825, ed. Cole, 1922, 52 sq.).

Yet though capital, as much as land, is certainly a technical, it is as little as land a social, factor of production. If land is a free gift made to men, capital is an unfree tool made by men : " The term Fixed Capital, includes some of the most noble inventions, which are indispensable to the success of labour. Without machines and tools the labourer could perform but few, and those very imperfect operations. . . . Machines, tools, and coals, undoubtedly facilitate labour ; but we must labour to prepare or obtain them. That the labour employed in preparing them facilitates subsequent production, no man can deny ; but when it is admitted that labour produces all things, even capital, it is nonsense to attribute productive power to the instruments labour makes and uses. All capital is made and used by man ; and by leaving him out of view, and ascribing productive power to capital, we take that as the active cause, which is only the creature of his ingenuity, and the passive servant of his will " (*Pol. Ec.*, 246 sq.).

If we translate the technical fact that the collaboration of land and capital enhances the productivity of labour, into the language of sociology, we are led to the statement that man increases his efficacy in producing wealth by subjecting the power of nature to his will. It is socially, i.e., humanly speaking, not the dead matter of the soil, however useful its physical and chemical properties, but the living knowledge and skill of utilizing them, to which the productive contribution of it must be attributed. " Land may be left entirely out of view, but labour, as it becomes enlightened by knowledge, giving birth in the progress of society to exquisite skill, whether employed in draining or cultivating the ground, constructing and using the machinery of manufactures, or anything else, is notoriously more and more productive " (*Ec.*, 1848, 1228). A social analysis of the technical achievement of capital leads to the same result : " After any instruments have been made, what do they effect? Nothing. . . . A ship, for example, is undoubtedly a noble instrument, as admirable and useful a portion of fixed capital as the hand of man ever created, or his skill ever employed. . . . But our navy would lie and rot unless care were taken to preserve it ; and the ships when turned adrift would be bruised by the waves, the winds or the rocks unless they were guided by seamen. . . . To conduct her safely from port to port, and from hemisphere to hemisphere, a great deal of knowledge of the winds and tides, of the phenomena of the heavens, and of the laws which prevail on the surface of the earth, is necessary ; and only when this knowledge is united with great skill, and carried into effect by labour, can a ship be safely conducted through the multitudes of dangers which beset her course. To have and to use this fixed capital, knowledge, labour and skill are necessary. Without these it could not be made, and then it would be less productive than the clod from which its material springs, or from which they are fashioned by the hand of man " (*Lab. Def.*, 58 sq.).

Thus the technical contraption contributes nothing, human ingenuity everything, towards social productivity and its promotion. " *It is not the instruments which grind corn, and spin cotton, but the labour of those who make, and the labour of those who use them. The co-operating labours of the millwright, for example, and the almost numberless other workmen who prepare his tools and the materials, of which the mill is fabricated, or who bring them* from remote parts of the earth—they themselves using very complicated machines for this purpose, which are prepared by the combined labour of a vast number of persons—in the first instance construct the mill ; and then the labour of the miller, assisted also by various instruments . . . which are made by some other labourers, *profiting by the force of the wind, and the natural hardness of the stones*, as compared to the hardness of corn, grinds it, sifts it, and prepares it for the use of the baker. So the united labours of the miner, the smelter, the smith, the engineer, the stoker, and of numberless other persons, and not the lifeless machines, perform whatever is done by steam engines " (*Pol. Ec.*, 250). The steam-engine is, in fact, the prototype of all machinery and capital : " Its vast utility does not depend on stored up iron and wood but on that practical and living knowledge of the powers of nature which enables some men to construct it, and others to guide it " (*Lab. Def.*, 61).

This then is the conclusion to which Thomas Hodgskin finds himself led : there is only one active factor of production—labour. The powers of the external world, embodied in soil and capital, are its servants and not its equals. In the state of nature, the productive contribution of the former is entirely free ; the latter is an element of costs merely in so far as labour was necessary to create it. Therefore, in economic analysis and social doctrine, " we have . . . [only] two species of labour to which it behoves us to attend ; viz. the labour of observing and ascertaining by what means the material world will give us most wealth, and the labour of carrying those means, when ascertained, into execution . . . Beyond observing the laws which regulate the material world [which constitutes mental labour], and carrying those observations into execution by manual labour, there is no other element necessary to produce wealth " (*Pol. Ec.*, 45 sq.).

The whole history of the human race is a living proof of this proposition. The advancement of knowledge, not the increase of capital, is the driving power behind material progress : " Naturally and individually man is one of the most feeble and destitute of all created animals. His intelligence, however, compensates for his physical inferiority. . . . He directs his course on the waters, he floats in the air, he dives into the bowels of the earth, and all which its surface bears he makes tributary to his use. The gales which threaten at first to blow him from the earth, grind his corn, and waft to him a share in the treasures of the whole world. He creates at his pleasure the devouring

c

element of fire, and checks its progress, so that it destroys only what he has no wish to preserve. He directs the course of the stream, and he sets bounds to the ocean ; in short, he presses all the elements into his service, and makes nature herself the hand-maid to his will. The instruments he uses to do all this, which have been invented by his intelligence to aid his feeble powers, and which are employed by his skill and his hands, have been called fixed capital." Yet this is only a word which conceals rather than exposes the agent that has led mankind from hunger to plenty and from savagery to culture : "All those numerous advantages, those benefits to civilization, those vast improve-ments in the condition of the human race, which have been in general attributed to capital, are caused in fact by labour, and by knowledge and skill informing and directing labour." Indeed : "All the benefits attributed to capital arise from co-existing and skilled labour " (*Lab. Def.*, 65 sq., 109, 19).

This sentence, Hodgskin held, contains a theoretical truth as sound, as certain, as undeniable as any statement of the physical sciences. Yet it is gross with the most far-reaching practical implications ; for " the utility of the instruments the labourer uses can in no wise be separated from his skill. Whoever may be the owner of fixed capital—and in the present state of society he who makes it is not, and he who uses it is not—it is the hand and knowledge of the labourer which make it, preserve it from decay, and which use it to any beneficial end " (*Lab. Def.*, 63). Therefore " the principle, that all wealth is the produce of labour . . . is the only safe basis . . . on which the legislator can establish a right of property—if he be at all called on to establish what exists naturally ; it is not only the source of all wealth, but the guide to just distribution, serving at all times to set straight the consciences of individuals when led astray by self-interest, and to rectify the policy of legislators when perverted by false views of expediency " (*Pol. Ec.*, 20 sq.).

This opinion, that labour is the only natural source of value, and therefore the only legitimate foundation of property, finds further support in its natural and legitimate destination : " The object in labouring is to supply the individual's wants. Nature gave him his faculties and powers for this purpose ; for this purpose only, and not for the purpose of supplying the wants of other men whom she equally endowed."

These words, and particularly these last words, clearly show what inferences Hodgskin drew from his theory of value for his doctrine of property : inferences which are, in fact, cogent and necessary. As his theory of value has two aspects, one positive and one negative, so has his doctrine of property. In its positive meaning, it asserts that the principle of private property —of private property as the product of individual exertion—is part and parcel of the great order of the universe. "Property itself, or a man's right to the free use of his own mind and limbs, and to appropriate whatever he creates by his own labour, is the result of natural laws " (*ib.*, 51, 237). On this fundamental conviction, Hodgskin based his political creed : " I look on a right of property—on the right of individuals, to have and to own, for their own separate and selfish use and enjoyment, the produce of their own industry, with power freely to dispose of the whole of that in the manner most agreeable to themselves, as essential to the welfare and even to the continued existence of society. . . . Believing . . . with Mr. Locke, that nature establishes such a right . . ." Hodgskin decidedly rejects the opinion of all " those who vituperate it as the source of all our social misery "—i.e., the socialists (*Right of Property*, 24).

But, as the positive statement that labour is the parent of wealth, is accompanied and supplemented by the negative postulate that the physical forces active in soil and capital goods should not be regarded as sources of value, so the positive statement that rightful property is the offspring of individual toil implies and leads to the negative postulate that the exclusive appropriation of what is a spontaneous gift of nature to all, cannot be acknowledged as legitimate. In developing his idea of natural property, Hodgskin makes it perfectly clear that it can have regard only to the outcome of man's industry and not to the offerings of God's bounty. As labour is the only source of value, so achievement is the only title to property ; before God the artificial monopolization of land and capital goods can give none : in its highest and purest, in its philosophical and social sense, property is in essence the expression of human personality, as distinct from, and opposed to, the productions of elements that are non-human, sub-human or super-human : " By the operations of nature . . . there arises in every individual, unwilled by any lawgiver, a distinct notion of his own individuality and of the individuality of others. By the same operations, we extend this idea, first for ourselves and afterwards for others, to the things we make or create, or have given to us." In this way, " the ideas expressed by the words mine and thine, as applied to the produce of labour, are simply . . . an extended form of the ideas of personal identity and individuality. We readily spread them from our hands and other limbs, to the things the hands seize, or fashion, or create, or the legs hunt down and overtake " (*Right of Property*, 29).

So understood, so confined, the principle of private property (selfish though it may appear at first sight) is in truth social at the same time. Far from being the cause of social disorder, it is the pivot of social order : a spontaneous product of nature, spontaneity is its natural product. By giving to each what is properly his, what is his according to the obvious will of our Maker, it is—when allowed freely to operate—the foundation of understanding and peace among men. " Without the intervention of any law, contract, or agreement between individuals, as to what shall belong to each, Nature produces in each the idea of individuality, which she extends to ownership, by bestowing on each individual, and exclusively, whatever he produces . . . And she begets antecedently to all law an expectation in every one that he shall be able to enjoy what he produces. All the fruits of industry she bestows on industry, and bestows them in proportion commensurate to the labour and skill employed."

What can be imagined more plain, more just, more sacred ? " The relation between labour and its produce . . . or the right of property, as thus explained, seems to me as much a creation of the Deity, as much a part of the universe as the great globe itself, or as the law regulating the course of the seasons. That it is essential to our happiness to regulate our conduct by the latter, clothing ourselves warmer in winter than in summer, and sowing in autumn the seed that is to ripen against the next harvest, no man doubts and it must, I presume, be equally essential to our happiness, to regulate our conduct by the relation which the Almighty has established between labour and its produce. To desire or enforce any other species of appropriation is a presumptuous interference with the laws of nature or of the Deity, not less absurd, or wicked in principle, than to decree a new course to the winds, or a different return of the seasons " (*Right of Property*, 34 sq., 41 sq.). Thus the scientific analysis of what is furnishes the ethical principle of what ought to be : science is not only a store of knowledge but also a guide to action. Its findings can and should decide the worth or worthlessness, the preservation or abolition, of all existing institutions.

The state of nature then, or, what comes to the same, the ideal

order of things, is a society in which the treasures of the earth are
everybody's for the taking : a society in which labour is the
only source of income, and achievement the only measure of
riches. Alas ! reality shows a very different picture : "Nature
or God, whichever the reader pleases, for the two words signify
the same everliving First Cause, commands, and always has
commanded, that industry should be followed by wealth, and
idleness by destitution. But political society is formed on the
principle of violating this command " (*Right of Property*, 57).
It is not difficult to find striking proof of this melancholy assertion.
Take the best example : the distribution and appropriation of
the soil. " The [natural] right to own land is in fact only the
right to own what agricultural or other labour produces." Yet
to-day " the mere land-owner is not a labourer. . . . He never
has been even fed but by violating the natural right of property."
Nevertheless " his right to possess the land, not to possess the
produce of his own labour, is as admirably protected as can be
effected by the law " (*ib.*, 36, 51 sq.).

How could it ever happen, it must be asked, that positive law
became so widely divorced from law divine ? Hodgskin based
his answer to this question on the doctrine of Saint-Simon, so
influential in contemporary France : there is, he taught, a fact
of history which destroyed the original order of happiness and
established the actual order of misery : the barbarian invasions
of the Dark Ages. Great and unfortunate wars divided mankind
into conquerors and conquered, masters and slaves, and from
the antagonism thus created between hostile nations sprang the
later antagonism between hostile classes.   Such was the origin
of the present artificial order of society, the present un-natural
distribution of wealth and incomes. " Labourers are . . . unfortunate in being descended from bondsmen and serves. Personal slavery and villanage formerly existed in Britain, and all
the living labourers still suffer from the bondage of their ancestors. . . . Without adverting to what we produce, which
seems the only criterion by which we ought to be paid, we are
instantly condemned as insolent and ungrateful if we ask for
more than was enjoyed by the slave of former times " (*Lab. Def.*,
22).

Yet, is it not false to charge our social constitution with the
existing inequality of wealth and income-distribution ? Are not
facts of nature its real foundation ? Has it not been proved, and
proved conclusively, by Ricardo, that the phenomenon of rent

arises from physical differences of fertility in different classes of
soil ? It is true, Hodgskin admits, that a part of what the landlord receives from his tenant can be characterized as differential
rent—a part, but by no means all ! The main ingredient of
the landowner's income is absolute rent : absolute rent which,
in the last analysis, is nothing but the old tribute of the conquered
Gaul or Saxon to the conquering Frank or Norman, transfigured
and transformed. " There can be no doubt . . . that diversities
of soil, and the necessity, as population increases, to have recourse
to poorer soils, are natural circumstances, influencing the increase of rent ; but neither can there be any doubt that the
appropriation of the soil of Europe by the sword, and the adapta-
tion of the institutions of Europe to enforce and maintain that
rude appropriation, was the original cause of rent " (*Ec.*, 1848,
604). One need not go far back through the centuries to find
convincing illustration : " Walter Scott has, in a graphic passage
in the *Heart of Mid-Lothian*, described the gradual conversion of a
great number of feudal exactions into money rent ; evidence of
such conversion is to be found in almost every page of history,
leaving no doubt whatever that the origin of rent was the ancient
appropriation of man with the soil " (*Ec.*, 1848, 1228).

To-day, not he who monopolized the soil but he who possesses
machinery holds the better part of the nation's wealth and receives the lion's share in the distribution of the social product :
yet his claim is not better. The capitalist profit rests on, and
springs from, the same fundamental fact as did the feudal
exactions. " Capitalists . . . have . . . reduced the ancient
tyrant of the soil to comparative insignificance, while they have
inherited his power over all the labouring classes. It is, therefore, now time that the reproaches so long cast on the feudal
aristocracy should be heaped on capital and capitalists ; or on
that still more oppressive aristocracy which is founded on wealth,
and which is nourished by profit." Do you require proof for the
contention that surplus-value is due, not to natural reasons, but
to artificial institutions ? Here it is : " The warmest admirers
of circulating capital will not pretend that it adds in the same
way as fixed capital to the productive power of the labourer. . . .
The degree and nature of the utility of both species of capital is
perfectly different and distinct. The labourer subsists on what
is called circulating capital ; he works with fixed capital. But
equal quantities or equal values of both these species of capital
bring their owner precisely the same amount of profit. We may,

from this single circumstance, be quite sure that the share claimed by the capitalist for the use of fixed capital is not derived from the instruments increasing the efficacy of labour ; or from the utility of these instruments ; and profit is derived in both cases from the power which the capitalist has over the labourer who consumes the circulating, and who uses the fixed capital. . . . This power . . . is derived from the whole surface of the country having been at one period monopolized by a few persons ; and the consequent state of slavery in which the labourer formerly existed in this country, as well as throughout Europe " (*Lab. Def.*, 67, 69–71).

These last words describe the essence of the social revolution wrought by the barbarian conquerors of Europe whose offspring are the capitalists and landlords of to-day : it consisted in the fact that " the whole surface of the country " was " monopolized by a few persons "—the whole surface of the country including what is above and what is below it : the treasures of the soil and the powers of the air : in short all the physical means of production which God and Nature gave to all men in common and to no man in particular. Formerly " it has been generally supposed that the whole world was given to the human race, with dominion over all other created things, for them to use and enjoy in every way, abstaining from nothing—restricted in nothing consistent with their own happiness—bound mutually to share the blessings provided for them, because mutual assistance begets mutual love—supplies physical wants easier and better, and promotes moral and intellectual improvement ;—that the rights and duties of men grow out of the great scheme of creation, which is sometimes misinterpreted, and rarely understood, by human sagacity—sometimes marred, and never mended, by human wisdom. But now . . . that we may find an apology for our own infirm and base submission, we must believe that men had naturally no right to pick up cockles on the beach, or gather berries from the hedge—no right to cultivate the earth, to invent and make comfortable clothing, to use instruments to provide more easily for their enjoyments—no right to improve and adorn their habitations—nay, no right to have habitations—no right to buy or sell, or move from place to place—till the benevolent and wise lawgiver conferred all these rights on them " (*Right of Property*, 19 sq.). Yet " many of the [positive] laws for the protection of property [of property in the spontaneous offerings of nature] had no better origin than game laws. They were intended to repress in the multitude actions of which the few set them the example. . . . There is no crime in ensnaring or shooting wild birds or animals. It is a primitive mode of obtaining subsistence common in the early ages to every people. . . . But, from their selfishness, or from pride, or from anger, that other men should interfere with their sport, the upper classes . . . make ensnaring wild animals and birds a crime, and punish it very severely. . . . The ancient usurpations of feudal chieftains were, and continue to be, hedged round by penal laws, which have never in like manner protected the [natural] property of the labourer " (*Ec.*, 1847, 836 sq.).

Indeed, the preservation and perpetuation of those original usurpations centring around the exclusive appropriation of the physical means of production is the essential purpose of the political organization, which, under the name of the state, the barbarian conquerors set up in defiance and for the destruction of the natural order of things : " The persons who appropriated the soil of Europe, did so by a right of conquest. . . . In appropriating the soil, they appropriated its inhabitants. . . . Power so acquired, and privileges so established, were the basis of the present political and legal edifice of Europe. These conquerors were the first legislators. By an almost uninterrupted succession, the power of legislation has continued in the hands of their descendants to the present day." So it is only a matter of course that " the great object of law and of government has been and is, to establish and protect a violation of that natural right of property they are described in theory as being intended to guarantee ". In fact, " the landed aristocracy and the government are one—the latter being nothing more than the organized means of preserving the power and privileges of the former ". As to " the capitalists ", they " have in general formed a most intimate union with the landowners " (*Right of Property*, 72 sq., 48 sq.).

Yet, state and law not only serve to protect the original but help to perpetrate ever new usurpations. The form has changed, it is true, but not the matter : masked exploitation has replaced open expropriation, but the difference between them is not a difference in essence : " A regular compact has here [in Britain] been entered into between the peaceable flock and the wolves, and the latter receiving a stated, and as large a quantity of the whole as they can possibly exact, promise to allow the remainder to fatten in peace and tranquillity. . . . They have ceased making open war on the flock, and only privately in the guise of shepherds, take as much as they can without terrifying and revolting the peaceable industrious people." In feudal times, the military power of the lord compelled the serf to submit to plunder. "The right of property . . . is now arming the landowner and the capitalist against the peasant and the artisan" (*ib.*, 132, 15).

In other words : state and law not only enforce an unnatural distribution of wealth but also an unnatural distribution of incomes. The same force-begotten institutions which bar the labourer from the treasures of the soil and the powers of the air, rob him also of the enjoyment of the full produce of his labour : "The power of making laws was long vested in those—and still is vested in their descendants—who followed no trade but war, and knew no handicraft but robbery and plunder." So "the law has always been, and is at present made, by men who are not labourers. It is actually made by those who derive from nature no title whatever to any wealth. But as law in fact is only a general name for the will of the law-maker, being the expression of his desire to have wealth, and retain power and dominion, it is clear that in making laws for the appropriation of property, he will not, consistently with nature, give to every one what he produces." On the contrary : "The law, to preserve which is said to be the first duty of communities, as to preserve life is that of individuals, is a set of rules and practices . . . intended to appropriate to the law-makers the produce of those who cultivate the soil, prepare clothing, or distribute what is produced among the different classes, and among different communities" (*ib.*, 32, 46 sq.).

Yet, enough of the colourful declamations ! Enough of the emphatic assertions ! Let us come to proof and demonstration ! In what manner, by what mechanism, have the positive, usurping place and power of the natural, laws changed the process of pricing and distribution ? In the state of nature, this is clear, where the treasures of the soil and the forces of the air are free, not monopolized, goods, where neither the one nor the other represents an element of costs, the value of commodities which forms the basis of incomes, is determined by labour alone. "As all commodities are exclusively the produce of labour, there is no other [natural] rule, and can be no other [natural] rule, for determining their relative value to each other, but the quantity of labour required to produce each and all of them . . . Natural or necessary price means . . . the whole quantity of labour nature requires from man, that he may produce any commodity. . . . Nature exacted nothing but labour in time past, she demands only labour at present, and she will require merely labour in all future time. Labour was the original, is now and ever will be the only purchase money in dealing with Nature " (*Pol. Ec.*, 185, 219 sq.).

The employment of machinery, the participation of capital in the process of production, cannot, by itself, produce any essential change. Machines are contrivances which serve to replace human exertion by natural agencies. In so far as they are products of labour, they represent, of course, an element of costs ; yet the co-operation of the physical forces which they bring about, is, under natural conditions, gratis. Now, it is obvious that every piece of fixed capital saves more labour (i.e., costs) when it is used, than it absorbs while it is being created : otherwise it would not pay to introduce it. What machinery and capital do (and all they do) is therefore to decrease *per saldo* the amount of labour, i.e., the amount of costs, required to bring forth a certain commodity ; even positive experience can prove this : " The successive improvements introduced into the manufacture of all metallic articles and most articles of clothing within the last century, having diminished the quantity of labour necessary to produce them, they have all fallen in value." Where capital co-operates, the value of an article is made up, it is true, of two elements : the labour directly, and the labour indirectly— through machinery—expended in its production : but both elements consist of labour, and so—where there is no monopoly in the physical means of production—the old formula remains true. " The natural or necessary price of commodities is only influenced by all those circumstances which make labour more or less productive " (*ib.*, 187, 233).

Since the laws of pricing are at the same time the principles of distribution, incomes, too, are, under natural conditions, exclusively regulated by labour : where artificial men-made laws have not interfered, a man's earnings are in proportion to his achievement ; if his productive power increases, because he has compelled the elements of soil and air to work with, or for, him, all that can naturally happen is that nominal prices fall, or, what comes to the same, real incomes rise. In the state of nature therefore labour is not only the sole determinant of prices but also the only title to income : he who does not work must starve.

In our artificial society this is not so : there are many who do not work and yet do not starve. "But how do those who do not labour pay for what they consume? All wealth, including gold and silver, is the produce of labour ; and those who do not labour cannot have any thing to pay their tradesmen with, which is not the produce of labour. They therefore obtain, having, in fact, a legal right to receive, the produce of some labourers, and this is what they give their tradesmen. But if they had no claim over this produce, the labourers would have so much the more . . ." (*Pol. Ec.*, 117).

Indeed, if they had no such claim, the labourers would have all : and this is what the law of nature ordains they should have. But the laws of society rule it otherwise : "The real price of a coat or a pair of shoes or a loaf of bread, all which nature demands from man in order that he may have either of these very useful articles, is a certain quantity of labour. . . . But for the labourer to have either of these articles he must give over and above the quantity of labour nature demands from him, a still larger quantity to the capitalist" (*Lab. Def.*, 75) who holds the raw materials and tools without which no labour, not even the most enlightened and most skilled, can maintain the labourer.

However, the capitalist must have some sort of claim to this "still larger quantity"—be it only an artificial one. What is his claim? Wherein does it consist? It is based on the un-natural appropriation of the powers of soil and air by the bar-barian conquerors and their descendants. Before the conquest the labourer received the full produce of his labour ; since the conquest his income has never increased, although his productivity has tremendously expanded through the constant subjugation and utilization of physical forces. It has never increased because all the increase due to technical progress has been—by means of their monopoly in the objective means of production—forcibly seized by the masters of society to whose claims, however extrav-agant they may be, the labourer has to submit because, by with-holding the raw materials and tools which alone make his labour useful and productive they can starve him into submission : "By our increased skill and knowledge labour is now probably ten times more productive than it was two hundred years ago ; and we are, forsooth, to be contented with the same rewards which the bondsman then received. All the advantages of our improvements go to the capitalist and the landlord" (*Lab. Def.*, 22 sq.). They go to the capitalist and the landlord because the artificial laws of society have set a price on, and allot an income to, what has neither price nor income according to the natural laws of the creation : the germinating power of the clod and the driving energy of the wind. " The accuracy of Dr. Smith's remarks on the beneficial effects of division of labour, must be perceptible to every man. . . . It is however indispensable to remark, that all the benefits of this practice naturally centre in the labourer ; belong to him, and contribute to his ease or add to his opulence. It increases *his* skill, by allowing his attention to be uninterruptedly fixed on a single operation ; it saves *his* time, by making no change of tools or of employment necessary ; and it facilitates *his* invention of those machines that are adapted to the single and simple operations, which, in consequence of division of labour, constitute the whole task of each individual. . . . But as all the advantages derived from division of labour naturally centre in, and naturally belong to the labourers, if they are deprived of them, and in the progress of society those only are enriched by their improved skill who never labour—this must arise from unjust appropriation ; from usurpation and plunder in the party enriched, and from consenting submission in the party impoverished " (*Pol. Ec.*, 107–109).

This theory of exploitation—a theory consistent in itself once its natural (we should almost say : theological) starting-point is accepted or admitted—stands in striking contrast to Ricardo's theory of distribution, and still both doctrines claim to be logical developments from, and intellectual improvements on, Adam Smith's labour theory of value. How can their opposition be explained ? It sprang from the fact that Hodgskin developed the social, Ricardo the technical implications of Smith's teachings. " In that early and rude state of society which precedes both the accumulation of stock and the appropriation of land, the proportion between the quantities of labour necessary for acquiring different objects seems to be the only circumstance which can afford any rule for exchanging them for one another ", the *Wealth of Nations* (ed. Cannan, 1904, 49, 66 sq.) had taught. Therefore " in that original state of things . . . the whole produce of labour belongs to the labourer ", and, " had this state continued, the wages of labour would have augmented with all those improvements in its productive powers, to which the division of labour gives occasion ". Yet " this original state of things, in which the labourer enjoyed the whole produce of his own labour, could not last beyond the first introduction of the appropriation of land **and** the accumulation of stock. . . .   As soon as land becomes private property, the landlord demands a share. . . .   Profit makes a second deduction " from the natural income of the worker, or, what comes to the same thing, a second addition to the natural price of the commodity.

This argument of Smith offers a key both to a technical explanation of the phenomenon of prices, and to a social critique of the distribution of incomes.   While Hodgskin made use of the latter, Ricardo availed himself of the former, perfecting it by the exclusion of the two " deductions " or " additions "—of rent as a differential, and of profit as a residual, income—as factors in the formation of prices.   Yet was this really a perfection ?   Only in a technical, not in a higher, sense, because by neutralizing rent and profit as elements of costs, Ricardo has excluded the social problem from economic theory and thus made it unrealistic :   " Mr. Ricardo is logically most accurate in ascribing, throughout, according to Smith's own doctrine, ' of labour paying all price,' every variation in price ultimately to variation in quantities of labour.   We must, however, say, that, in one sense, Smith's verbal variation from his own principle [i.e., the description of rent and profit as elements of costs] serves better to explain some social phenomena than Mr. Ricardo's technical adherence to it.   Clearly the increase of price which Smith indicated to be caused by rent and profit, meant the increase of labour, which the labourer, who originally possessed [what] the whole community produced, had to give for the same, or an equal commodity, when he, not other men, not certainly the capitalists and the land-lords, had to pay profit and rent, or share that commodity with others.   Substituting labourer for labour, in Smith's doctrine, it is a truer representation of what actually occurs in society than Mr. Ricardo's, which, after all, is of comparatively little import-ance, because it is limited entirely to the exchangeable variations in the value of commodities, and takes no notice of the exchange between the different classes of labourers, capitalists, and land-owners, which it was partly Smith's object to explain.   Admitting the greater verbal or logical accuracy of Mr. Ricardo, it was obtained, we apprehend, by shutting entirely out of his science those important relations of the labourer to other classes, which Smith, by a change in his terms, really discussed " (The Economist, 1846, 1557).

In the same vein Hodgskin, in a letter to Francis Place of May 28, 1820, described as the greatest fault of the Principles of

Political Economy "the want of an accurate distinction between natural price and exchangeable value. Natural price is measured by the quantity of labour necessary to produce any commodity ; its exchangeable value, or what another will give, or is obliged to give, for this commodity when produced, may or may not be equal to the quantity of labour employed in its production. Mr. Ricardo has, I think, made a mistake by supposing these two things to be equal. They are not, or the wages of labour would always be equal to the produce of labour. It requires, for instance, a certain portion of labour to produce a quarter of corn. This quarter of corn, however, when produced, and in the possession of a man who is at the same time both landlord and farmer, will at present exchange for a prodigious deal greater quantity of labour than it cost to produce it. There is, therefore, a great difference between real natural price and exchangeable value " (cit. Graham Wallas, *The Life of Francis Place*, 1898, 267). The difference between them is the difference between natural and actual society, between the Ought and the Is, between social justice and economic exploitation, or, to speak more soberly and still in Hodgskin's vein, between freedom and monopolization of the physical means of production, for where the physical means of production are free there is only one element of costs and consequently only one class that receives the whole social product, while where they are monopolized, capital and land appear as additional claimants, and labour has to share the national income with them.

How can it be explained that the great economists who came after Smith were not sensible of this truth ? They failed to distinguish between natural conditions and man-made institutions, regarding both as equally necessary and lasting : "These philosophers [Malthus and Ricardo] did not confine their researches to the law of population, to human nature and its attributes . . . which comprise all the phenomena to be considered . . . but . . . they left man . . . and passed to some certain qualities in a *monopolized soil*, which they called fertility, and from that shaped out laws for the progress of man in society " (*Ec.*, 1854, 1269). Indeed, "Political Economists . . . describe as a natural phenomenon the present distribution of wealth ; though it is in all its parts a palpable violation of that natural law which gives wealth to labour and to labour only. . . . They stop short of first principles, and draw conclusions when they are acquainted with only half the circumstances on which a correct opinion can be founded " (*Pol. Ec.*, 267 sq.). Yet, " without including property in the discussion, the great natural science, miscalled political economy, of the application of industry to produce and distribute wealth, can never be fairly nor fully treated " (*Ec.*, 1855, 371). On the contrary, " the whole doctrines of the distribution of wealth, embracing all that can be said about rent, profit, and wages, depend altogether on the right of property. I defy any man to explain either of those without assuming, as the basis of his argument, the present legal right of property, and I am sure that no man can be acquainted with the modern doctrines on these subjects, without being thoroughly sensible, that, by assuming the present legal right of property to be the natural right, the whole of those doctrines are founded on a false basis, and give a false notion of the natural laws which regulate the progress of society " (*Right of Property*, 171).

Let us, in order to prove that the present distribution of income rests on force and force alone, investigate the two most essential points of detail : the formation of profits, and the formation of wages. Profits, and especially interest, the orthodox economists hold, are justified because they are the natural reward of a necessary achievement, abstinence from consumption, or saving. Yet " it is a miserable delusion to call capital something saved. Much of it is not calculated for consumption, and never is made to be enjoyed. When a savage wants food, he picks up what nature spontaneously offers. After a time he discovers that a bow or a sling will enable him to kill wild animals at a distance, and he resolves to make it, subsisting himself, as he must do, while the work is in progress. He saves nothing, for the instrument never was made to be consumed, though in its own nature it is more durable than deer's flesh. This example represents what occurs at every stage of society, except that the different labours are performed by different persons—one making the bow, or the plough, and another killing the animal or tilling the ground, to provide subsistence for the makers of instruments and machines. To store up or save commodities, except for short periods, and in some particular cases, can only be done by more labour " [1] (*Pol. Ec.*, 255 sq.). Labour, therefore, and not saving, is the source of capital.

---

[1] In the course of this discussion Hodgskin shows that the idea of a wages-fund is unsound, and this is perhaps his best contribution to economic science in the narrow and technical sense of the word : " The real wages of the labourer do not consist in money, but what the money buys," he writes (*Pol. Ec.*, 247). " When a capitalist therefore, who owns a brew-house and all the instruments and materials requisite for

Hence it follows that " fixed capital . . . does not bring its owner a profit because it has been stored up ". It yields an income, Hodgskin maintains, " because it is a means of obtaining a command over labour " (*Lab. Def.*, 55). We may use an example to make this clear : " A road is made by a certain quantity of labour, and is then called fixed capital. . . . The road facilitates the progress of the traveller, and just in proportion as people do travel over it, so does the labour which has been employed on the road become productive and useful. One easily comprehends . . . why the roadmaker should receive some of the benefits accruing only to the road-user ; but I do not comprehend why all these benefits should go to the road itself and be appropriated by a set of persons who neither make nor use it, under the name of profit for their capital " (*ib.*, 59 sq.). In other words : that the labour spent in building the road must be paid, is a matter of course. But if the labour saved by using this piece of capital is greater than the labour spent in its production, to what cause is this due ? Simply to the physical fact that a smooth surface offers less resistance to the locomotion of heavy bodies than a rough one. Yet whose merit is this ? Nobody's ! So who should be paid for it ? Nobody, indeed—but the capitalist is, in fact, being paid for it, because, by forcible means, he has succeeded in usurping an exclusive right in the utilization of the physical fact in question—an exclusive right which he sells piecemeal to those who stand in need of his capital, although he has not given anything in acquiring it.

Now, what is true of the road is true of all machinery. Instruments and tools " are made only for the use of the labourer, and directly they come into his hands they return or repay the capitalist the sum they cost him ; and [still], over and above this the labourer must give him an additional sum corresponding to the rate of profit in the country " (*Lab. Def.*, 54 sq.). Therefore " capital seems to mean, when ultimately analysed, little more than, or be very little different from, the power of one man, however obtained, over the labour or produce of the labour of another " (*Ec.*, 1854, 1454). Thus Hodgskin believes he has

---

making porter, pays the actual brewers with the coin he has received for his beer, and they buy bread, while the journeymen bakers buy porter with their money wages, which is afterwards paid to the owner of the brew-house, is it not plain that the real wages of both these parties consist of the produce of the other ; or that the bread made by the journeyman baker pays for the porter made by the journeyman brewer ? But the same is the case with all other commodities, and labour, not capital "— current labour, not hoarded capital—" pays all wages ". Cf. also *Labour Defended*, ed. Cole, 1922, 38–52.

proved the thesis put forward in his first publication : " The landlord and the capitalist produce nothing. Capital is the produce of labour, and profit is nothing but a portion of that produce, uncharitably exacted for permitting the labourer to consume a part of what he has himself produced " (*Travels in the North of Germany*, 1820, II, 97).

Since this is so, a special theory of wages seems superfluous. The labourers receive what is left of the social product after the ruling classes have subtracted their part : " Wages vary inversely as profits ; or wages rise when profits fall, and profits rise when wages fall ; and it is therefore profits, or the capitalist's share of the national produce, which is opposed to wages, or the share of the labourer " (*Lab. Def.*, 27. sq.) [1]. The only question which remains is the question of measure. How much do the capitalists engross, and how much do they leave for the working men ? But even here the answer is obvious : the capitalists will take as much as they can and give to the working men as little as possible : " The capitalist must allow the labourer to subsist, and as long as his claims are granted and acted on he will never allow him to do more " (*ib.*, 77).

This, then, is the truth about capitalist distribution : " The labourers do only receive, and ever have only received, as much as will subsist them, the landlords receive the surplus produce of the more fertile soils, and all the rest of the whole produce of labour in this and in every country goes to the capitalist under the name of profit for the use of his capital. Capital . . . thus engrosses the whole produce of a country, except the bare subsistence of the labourer, and the surplus produce of fertile land " (*Lab. Def.*, 31).[2] " We may distinguish ", Hodgskin explains,

[1] When Hodgskin grew older, he considerably modified his views. It was especially this doctrine, the doctrine of a necessary opposition of interests between capitalists and workmen, which he abandoned. The following quotation shows how near he came to the opinion of such writers as Bastiat, who believed in a necessary harmony of interests : " Mr. Ricardo . . . puts the wages of the labourer and the profits of the capitalist in opposition, and regards the one as a deduction from the other. These are fatal errors. We are now fully satisfied by experience that the invention of machinery and the use of canals and railroads raises profits, though they may, after a season, gravitate again to zero, and we know from experience that the same causes raise the rate of wages, and that capitalists and labourers may both get more and become better provided for by means of an improvement in productive power, which Mr. Ricardo denies " (*Ec.*, 1846, 1558). Similarly, while in 1825, in his *Labour Defended against the Claims of Capital*, he had advocated trade-unions as appropriate weapons in the struggle for higher wages, he wrote in 1854 in *The Economist* (459) : " Interference between capital and labour by Communists, Socialists, and combinations—they are all evil ".

[2] This passage reveals that Hodgskin was not quite sure of his theory. Two inconsistencies are obvious : firstly, with regard to the relation of wages and profits. While he suggests in some connections that the worker's income is still the same as the

systematically surveying the conceivable possibilities, " three classes of circumstances under which the effects of an accumulation of capital will be very different. First, if it be made and used by the same persons ; second, if it be made and used by different classes of persons, who share between them in just proportion the produce of their combined labour ; third, if it be owned by a class of persons who neither make nor use it " (*Pol. Ec.*, 243). The first case is the case of primitive society ; the second case is the case of a developed society with division of labour, as it would have emerged, had not force intervened ; the third case is the case of class society as it has been created by the barbarian invasions :

" First. If the instruments . . . intended to promote production be made and used by one and the same individual, we are bound to suppose that he finds these labours advantageous, or he would not perform them ; and that every accumulation in his possession of the instruments he makes and uses, facilitates his labour. . . . When capital, therefore, is made and used by the same persons, when all which they produce belongs to themselves, too much cannot be said in its favour " (*Pol. Ec.*, 243 sq.).

" Second. Capital may be made by one labourer and used by another, and both may divide the commodity obtained by the labour of making and of using the capital between them, in proportion as each has contributed by his labour to produce it. He who makes the capital finds this employment productive to him, or he would not continue it ; and he who uses the capital finds that it assists his labour, or he would give nothing for it. Under these circumstances, the accumulation and employment of capital is advantageous. . . . As long as the produce of the two labourers—and speaking of society, of the two classes of labourers —be divided between them, the accumulation or increase of such instruments as they can make and use, is as beneficial as if they were made and used by one person " (*Pol. Ec.*, 244). For, surely, " he who makes the instruments is entitled . . . in proportion to the labour he employs, to as great a reward as he who

income of the average Saxon or Gaul of pre-conquest days, in others he seems to assume that it is determined by the—physical or cultural—minimum of subsistence. Yet these two things are not the same ; secondly, with regard to the relation of profits to rent. On the one hand he states that the better part of the landlord's income is absolute, not differential, rent, on the other he expresses the view that the whole result of exploitation but differential rent is pocketed by the capitalists. These flaws in Hodgskin's system are, however, of comparatively small importance. Had he ever had leisure enough to develop his theories more systematically (he longed to do so all his life) he could have easily removed such blemishes.

uses them ; [only] . . . he who neither makes nor uses them has no just claim to any portion of the produce " (*Lab. Def.*, 71).

While these two forms of social production are equally beneficial to all that take part in it, the same cannot be said of the " Third. One labourer may produce or make the instruments which another uses to assist production—not mutually to share in just proportions the produce of their co-operating labour, but for the profit of a third party. The capitalist being the mere owner of the instruments, is not, as such, a labourer. He in no manner assists production . . ., He employs or lends his property to share the produce, or natural revenue, of labourers ; and every accumulation of such property in his hands is a mere extension of his power over the produce of labour, and retards the progress of national wealth. In this which is at present the case, the labourers must share their produce with unproductive idlers, and to that extent less of the annual produce is employed in reproduction " (*Pol. Ec.*, 245).

Yet, the spoliation of the working class is by no means the only dismal result of the monopolization of the physical means of production. Capitalism is not only socially unjust but also economically vicious : vicious in so far as it is indissolubly connected with the trade cycle—the regularly recurring cycle from order to chaos and happiness to misery. " To our legal right of property we are indebted for those gleams of false wealth and real panic, which, within the last fifty years, have so frequently shook, to its centre, the whole trading world " (*Right of Property*, 156). Say's optimistic and apologetic *théorie des débouchés* is not true : " It is a maxim with political economists, that products always create their own market ; but this maxim is derived from the supposition that no man produces but with the intention of selling or enjoying, and it does not therefore hold good with our labourers who are compelled to produce but are not permitted to enjoy. . . . Dearth and famine were formerly the evils nations had to dread, but since a means has been found of muzzling the labouring classes while they are goaded on in the great work of production, the earth has become encumbered with the fruits of their exertions. Plenty of corn, and an abundance of cloth, are now the ruin of a country ! " (The Spitalfields Acts, *Mechanic's Magazine*, Sept. 6, 1823). How could it be otherwise ? " The wants of individuals which labour is intended to gratify, are the natural guide to their exertions. The instant they are compelled to labour for others, this guide forsakes them, and their exertions are dictated by the greed and avarice and false hopes of their masters. The wants springing from our organization, and accompanying the power to labour, being created by the same hand which creates and fashions the whole universe . . . it is fair to suppose that they would at all times guide the exertions of the labourer, so as fully to ensure a supply of necessaries and conveniences, and nothing more. They have, as it were, a prototype in nature, agreeing with other phenomena, but the avarice and greed of masters have no such prototype. . . . Nature disowns them as a guide to action, and punishes us for following them. By this system the hand is dissevered from the mouth . . ." (*Right of Property*, 155), while " in the system of nature, mouths are united with hands and with intelligence " (*Lab. Def.*, 108). Therefore, in the spontaneous system of nature, there reigns harmony and order, in the artificial system of class-society dis-harmony both social and economic.[1]

However, not even the constant poverty of the working classes and the recurring depressions of economic activity are the only evils springing from the forcible appropriation of the physical means of production by the barbarian conquerors and their des-cendants. " Laws and constitutions, political organization alto-gether, being founded on a violation of the natural right of prop-erty, is the source of most, if not all the evils, moral and physical, which yet afflict our race " (*Right of Property*, 57). Does not the most important department of social pathology furnish conclusive truth of this all-important fact ? " Somewhat more than four-fifths of all the crimes punished by the laws of Europe are viola-tions of the artificial right of property " (*Travels*, II, 68).

Thus the happiness and misery of mankind depend entirely on the preservation or abolition of the artificial, force-begotten and force-defended, monopoly in the powers of soil and air : " The contest now going on in society, the preternatural throes and heavings which frightfully convulse it from one end to the other, arise exclusively and altogether from the right of property, and can be neither understood nor relieved, but by attending to the great distinction . . . between the natural and the legal right of property " (*Right of Property*, I). Yet—and this is the crux of the matter—is there a way from distribution as it is, to distribution as

---

[1] In a later context (the critique of Lalor's *Money and Morals, Ec.*, 1852, 796) Hodgskin described as the cause of economic crises not only " improper and erroneous relations of property " but also " bad governments " and " times of war "—hence, exogenous besides indigenous factors ; yet this does not change his fundamental thesis that the phenomenon of the trade cycle has " an artificial origin ".

it ought to be ? This vital question, Hodgskin unhesitatingly answered in the affirmative.

It is the change in the past from the natural to the artificial order of society which shows the way to the future change from the artificial back to the natural system. What has been done by the Norman and Frankish conquerors of England and Gaul must be undone : the instrument which established and perpetuates their rule, must be destroyed. This instrument, it is plain, we perceive in the law : in those man-made commands which, secured by brute force, have, since the invasions, replaced the God-given ordinances which spontaneously reigned before. For " the object of the law, generally speaking, has been, and is, to prevent the natural principles from which the rule of appropriation is deduced, from coming into full operation " (*Right of Property*, 68). And, indeed, it could not be otherwise. It is a matter of course that the triumphant barbarians used their power to protect what they had acquired : " The inherent and undeniable desire in all men to secure and promote their own welfare [naturally] induces those who have the making of laws . . . to make them for their own advantage. . . . The whole of our penal legislation which relates to property is [therefore] intended to protect the peculiar property of one portion of the community [the possessing classes] from the assaults of the other [the dispossessed]. . . . In other words, our penal jurisprudence, so far as property is concerned, is a species of class legislation " (*Ec.*, 1856, 982).

Yet not only class legislation but all legislation would to-day necessarily tend to preserve the artificial distribution of fortunes and incomes which robs the have-nots of society of part of what is theirs. The great mission of the law, the defence of peace and order, can only be achieved if social struggles are quelled and social changes prevented. Thus " the legislator . . . always aims at preserving the institutions of a past age " (*Right of Property*, 2). Penal jurisprudence which " may be truly said to lie at the foundation of all political power " because " punishment is relied on to enforce obedience to law " (*Ec.*, 1856, 448), proves this beyond all doubt : " In all States of antiquity and the middle ages, slavery prevailed in Europe, and the principles of our penal legislation were adopted in, and adapted to, such a condition of society. . . . We have inherited the laws of our ancestors, and continue to act on the principles they acted on, though our cir-

cumstances are different and our knowledge much enlarged "
(*Ec.*, 1855, 1428). Nor is this all : for even if we abstract for a
moment from the fact that the possessing classes hold the power
of legislation, and that the law, by its very function, is bound to
be conservative, we see that it is not the interest of the people, but
always an interest opposed to that of the people, which inspires
all legislative measures : " When we inquire, casting aside all
theories and suppositions, into the end kept in view by legislators,
or examine any existing laws, we find that the first and chief
object proposed is to preserve the unconstrained dominion of the
law over the minds and bodies of mankind. . . . Perish the
people, but let the law live, has ever been the maxim of the
masters of mankind " (*Right of Property*, 44 sq.).

This anti-legislative, truly anarchist attitude reveals one of
Hodgskin's fundamental axioms. It overruled in his mind all
other considerations : " Men had better be without education
than be educated by their rulers," he says (to quote but one
example), " for then education is . . . the mere breaking in of
the steer to the yoke ; the mere discipline of a hunting dog, which,
by dint of severity, is made to forego the strongest impulse of his
nature, and instead of devouring his prey, to hasten with it to the
feet of his master " (*Mechanic's Magazine*, Oct. 11, 1823). " The
education of a free people, like their property, will always be
directed most beneficially for them when it is in their own hands.
When government interferes, it directs its efforts more to make
people obedient and docile, than wise and happy."

The basis of Hodgskin's theory of the state is liberal, in the
sense of economic liberalism, but the conclusions which he draws
from it are anarchist, in the sense of political anarchism :
" Government, as such, produces nothing," he says (*Right of
Property*, 50). " The hand of the artisan, while he is fed, produces
more value than his food ; the hand of the policeman produces
nothing, and he must be fed by rates levied on the people. What
is true of the policeman is true of all the administrators of the
law " (*Ec.*, 1846, 660 sq.). " It is certain that every policeman
must be paid from the produce of the labourer, and because his
occupation is disgraceful, he must be well paid, and in proportion
as a police is numerous, so is the labourer reduced to poverty ;
the inequality of his condition is farther augmented, and this
causes more crimes than the best organized police can suppress."
Thus, the police are not only useless but even harmful. In any
case they are superfluous : " Probably all the now hateful duties

of a police might be better performed by the individuals of the society taking on themselves, as every man now partially does, the duty of learning what his neighbour's conduct is, and speaking of it freely and openly, and treating him according to his behaviour " (*Travels*, I, 333, 73). Indeed, not even the right of property needs public protection " on account of its being at all tin.es more difficult to take from one another than for each to make for himself " (*Right of Property*, 145). And a system of civil laws is just as senseless as a system of public institutions : only think of the law of inheritance and succession ! " All . . . general regulations, however apparently wise, can never equal individual wisdom in judging of all the different circumstances which ought to influence its decision in the disposal of its property, nor supply its place when it may chance to fail " (*Travels*, I, 262 ; cf. also II, 152).

From this point of view every act of the state, however harmless it might seem in itself, must appear as a gross violation of common sense and common liberty : " The regulations of the police . . . oblige every man to notice every alteration in his family to it. When a child is born to him, or one dies, or he brings home a wife, or discards a mistress, he must give official notice of the alteration in the number of his family to the police. This seems to be treating men something like beasts, in whom their rulers have a property. . . . To gratify the impertinent curiosity of the magistrate or his nonsensical regulations, neither the griefs nor the joys of the heart are allowed to be secret and sacred. They must all be open to his inspection and registered in his book. The art, or science, or craft, or knavery, whichever it may be, of government, considers man as a sort of machine, that can be wound up, and made to point with its index to some events the magistrate wishes to be acquainted with " (*Travels*, II, 441 sq.).

Since Thomas Hodgskin is so hostile even to trivial interventions of the state in the life of its citizens, it goes without saying that he decidedly rejects any interference of the public power with the great concerns of society. In a sweeping statement which covers all possible fields of action, he says : " The state can have no right which the individuals who compose it have not. . . . Morality is the rule for individuals ; and all the rules applied to the conduct of governments are necessarily derived from the rules laid down for individuals. What individuals are prohibited from performing, that is also prohibited to governments " (*Ec.*, 1846, 629). Indeed, he doubted the very right of the state to organize the fight against external enemies : " It is commonly said that every man is bound to defend his country, but this can only mean that every man is bound to defend himself " (*Travels*, I, 484). And he is still more outspoken with regard to the internal enemies of peace and order : As criminal statistics prove, " 1 out of 65 of the responsible agents in the community is always, as the inmate of a gaol or in felon slavery, brought up to be a criminal. It is an easy matter for the 65 to bind the one, particularly as they have an organization for this very purpose. They have undoubtedly might, and, according to Mr. Carlyle, right, on their side. . . . But, though it be not possible for the one to escape from the might of the many, he forms with them part of a great whole, and thus the right to inflict this terrible and great calamity because there is the might, is only the right of the philandering soldier to maim, or of the suicide to destroy himself. The individuals punished are members of the community, having equal claims with others on its protection and advantages, and in punishing them in this manner the majority acts wrongfully and mutilates society " (*Ec.*, 1856, 924).

Thus the state, which is the fruit of the great misdeed of the barbarian hordes against the happiness of mankind and perpertuates its unhappiness, is the core of all evil. It is the bar across the way back to well-being and harmony : " The affairs of every society can never be well managed by a class of men set apart for that purpose " (*Travels*, I, 416).

Yet, is this not going too far ? Is it not necessary to distinguish between the authoritarian state of king and nobles and the libertarian state of the nation at large ? Granted that the former was an organization instituted by the victorious Francs and Normans for the defence of their spoils, has not the latter, in which the offspring of Gauls and Saxons form the majority, an entirely different character ? Hodgskin, in opposition to his master Saint-Simon,[1] sees hardly any difference : " Men boldly arraign and censure the laws of an individual sovereign or his minister, or the actions of any single man, when they patiently

---

[1] Not to have noticed the decisive influence which Saint-Simon exerted on Thomas Hodgskin is the great shortcoming of Elie Halévy's monograph on the latter (1903). This defect is probably due, not to an insufficient analysis of Hodgskin, but to a total misunderstanding of Saint-Simon, whom Halévy, it seems, regarded, with the *communis doctorum opinio*, as a socialist. Cf. the introduction to the new edition of the *Doctrine de Saint-Simon* (Collection des Economistes et des Réformateurs Sociaux de la France, 1924) by Halévy and Bouglé. I have advanced a different interpretation of Saint-Simon's work—proving its essentially liberal character—in two articles which are to appear in the *Journal of Economic History* (cf. May issue, 1943.)

submit to those laws which emanate from a body of men, and they deem those actions right which are performed by a multitude. The decrees of a congress, or of a parliament, though as unjust as the decrees of a single man, are much more respected." Yet " the wisdom of a few men is but little better competent to govern nations than the wisdom of one. Both are inadequate " (*Travels*, I, 464 sq.). The call for democracy is the call for a new form of the state. Yet the decisive question is whether there should be any state at all. " Creating a legislative assembly supposes a necessity to make laws, and it encourages that desire to legislate which has already been so productive of evil. The doctrines of political economy have taught us that there exist laws made by nature which are eminently productive of prosperity. . . . Nature has, therefore, already made laws for the conduct of individuals and of nations, which cannot be violated without prejudice, and which teach us that there is little or no necessity for human legislation. For the people to demand legislative assemblies, supposes them ignorant of this most important fact, and to create legislative assemblies can only tend to oppress future generations, even more than we are oppressed with the unwise regulations of a more ignorant age " (*Travels*, I, 466 sq.).

Legislative interference has been evil in all times past : legislative interference will be evil in all times to come. No legislator can turn to good account what is bad in its essence. His intentions may be pure, but what is will without wisdom ? " Much has of late been very needlessly written about the greatest happiness principle, the basis of all Mr. Bentham's philosophy. There can be no doubt that the Deity wills the greatest happiness—no doubt that the legislator, whenever he speaks of the good of the country, pretends to mean the greatest happiness of the greatest number of inhabitants ; and no doubt that the faculties of individuals, admirably adapted to secure their own preservation, are not competent to measure the happiness of nations. Admitting therefore that the legislator ought to look at the general good, the impossibility that any individual can ascertain that which will promote it, leads directly to the conclusion that there ought to be no legislation " (*Right of Property*, 22). Surely, a legislator, to be successful in his benevolent design, would not only have to possess perfect knowledge of the present state of society, but also some insight at least into the future course of development : " The mutual action of responsible individuals in society —sometimes in subserviency to law, sometimes independent of all law, and sometimes in direct opposition to law, so as to lead, as at present, to condemning, reforming, and overturning it—is the means of settling and determining at every moment all the rights of individuals as society is developed. . . . Their rights are always undergoing modification. If the law be made to conform to them now, to-morrow, next day, next week, next month, next year, there will be . . . new relations and different rights established and acknowledged. Human prescience is quite inadequate to provide regulations for the future. There is no criterion, then, for making new laws about which men can agree as they agree in condemning the old laws " (*Ec.*, 1856, 1371). In short, " the public good is not cognizable by human faculties ; and he who pretends that his actions are guided by a view to that, is an impostor, who looks only to his own interest and ambition " (*Right of Property*, 77).

Thus Hodgskin rejects *a limine* the idea to use the machinery of the state for the reintroduction of the natural system of social and economic relations among men. Legislation in the service of ideals appeared to him as a contradiction in terms. It was, he thought, like feeding a sound man with drugs that make him sick while nothing is required to restore his health but to leave him alone. Why make laws for society ? " The government of the whole moral world, even to its minutest part, is carefully regulated by Divine Providence," and therefore " society can exist and prosper without the lawmaker " (*Right of Property*, II, 148). It has its natural order and does not require an artificial one : " The dependence of men on men, whether they live under the same government or not, is the necessary conse-quence of the beneficial practice of division of labour . . . So dependent is man on man, and so much does this dependence increase as society advances, that hardly any labour of any single individual, however much it may contribute to the whole produce of society, is of the least value but as forming a part of the great social task " (*Pol. Ec.*, 157 ; *Lab. Def.*, 84).

It is plain what practical conclusions Hodgskin must draw from this theoretical conviction : " The more the legislature adopts the principle of *laissez-faire*, the more prosperous and happy will be every community " (*Ec.*, 1848, 1227). And there-fore " all law-making, except gradually and quietly to repeal all existing laws, is arrant humbug " (*Right of Property*, I). Indeed, not even legislation for the abolition of legislation is desirable : " Bad laws . . . should not be swept away by new laws, but be suffered to fall into desuetude, which is for all parties a gradual and safe extinction of evil " (*ib.*, 123).

This extreme language forces upon us the question whether the consistent and uncompromising rejection of all legislative measures, even negative ones, does not necessarily imply the renunciation of all changes in the social constitution—even the change back from the artificial to the natural order of things ? How can society as it is be replaced by society as it ought to be, real society ousted by ideal society, if all conscious action is in principle rejected ? Here, surely, lies Hodgskin's main problem. Was not the world for which he longed the exact opposite to the world in which he lived ? " I am far from thinking that large capitalists and numerous destitute workmen are desirable ", he protests. " A large quantity of useful machines, and of necessaries, and luxuries, divided into tolerably equal proportions, are much to be desired, but when they are collected in the hands of a few, they neither minister to greater production, nor to happiness and morality." Indeed, he held, " every society is prosperous, flourishing, moral, and happy, [only] in proportion as wages are high, and approximate in amount to the value of the products of labour." Therefore he envisaged and demanded a society which would rest on the principle contrary to that of liberty which the industrial revolution had just made paramount : " Philosophy regards . . . the greatest possible approximation to equality . . . as the surest means of promoting the happiness of all." And yet ! In spite of this conviction, Hodgskin rejected all conscious interference with matters social—even interference with the aim of establishing his ideal : " We are of opinion, in common we believe with many other persons, that the means of subsistence are unfairly distributed . . . but . . . we do not conclude that the Government should equalize the means of subsistence " (*Travels*, II, 174, 461 ; " Remarks on the Spitalfields Acts ", *Mechanic's Magazine*, Oct. 4, 1823 ; *Ec.*, 1847, 381).

This somewhat paradoxical conception Hodgskin held in all earnestness and consistency. He went so far as to oppose all philanthropic endeavour : " The success of one or two agitations amongst ourselves to effect good objects, such as the emancipation of the Catholics and the reform of Parliament, . . . has had a pernicious effect, in encouraging benevolent schemers and projectors to have recourse to political agitation to attain their ends. It is quite possible that each and all of these objects would have been more advantageously attained by awaiting the slow but sure progress of opinion, which throws down all kinds of errors harmlessly, like decayed leaves, when their functions are at an end. But reliance on opinion, faith in truth and right seem to have forsaken even those whose very existence depends on maintaining the almighty power of reason [—the literary classes]. They cannot wait for the progress of events. They must work at a little winch' of their own, to quicken the revolving of the globe and hasten the coming 'day. . . . By some kind of clamour, or reproach, or appeal to passion, or the mob, they insist on having their plans embodied into laws. . . . They vehemently demand the help of the demagogue or the oligarch to give their fancies all the force of a solemn enactment " (*Ec.* 1848, 1191).

This point of view also determined Hodgskin's attitude to the socialists. Even the scheme of Louis Blanc, although wholly in the line of his thought, did not find his approval : he stigmatized it as characteristic of the ." presumption of the literary classes ". All through 1848 he remained openly hostile to the attempts to reform or reconstruct society—to reform or reconstruct it in the sense of an approximation to, or a realization of, the principle which he himself had annunciated : " The literary heroes of the day, who have superseded other heroes, are mistaken in supposing that they can, any more than effete sovereigns and secular churches, give a form to society, or prepare it for those future and unknown changes which we may suppose it is destined to undergo. . . . They were nowhere content with detecting and exposing the old errors, obtaining a victory over them, and relying on the gradual progress of knowledge to provide proper substitutes ; they went far beyond that, and assuming a wisdom they never possessed, they recommended or prescribed constitutions and laws for society that . . . being the mere offspring of their own imaginations, are perfectly preposterous, and more mischievous than the old rules and the old rulers they had so much helped to subvert. . . . Governments may preserve peace, see justice done between man and man, enforce obedience to the laws, give security to property and life, but they only do mischief when they step beyond these limits, and pretend, whether administered by ancient dynasties or new *literateurs*, to rule it by their intellectual, political, and social ideas " (*Ec.*, 1848, 1190 sq.).

It is only natural that Hodgskin, who did not accept a single action of the public power as a means, should have rejected a state in which the government would be in charge of all economic activity, as an end. Communism, as a system of authoritative planning, therefore went against the grain with him : " A complete community of goods, of food, clothing, dwellings, instruments, weapons, and utensils, or of all the produce of labour, never has existed, and never could exist, even in any family, much less in any community. The use of such things, like the making of them, must be individual, not common, selfish, not general. The approximations to a community of goods among some religious and some political societies, have always been the constrained and unhappy results of positive [i.e. unnatural] institutions, which have neither been of long duration, nor generally advantageous " (*Right of Property*, 41). And as he judged of general socialization, so he judged of all partial measures of this cast : The " plan of giving the land to the public, and making those who cultivate it pay for its use, would be in fact to take away from the cultivators a part of the produce of their labour—for it is an error to suppose [that] the land produces anything ; what is usually called the produce of land, is the produce of individual labour applied to the land—and would be to bestow that on other men, alias the public " (*Ec.*, 1851, 151). His aversion to all forms of socialism was very deep : his theory of the state (or perhaps it would be better to say : his theory against the state) had its roots in a profound adherence to, and radical conception of, individualism and democracy : " In proportion as the State charges itself with the duties of individuals, it exonerates them from the performance of their duties. . . . It substitutes the State for the order of Nature. Now, as the State comes in the end to mean the one only mind which con- ceives the law, and the one or two persons only who carry it into execution, this contrivance really, in the end, substitutes the skill and wisdom of one or a few for the skill and wisdom of the many. But it is clear that the skill and wisdom of the few never can equal the skill and wisdom of the whole, of which they form a part. This contrivance, then, necessarily substitutes com- parative ignorance for wisdom. It destroys in the many natural motives for exertion, and makes them the slaves of a system devised and carried out by a few " (*Ec.*, 1847, 324).

Thus Hodgskin saw only the negative, and refused to see the positive, side of socialism. He believed indeed that men can destroy, but he declined to believe that men can construct : " To detect the faults of an existing political constitution, or the vices of a reigning sovereign, no more suffices to direct society . . . than the skill of a surgeon, which detects the cause of a disease, and can perhaps remove it, suffices to regulate the growth, formation, and functions of the human body. Between finding out the errors of a Louis Philippe, a Guizot, and a Metternich, and prescribing suitable rules for that great and growing society which has rent asunder their frail bands [in the revolution], there is as great a difference as between the offices of a surgeon and the functions of nature " (*Ec.*, 1848, 1190). Therefore his last word on all human attempts to re-make and re-mould the form of their social co-existence is negative : " Society is the offspring of the instincts of the human animal, not of his will, and . . . man cannot organize it. . . . The regulation of society is as much beyond individual skill, as reining in the storm " (*Right of Property*, 178 sq., 186).

This then is the final result to which all Hodgskin's political speculation was leading : a wilful act of men has led from the beneficent order of nature that was, to the dismal system of society which is, yet a wilful act of men is not able to lead back from the dismal system of society which is to the beneficent order of nature that should be ; for one evil cannot compensate the other ; one law cannot undo what another law has done. And still he believed that the state could and would be restored in which the labourer would receive the full produce of his labour and thus income and wealth be distributed according to merit and achievement. Yet—how can this change of things take place if it is not brought about by conscious action ? Should we assume and believe that it will happen by itself ? This was indeed what Hodgskin assumed and believed. This was what he tended to demonstrate and prove. It is not his theory of the state but his doctrine of development [1] which furnishes the key to his practical philosophy.

While both the physical and the moral world are governed by beneficent laws divine, Hodgskin taught, the laws of the

---

[1] The principle of evolution has twice found classical expression on English soil : in Cardinal Newman's *Essay on the Development of Christian Doctrine* (1845) and in Charles Darwin's *Origin of Species* (1859). In the social sciences it is, by the middle of the nineteenth century, implicitly taken for granted rather than systematically set forth. It is Hodgskin's outstanding merit to have clearly understood and presented it as early as 1832 in his book *The Natural and Artificial Right of Property Contrasted*—a merit which should secure him a lasting place in the history of English social theory. It must not, however, remain unmentioned that Hodgskin was not quite sure of the import and importance of the idea which he had adopted. " There is a progress in society, a successive development of human nature physically and morally—there is or can be a history of that development ; but man, its subject, cannot have a science of that. . . . There can be no science except of what is permanent ", we read in one place (*Ec.*, 1852, 1326 sq.).' And again : " Human nature may have been identical at different epochs, though this is doubted " (*ib.*).

physical world are static in their beneficence, while the laws of the moral world are dynamic : " The vital principle of society ", he says, the principle " which distinguishes it from every other part of the earthly creation [is] that of steady progression in improvement " (*Right of Property*, 3). And he indicates the moving force which drives society forward on its way of ever-increasing welfare : " The laws of population ", he boldly states, defying the authority of Robert Malthus, are the " clue to the whole " (*Ec.*, 1848, 604). " The increase of population . . . carries with it all the necessities for increasing subsistence, increasing knowledge, and increasing art, which are at all times observed [1] . . . It is the germ and essence of all civilization " (*Ec.*, 1849, 1060).

These words are not only characteristic of the contrast between the dynamic conception of Hodgskin and the essentially static view of Malthus : they also express the opposition between the idealistic attitude of the eighteenth century which Hodgskin never outgrew, and the materialistic outlook of the nineteenth century which announced itself in Malthus. " Nature every where provides some sort of compensations for apparent evils ", Hodgskin contends, in the vein of Locke and Smith (*Travels*, II, 188), and it is still the deistic creed which forms the basis of his optimism. " It does, indeed, seem something like impiety to recognize the fertility of the human race as we recognize the fertility of plants and animals, and infer that alone this great principle or portion of creation is not in all its consequences regulated by the highest wisdom " (*Ec.*, 1846, 1652).

It was, however, not a religious sentimentalism but a rational

[1] The conviction that the increase of population is, not the source of all evil, but the source of all good, was, in Hodgskin, the result of a definite scientific theory and not of a blind preconceived belief. Yet, he never and nowhere explicitly stated and developed his doctrine, which would have been a complete refutation of Malthus's *Principle of Population*. The reason is simply this, that Hodgskin, in the 82 years of his life, never was in a position to devote the necessary time to his higher pursuits. A contemplated *magnum opus*, " The Absurdity of Legislation Demonstrated ", meant " to explain his views in a connected didactic form " (*Our Chief Crime : Cause and Cure*, 1857, 26), never got as far as the printer. It was poverty that made the story of Hodgskin's life " l'histoire d'une carrière manquée " (Halévy, *Thomas Hodgskin*, 1903, 191). In reading his scattered literary remnants, especially his book-reviews, in which the great capital of his ideas is given away piecemeal, one is impressed with the strength of his personality. He had all the gifts of a great philosopher, a great economist, a great historian, a great theorist of law. That he was unable, for purely material reasons, systematically to set forth his opinions on any of these subjects, not only robbed him of the supreme happiness which spiritual work entails, but also—what is worse—mankind of the great contribution of culture which it would have represented. Halévy's biography, through which alone Hodgskin's name has been preserved, is, incidentally, incomplete. He did not know the following three publications of his author : *The Word Belief Defined and Explained*, 1827 (a philosophical attempt in the vein of Locke, Hume, Stewart and Thomas Brown) ; *On Free Trade and Corn Laws*, 1843 ; *A Letter on Free Trade and Slavery*, 1848.

argument which Hodgskin set against the theorists of economic pessimism. He pointed to the rapid increase of wealth which England—and not only England—was then experiencing, and asked how this obvious fact, this happy development, agreed with the ever ill-boding Malthusian law of population. " According-ing to it ", he argued in 1820 in his first book, " we might expect with an increase of population great absolute poverty. We see, on the contrary, however, absolute wealth and only comparative poverty ; or the capital of Europe has increased faster than its population. So that, if the means of subsistence or the capital, now possessed by every European society, be compared with the absolute amount of its population, it will be found greater than at any former period " (*Travels*, I, xii). The observations of a life-time confirmed Hodgskin in this view. " With the increase of the people there is no deterioration in the general condition of society ", he asserts in 1851 in the *Economist* (895), adducing ample evidence from recent statistics. " On the contrary, with the increase of the people pauperism has decreased, and the condition of all the classes above paupers has been improved." And again five years later (31) : " Much as the population has increased since 1800, and in no other 56 years did our population ever increase so fast, wealth has increased faster."

Yet, on however firm factual foundations this argument may have been based, Hodgskin realized that it was insufficient to refute Malthusianism. For he knew that the gradual improve-ment of the general level of subsistence was not a slow and harmonious process but a process interrupted by awful spells of hunger and misery. The Irish famines of the 'forties furnished an impressive example. Were they not due to over-population ? Indeed not, answered Hodgskin, and he appeals again to facts and numbers for the support of his opinion : " The Irish . . . densely as they were supposed to be crowded . . . no person would conclude that amongst them there was not a single acre which could be cultivated. On the contrary, it is quite certain that much of the uncultivated land—in 1851 there still remained 5,023,984 acres uncultivated—is quite as susceptible of culti-vation as some of the land already cultivated. It is, therefore, manifest that it was not for want of space, or of natural means to employ industry and obtain subsistence, which made Ireland over-peopled and led to the disasters of 1846, 7, and 8. It was the vicious artificial system of society . . . which doomed the people to terrible starvation " (*Ec.*, 1856, 1006). Hence, in spite of the crises, Malthus is wrong. The recurring interruptions in the upward development of social welfare are due, not to the spontaneous laws of nature, but to the unfortunate interference with those laws : " The [artificial] limitation of the soil—the appropriation and monopoly of it—have always supplied the practical and immediate barrier to progress " (*Ec.*, 1854, 1270). The crises then are unnatural interruptions of progress, and progress is a natural phenomenon. It is a natural phenomenon in the strict sense of the word, for a fact of nature is its basis : the very fact which Malthus had discovered : the steady tendency of the human race to increase in numbers. How does this tendency work ? How does it become the source of all improvement ? One sentence is enough to state Hodgskin's thesis in all its simplicity : " Man becomes skilful as the species become numerous." For this reason " the history of civilization is the natural history of man " (*Ec.*, 1848, 1228, 1481).

This view is a logical deduction from, or rather development of, the grand principle enunciated by Adam Smith : the principle of the social division of labour. The more divided labour is, the more productive it becomes, Smith contended. And Hodgskin added : the more the population is expanded, the more can the division of labour be extended. " As the world grows older, and as men increase and multiply, there is a constant, natural, and necessary tendency to an increase in their knowledge, and consequently in their productive power ", for " there have been more eyes to see, more hands to practise, and more minds to treasure up and record observations and practices " (*Pol. Ec.*, 94 sq.). It is this theory which is in harmony with historical experience, and not the contrary one of Robert Malthus : " As men have been multiplied, industry has become productive in the compound ratio of their numbers. . . . The industry of a small part of every civilized society suffices to feed the whole, but in a savage community almost every man and every woman must be a food provider " (*Ec.*, 1854, 1269). Thus the principle of population, far from invalidating the deistic creed, is in truth its firm foundation : " I look upon the increase of people as the great physical cause of all the moral changes in society. The several [other] causes . . . leading forward improvement, such as inventions in the arts, discoveries of science, the rise and growth of the middle classes, the influence of the press, are all subordinate to, and dependent upon, the increase of population " (*Right of Property*, 91 sq.).

D

Applying this theory of history to history itself, to historical reality, Hodgskin put forward the idea (later reappearing in Friedrich List) that (before the barbarian invasions) three stages of development must be distinguished which, in succession, show the spontaneous tendency of natural evolution : " In the earliest known periods mankind were few in numbers, and equally ignorant and destitute. . . . The first known condition of society is that of scattered and wandering savages ; destitute of arts, of knowledge, and of skill. Man was everywhere originally . . . a wild *hunter or fisher*. . . . When the earth was thinly inhabited, each individual, or each tribe . . . might travel over many· square leagues of land, using the whole of its produce . . . without encountering any other individual or tribe, and of course without infringing on any other person's rights. Under such circumstances, though no individual could possibly care much for any particular spot of ground, yet to each one it must have appeared, and in fact it was, necessary to have an extensive district, wherefrom to obtain wild animals, or wild fruits. In the early stages of society, all men must have found, just as the Indians of America now find, that hunting grounds, which we know to be large enough to subsist many thousand agriculturists, were necessary to supply a few hunters with the means of subsistence; and, like the Indians, being in a similar condition of society, they might appropriate, as theirs, all the land over which they roamed and hunted " (*Right of Property*, 63 sq.). But the principle of progress drove mankind onward and forward : " From rude and savage hunters, men became *shepherds*, feeding flocks and herds which they had previously tamed ; but even in this condition they required extensive territories, though not equal to those required by the hunters, to nourish their cattle and themselves. . . . In this state of society, the right of property in land would not be limited by the quantity which a man could dig and cultivate, but by the quantity necessary for the pasturage of his cattle including a large portion to lie continually fallow, and recover its natural herbage " (64 sq.). The shepherd stood both economically and culturally on a much higher level than the hunter, but the beneficent laws of evolution led mankind even beyond this second stage : " Subsequently men became *agriculturists*, and then a comparatively small space sufficed to supply each one with the means of subsistence. They fixed their habitations, and around them they fixed landmarks, each one appropriating as much land as he was able, consistently with the rudeness of original agriculture, to till, plant, and cultivate, and as he deemed necessary to supply his family with food." And so " each individual found a decreasing extent of surface suffice to supply his wants, as the condition of mankind was changed from that of hunters to shepherds, and from that of shepherds to agriculturists " (65). This fact convincingly demonstrates the great progress in material production that had been made, and it also indicates the great progress in social organization that had been made possible : the natural process of evolution taught mankind that " the right of each individual to own land . . . as he requires a less space to supply him with food . . . ought to be gradually limited to an ever narrowing, ever decreasing space " (66 sq.). Had this simple and natural principle always been acted upon, as it spontaneously was in the early stages of history, material welfare and social harmony would always have developed side by side and hand in hand. But alas ! it was not to be.

The barbarian invasions of the dark ages substituted the principle of preservation for the principle of evolution, i.e., the rigid artificial right of property for the progressive natural right that reigned before, and thus stopped the spontaneous development of society towards greater happiness and harmony. Indeed, they turned the wheel of history back : " The rude tribes, who, on the destruction of the Roman empire, overran and appropriated Europe, knew much less of agriculture than the Romans. . . . Their ideas of property in land were derived from a state of society in which men were hunters or shepherds, and when each man required a comparatively large quantity of land to provide the means of subsistence. . . . Accordingly all Europe was parcelled out by the German tribes, in what are now become princely portions. . . . The appropriation of the land in such large portions was, for our subject, the original sin. . . . An opinion derived from times when men were hunters and shepherds, viz. that a considerable quantity of land is a great benefit, and necessary to enable each man to provide himself with the means of subsistence, even now dictates our conduct." To have thus arrested the motor of progress is the crime of the barbarian conquerors, the crime which is embodied in the state and perpetuated by legislation : " The law has always been made with a view to preserve, as much as possible, that appropriation of the soil, that artificial right of property, and that system of government, which the northern barbarians, under the blind impulse of previous habits, utterly ignorant of the form society was destined to assume " forced upon the nations of higher culture which they overcame by the sword (*Right of Property*, 69 sq., 72, 74).

And yet ! All artificial institutions were unable to bring evolution to a complete standstill. In spite of its legal, force-protected obstacles, progress has gone on : the facts prove it. For " none of the districts appropriated by the Norman barons have descended unbroken to their present heirs. They have all been divided and subdivided, and the portions have generally passed into the hands of bankers, clothiers, stock-brokers, merchants, money-scriveners, and their descendants. . . . In fact, the absolute property even of these fragments of princely domains, does not belong to the nominal owner. . . . The nominal land-owner is only the receiver for two, three, four, or perhaps half a dozen creditors. The great object, therefore, at which the legislating land-owners have always aimed . . . has been completely frustrated. They have not succeeded in keeping estates undivided, and in securing the possession of them in their own families. Through the greater part of Europe, not only has the land been divided into diminishing portions, but it has passed from the descendants of warlike barons, and come into the possession of the children of their once much-despised vassals and slaves." As before the great social catastrophe, so even now it was the increase of population and the extension of the division of labour connected with it which wrought the change for the better : " The multiplication of traders, manufacturers, and artisans, and generally of the inhabitants of towns, has worked a most conspicuous alteration in all the moral relations of society, gradually mastering the landed aristocracy, and gradually tending to extinguish it. As men multiplied, new businesses and new arts came into existence ; new wants were formed, and new luxuries found to gratify them ; new classes of men arose ; wealth new in form, and different in kind from any thing our ancestors were acquainted with, was created, and new rights of property to the new wealth were continually developed " (*Right of Property*, 83 sq., 95).

These words contain the positive counterpart to Hodgskin's negative doctrine of political action. All conscious interference with the course of events is senseless and needless. History achieves by a slow but irresistible process what men strive and struggle for in vain. Has this not been proved by the development that has taken place since the Normans conquered England and the Franks Gaul ? " No fact seems more certain, than that the inhabitants of towns, the middle classes of Europe, grew into influence and power, altering all the political relations of individuals and of states, in spite of the land-owners, who were the legislators of Europe. . . . The feudal law-giver was every where the enemy of that trade which gradually subverted his power. He was slow and unwilling even to acknowledge the rights of his emancipated slaves. When they had congregated in towns, and were able to enforce their claims, a sort of compromise ensued, and the legislator or sovereign ceased his hostility in exchange for a tribute. The inhabitants of towns purchased of the feudal law-maker an exemption from his vexatious oppressions ; though his continual and ever frustrated aim was to maintain them in submission and slavery." Thus " the emancipation of villeins . . . and the comparative decay of the landed aristocracy throughout Europe, altering the legal right of property, and altering the political relations of all classes, were brought about in spite of the law ". Indeed : " The law-maker, instead of facilitating the emancipation of villeins, did what he could to prevent it, but his ambition and his greed were overpowered by the beneficent operation of natural laws. Improvements in art and science, the introduction of commerce and manufactures, consequent upon multiplication of the species . . . brought about the abolition of personal slavery " (*Right of Property*, 94–7, 92).

Greed and ambition of the law-maker have been overpowered : they have been overpowered by the beneficent operation of natural laws. These words, it seems, contain the fundamental idea of the materialistic conception of history,[1] later classically developed by Karl Marx. For what Hodgskin means to say is this : the social and economic substructure of society has been changed, and therefore the legal superstructure had, in the end, necessarily to undergo a corresponding transformation.

---

[1] In one place, Hodgskin expresses himself in the following terms on the formation of ideas in society : " It is plain that every individual, be his singularities and his intellectual powers what they may, has his character, his sentiments, his thoughts, his passions—yea, even his intellect itself—fashioned by the time at which he lives, and by the society of which he is a member ; so that any thing which is peculiar to himself forms but the smallest part of the whole man. Whatever may be his natural endowments, and some philosophers have doubted if there be originally any difference among men, every man is chiefly indebted for whatever he possesses of knowledge, of skill, of inventive power, to the knowledge and skill of other men, either living or dead. The influence of society over every individual mind, is paramount to all other things " (*Pol. Ec.*, 87). For another and still more striking anticipation of the basic idea of the materialistic conception of history, cf. Hodgskin's review of Mackinnon's *History of Civilisation and Public Opinion*, *The Economist*, 1848, 1480 sq.

Legislation is not free : it must submit to the exigencies of the times, and that is to say, of changing times. Past experience proves it : for in the rule " the legislator has only confirmed by his declaration, or acknowledged by his forbearance, rights that have grown into existence without his permission, and frequently in opposition to his will " (*Right of Property*, 112 sq.). Nor can it be otherwise, considering the essential tasks of the law in the life of state and society : " When the legislature fulfils its functions in the best possible manner, it only embodies the customs of the community in a legal and precise form of words, lending the sanction of its clear and delightful phraseology to the opinions and rights already existing among its subjects " (*ib.*, 113).

Yet if the legal superstructure cannot for ever remain at variance with the progressive socio-economic substructure, it can do so for a considerable time. It is this fact—the fact that legislature always lags behind the material and intellectual development of society at large—which makes the law so hateful : " The sentiments of men are formed by their gradual progress in knowledge, while . . . the laws are the remnants of times of ignorance and barbarity. Though institutions do not stop, they impede our progress " (*Travels*, II, 70). Thus, " the morality of law . . . is stationary ", while " the morality of trade " is all the time " improving " : " The great principle which induces alike Government and subjects to retain or place obstacles in the way of advancement is respect for antiquity. Opinions cling to men long after the circumstances which gave birth to them have passed away, and then they become prejudices and formidable obstacles to introducing the improvements which present circumstances dictate. In the earliest known periods of society, for example, mere brute force—the strength of a Hercules or a Sampson—of all qualities was the one most admired and honoured. Man had wild beasts to conquer and numerous physical obstacles to overcome, and he then venerated the brute force or the muscular violence which was the means of his success. Then it was natural that he should regard this commanding quality as the means of obtaining success on all points, and he sought moral ends by similar physical means. Brute force was embodied into laws, and success was expected in the moral as in the physical world from the use of violence. . . . In spite of much experience to the contrary . . . we still venerate the principle of violence as the basis of our present code " (*Ec.*, 1855, 1205, 1260).

These last quotations make it perfectly clear how in Hodgskin a pessimist theory of the law combines with an optimist doctrine of development : the law retards development, but development overcomes the law.   In the end, all will be as it should be : " In the long run, the material world is sure to correct all opinions. The mind, in fact, is a copy of that world, more or less complete and accurate.   Thus we go to the fountain head, when we seek to ascertain those material circumstances, such as changes in the numbers and wealth, and social relations of mankind, which determine first, the general opinions of society ; and secondly, the actions of the legislator and the judge " (*Right of Property*, 112). Thus the progress of population leads to economic progress, economic progress, in its turn, engenders intellectual progress, and intellectual progress, in the end, brings legislative progress in its wake.   And since the progress of population follows a law of nature, there is a strong necessity in the forward move of the whole moral world : " With and by time the mind enlarges or expands.   Scientific discoveries and the arts built on them are neither made fortuitously nor by man's design ; they are a regular and progressive development which no conduct of the human understanding could ever bring about.   The improvements in knowledge, skill, and wisdom that are continually dawning on mankind come quite contrary to our expectation, and very generally in direct opposition to the wishes and will of those who assume to guide society.   We must wait patiently, therefore, for the discoveries which are to ennoble man, and, in the meantime, lay no hindrance in the way of human development " (*Ec.*, 1854, 1021).

Thus the principle of *laissez-faire*, built on an optimistic view, not only of the social system, but also of the development of the social system, governs all Hodgskin's thought.   It is the spontaneous course of events from which he expects even the restoration of the original order of human coexistence in which the good things of the earth were distributed according to merit and justice, that is to say, in a way which guaranteed universal harmony : " The right of property . . . does not spring from the brain of the law-giver, and is not modified by him.   It arises from physical circumstances, and as they modify the customs of men, the law-maker alters his decrees. . . . The principles which have already produced the changes noticed, are still in active operation, and still tend to the same results . . . ordained by nature, in gradually restoring the natural right of property." As we have seen, " the land of Europe has been gradually divided, since it was first appropriated by the northern barbarians, into smaller portions than they seized on, notwithstanding the attempts to prevent such a division, by the laws of primogeniture and entail ". The same agency which before the great breach in history led to a progressive diminution in the size of the individuals' landed property—the increasing productivity of labour following upon the transition from hunting to cattle-breeding and from cattle-breeding to the tilling of the soil—has, triumphing over all artificial obstacles, been at work again. For it is obvious " that skilful agriculture obtains more produce from a given space than rude agriculture. Thus, as agriculture is improved, the quantity of land necessary to supply each individual with the means of subsistence diminishes. As mankind have multiplied, and as time has flowed on, knowledge has been extended, and the arts improved. Agriculture, sharing the general fate, has also been improved, and is continually improving ; so that a less and less quantity of land gradually suffices for the maintenance of indi-viduals. The same process, then, after the introduction of agriculture, goes on as before, and the same principle is found continually to operate, it being dependant on the increase of mankind " (*Right of Property*, 125 sq., 129, 82, 65 sq.).

Indeed, a comprehensive view of the past seemed to Hodgskin to augur well for the future. " There seems no reason why society should be clogged in its progress," he says. " It is not like a machine made by man, which friction speedily brings to a still stand. On the contrary, the longer it continues the more are the means multiplied for its rapid advancement. . . . From the time that Caesar first landed in Britain, till the era of William the Conqueror, nearly eleven centuries elapsed, and this country, during that long period, hardly made any sensible progress in wealth and population. If the inhabitants doubled their num-bers in these eleven centuries, they did no more. Subsequent to the conquest the people doubled their numbers, probably in about 400 years. Between the termination of the war of the Roses and the Revolution of 1688, a period of two hundred years, the people more than doubled themselves. During the last century, the average of the increase was a doubling in 80 years, and now, that is since the beginning of this century [up to 1832], they have been doubling, in most places, at the rate of 40 years. This proves that the progress of society takes place in an acceler-ating ratio. Instead of its being clogged . . . it only moves the faster the longer it continues " (*Right of Property*, 149 sq.).

The present, Hodgskin contended, fully confirms this conclusion and expectation : " With that increase of population [from 16 millions in 1801 to 27 millions in 1841] . . . attended as it has been with more than a commensurate increase of wealth, though it be not so well distributed as we must all wish, there has also been a wonderful progress in humanity. As the population has multiplied, they have not only become more productive, but more humane. . . . At present the sanatory condition, the moral instruction, the extensive and dangerous poverty of the masses, being the points of friction which obviously prevent the smooth motion of society, are all receiving the attention of the wisest, the most philanthropic, and the most earnest of our leaders ; and it would be treason to the human understanding, a total want of faith in man and nature now to doubt that a satisfactory solution of these great problems will soon be arrived at. The cheering fact . . . of a great increase of people [is] continually attended . . . by an increase of productive power, of material wealth and comfort, of ingenious inventions, and of manual skill, and, above all, continually attended by an equally rapid increase, in a tender regard for life, a profound respect for the rights of individuals, and in all the humanities " (*Ec.*, 1846, 1652). Indeed, Hodgskin thought, the final aim of development could not be far off : " We see the progress of knowledge in our own country, or in the whole of Europe, gradually knocking off the shackles of slavery, gradually overturning feudal tyranny and shaking off debasing superstition, gradually setting commerce free, and extending it over many lands . . . gradually increasing mutual services and mutual kindness, by an ever increasing dependence of man on man, as division of labour extends. . . . We are informed, from the beginning of history, of a gradual progress in knowledge naturally and necessarily evolved as population increases, bringing with it civilization, and we hope, certainly, that it may in the end, or at no distant day, teach mankind how to do without constables, soldiers, and gaolers " (*Ec.*, 1847, 439).

Armed with this unshakable optimism, Hodgskin was little disturbed when he saw the class struggle between factory-owners and factory-hands spring up and expand : " That great differences profoundly agitate these classes ", he coolly says, " is known to every observer, however calm at times the surface may be. Capital and labour make conflicting claims . . . [yet] by the natural and gradual progress of society they may be brought to a quiet conclusion " (*Ec.*, 1847, 381). In any case " all we are afraid that can be done is slowly to efface, or rather allow the benignant process of nature . . . slowly to efface the corroding evils of former mismanagement. . . . By the recognition of free trade, by allowing capital and labour to draw the means of subsistence whence they can be most easily obtained, and by that species of industry which is most productive, we adopted the principle of *laissez-faire* as the guide of our future policy. Let us follow that consistently till we are convinced it will not correct the evils of false appropriation " (*Ec.*, 1848, 480). Hodgskin felt certain that liberalism would not disappoint mankind, and he shaped his opinion of the social struggle and of social policy according to this conviction : " We doubt . . . whether it be desirable at present to enter into the important question of the original appropriation of the soil, by which the free use of the natural resources of the earth is necessarily denied to all those who have no share in the appropriation. . . . There is, however, little necessity for it, because the principles of free trade or free industry, now begun to be acted on, if successfully and effectually carried out, may, we think, correct many of the evils . . . without the direct and violent interference of the legislator with the appropriation of the soil, as made in past times, and inherited by us. We are ", he adds, and is entitled to add, " not blind to the consequences which we at present suffer from that original sin, but we are inclined to think that it will be better to permit society to outgrow them, than to interfere by new theories and new legislation to correct them " (*Ec.*, 1848, 480). New theories and new legislation are, in fact, unnecessary, for " the natural right of property is even now rapidly subverting the legal right of property " (*Right of Property*, 86).

This is, indeed, a strong statement. But Hodgskin thought it could be proved. The natural right of property is the right which secures for everyone the full produce of his labour : the full produce of labour is secured to everyone whose physical power to work is combined with the control of the material means of production necessary. Yet a class of this description, Hodgskin contended, has lately made its appearance and is visibly gaining in breadth : the feudal antagonism between lord and serf is dead, and the capitalistic antagonism between employer and wage-earner is dying. " The serf gradually outgrew his bondage, ceased to be the property of the warrior noble, and acquired a right of property in what he created, acknowledged by his master.

The capitalist then emerged into notice, and, obtaining from the landlord interest or profit on his property, shared his power. Now we find, in consequence of the respect for the natural right of property, that a *large middle class*, completely emancipated from the bondage and destitution which the law, by fixing the rate both of wages and interest, sought to perpetuate, has grown up in every part of Europe, *uniting in their own persons the character both of labourers and capitalists*. They are fast increasing in numbers ; and we may hope, as the beautiful inventions of art gradually supersede unskilled labour, that they, reducing the whole society to equal and free men, will gradually extinguish all that yet remains of slavery and oppression."

It was the spontaneous progress of material production which initiated this fortunate development : it is the spontaneous progress of material production which will lead it to its logical conclusion : " One of the distinguishing circumstances of this age is the great extent of mechanical improvements, and one of the moral consequences, least noticed, is the prodigious, comparative, multiplication of the middle classes ; that is, of men who labour a little, by, or in conjunction with, this machinery, who are at once labourers and capitalists, who do not suffer from the stigma which is cast on ordinary or long practised labour, because that was done formerly by slaves (new occupations, as they arise in society, being exempt from that stigma) and who, without being relieved from the necessity of labouring, are placed far above the condition of the great majority of slave-labourers and their descendants. On that class of men . . . I place my best hopes. That class has multiplied amazingly within the last fifty years, that class must multiply still more extensively, with new occupations and new machinery, and that class must gradually extinguish both the mere slave-labourer and the mere idle slothful dolts, who live on the rent of land or the interest of money " (*Right of Property*, 101, 180 sq.). For " the great and increasing use of machinery has a tendency to increase the middle classes more than either of the other classes, and is thus bringing about the ascendancy of a [real social] democracy placed, as it were, on a high level of civilization " (*Ec.*, 1848, 1481).

Alas ! This theoretical prophecy did not find practical fulfilment. Soon it became obvious that the prodigious advancement of technique, far from favouring the independent artisan, rather tended to destroy him, and thus led, not to a slow conquest of the class contrast, but to its rapid aggravation. It was not long before Hodgskin was confronted with emphatic and authoritative statements to this effect. " In the early part of the Session ", he writes on Aug. 10, 1850, in the *Economist*, " Mr. Gladstone was reported to have stated in Parliament that in the progress of society at present, the rich became richer and the poor poorer. . . . The phrase found very general favour ", he admits, but he was not convinced. For he believed in the 'fifties as he had done in the 'twenties that " general competition, if left free, will render large accumulation not possible " (*Travels*, II, 87), and so he insisted on his optimistic doctrine. " The fears entertained and expressed by many as to the probable disappearance of the middle classes from among us are unfounded. . . . It is far from being true that the rich are growing richer, and the poor are becoming poorer ; but . . . on the contrary, those who occupy a middle station—perhaps the safest station as regards personal respect-ability, and that which offers the surest guarantee for the progress and continued well-being of the country—are progressively increasing in number and in the proportion which they bear relatively to the population of the kingdom " (*Ec.*, 1850, 873 sq.).

Yet, half a decade later, Hodgskin no more denied the fact " that the rich have become richer, as Mr. Gladstone stated, and the poor have become poorer ". To be sure, his optimism was unshaken : " It is not the natural, necessary consequence of the increase of population and wealth," he protested ; " it is the consequence of certain ancient laws or ancient prejudices " that must be held responsible for the unfortunate course of events. But the awful fact remained, and he had to face it : " The labouring classes, or the great multitude, are not ' self-standing '. . . . They depend exclusively for their subsistence on the employment provided for them by the others. They are no longer . . . each one an isolated independent unit, wholly and exclusively responsible for his own condition. No one, as the rule, can get an honest livelihood and support a wife and children, except the owners of capital and land engage his services and pay him wages " (*Ec.*, 1856, 32, 645).

Thus, at the end of his life, Hodgskin could not but realize that his sublime theory had been a complete failure. In his last pamphlet he, indeed, repeated his favourite slogan with the obstinacy of an old and bitter man : " I am not for making new laws. Let the old ones perish ! " (*Our Chief Crime : Cause and Cure*, 1857, 25). Yet he no longer meant what he said. " There is, at present, a general and urgent demand for an alteration in the laws concerning landed property," he states, and his reaction to this cry for legislative interference is not negative now but positive. "The demand is not confined to visionaries, looking to spade husbandry for social improvement ; it is made by active practical men. . . . All the land which nature freely bestows for the use of the 20,000,000 people who now inhabit England, and who, to be prosperous, must for ever increase, is monopolized by about 35,000, land-owners, the true heirs and continuators of old oppression. . . . The growth of population, with the increase of other property, has made their monopoly glaring and intolerable. As every inquirer is aware, it is now a great obstacle to the creation of wealth. . , . Land cannot be easily acquired in small portions suitable to our crowded condition. Hence the demand for alterations in the law, which seems just to the bulk of the community. The laws concerning land must be altered. . . ." (ib., 6, 13).

Yet it was not only his anarchist doctrine of the state which Hodgskin found himself forced to abandon : unwillingly he changed even his theory of development, of a spontaneous development towards social equality. His words indeed remained the same, but not the spirit behind them : "All changes," he said in 1857, " whether for good or for evil, [indeed] necessarily originate in some one mind, however ready may be contiguous minds to explode by the same spark. . . . [But] the select few who first catch the light of coming knowledge, cannot use their advantages without passively, on their part, communicating a knowledge of them to others. . . . By the instinct of imitation and the laws of production, the conveniences and luxuries of the opulent in one generation become after a time the stringent necessities of the multitude. ᵪ . . Enjoyments are continually equalized. The toe of the peasant is for ever galling the kibe of the courtier. . . . No individual, and no class, can, under this dispensation, secure a monopoly of enjoyment, advantage, or power. There is a constant tendency to revert to the original equality of mankind, and always to preserve it, while all are improved " (ib., 1 ; What Shall We Do with our Criminals ? 30, 17).

These sentences cleverly conceal the deep change of mind which had been forced upon Hodgskin, but it is obvious none the less : in his early years he had taught that the pursuit of economic progress leads society to social equality ; in his old age he taught that the pursuit of social equality leads society to economic progress. Means and end had changed their places. To the young Hodgskin the urge to economic progress had been the means, and social equality the end ; the old Hodgskin conceived the urge to social equality as the means, and economic progress as the end. Thus in 1857 social equality was to him no longer the supreme ideal, as the following description of how society is at present improving convincingly demonstrates : " In England wheaten bread has, as the general rule, replaced the barley bread and oaten cakes which were still the chief food of the people of the North of England in my youth. At present the better sort of cereals, or fine wheaten bread, are displacing the coarser sort, the black rye bread. . . . How the change is brought about is plain. The opulent . . . prefer wheaten bread . . . to the bread commonly consumed by the multitude. The cultivators find it for their interest to grow an increased quantity of the finer cereal. In favourable years the quantity thus grown exceeds the limited demand, and then it becomes proportionably cheaper than the coarser cereals. It is offered to the lower classes ; they acquire a taste for it, and thus they are driven by this kind of necessity—cheapness in the end governing us all—to live on better bread. . . . Then as to meat : the opulent classes buy the prime joints, and the coarser pieces would be wasted unless the lower classes could buy and consume them. This occurs. The coarse meat becomes the chief meat the poor can get, and thus their diet, sorry though it continue to be, as the diet of the upper classes is improved, necessarily becomes better " (*ib.*, 19 sq.). Nothing can be more characteristic than these last words. Progress is still praised as improvement, yet what appears as promoted is no longer the social harmony among men, but only their economic productivity. The egalitarian liberal had become a liberal pure and simple. The impressive increase of material wealth had made him ready to forget that there would be richer and poorer—people who eat the prime joints and others who must be contented with the coarse meat—even in times to come.

Hence Hodgskin in the end solved the great conflict that had arisen between liberty and equality by preserving the libertarian and discarding the egalitarian principle. " Inequality of condition, and not a want of mere luxuries, renders men harsh, uncivil, and sometimes brutal," he had written in his first book (*Travels*, I, 307). Yet in his last we read : " Society requires look-out men and pilots as well as working hands. The upper classes are the former. . . . The superiority of a few, therefore, which has always existed, seems necessary, if not for the continuance, for the increase and improvement of the species " (*What Shall We Do with our Criminals?* 1857, 28 sq.). So Thomas Hodgskin, who had started from the egalitarian ideal of Locke and Smith, came in the end to be reconciled to the class society of capitalism which the industrial revolution had brought to life.

II. THE EGALITARIAN ALTERNATIVE : WILLIAM THOMPSON

Like Thomas Hodgskin, William Thompson shared the great conviction which François Quesnay and Adam Smith had inherited from John Locke : the conviction that there is a set of social and economic laws founded on the very nature of things which, if allowed freely to operate, would unveil the boundless benevolence of the Creator towards His creation. He, too, therefore envisaged a science of society and economy that would be at once realistic and idealistic : realistic in describing and analysing the actual order of society, the order that exists ; idealistic in announcing and advocating the perfect order of nature underlying it, the order that should prevail. The predominant economic theory of his time, never looking beyond the historically given form of social organization, seemed to him narrow and prejudiced, nay, misconceived and insufficient : " Of all the sources of error in reasonings respecting wealth ", he says (*An Inquiry into the Principles of the Distribution of Wealth most conducive to Human Happiness, applied to the newly proposed System of Voluntary Equality of Wealth,* 1824, 581 sq.), " none have been more frequent . . . than assuming that the circumstances surrounding the writer . . . were unavoidable and necessarily permanent. . . . The writer, surrounded all his life with certain moral features, accustomed to witness certain restraints and certain peculiarities of distribution, is apt to regard them as equally stationary with the natural features of the scenery around him. . . . Explaining the way in which wealth had been hitherto produced and distributed, inquirers thought their work was done." But this is not enough. Certainly, " as in physical, so in moral inquiries, we must first ascertain facts. . . . This step, however, [is] only preparatory to real knowledge " in matters social. For there is this deep and essential difference between the physical and the social sciences, that the physical sciences can only teach one to understand the laws of nature, while the social sciences teach one both to understand and to change the laws of society. They have therefore two missions : realistic description and idealistic critique of existing conditions. They must show not only what is, but also what ought to be.

Now, to the knowledge of what ought to be, the knowledge of what actually is affords only a humble preparation. Surely, " it is evident that the best past construction of windmills . . . would be no better guide in solving the question as to the best possible way of making these machines, than . . . the past expedients of creating or distributing wealth, could be conclusive as to the best mode of creating or distributing it. As a matter of history, of curiosity, of necessary information to guide our inquiry, nothing can be more useful : to proceed in the inquiry without such information, would be working without tools, building without materials. But neither the tools nor the materials are the finished fabric. . . . 'Tis not the explanation of the working of an actual machine, but the best mode of pro- ducing the effect, for the production of which alone the machine ought to be worked or supported, that we are inquiring after." This then is the ultimate task of social thought, a task which orthodox economics has not performed : . " to ascertain that mode of distributing wealth which would lead to its greatest reproduction and to the greatest preponderant happiness " (582).

Setting out to solve this interesting problem, Thompson is anxious to emphasize that his system does not rest on any wilful assumptions or tacit postulates : " The *materials afforded by nature*, out of which the mental and muscular *powers of mankind* must fabricate all those means of happiness which wealth affords ; such are our simple elements " (583). It is they, and they alone, which should determine the fundamental concept of economic science : for, properly understood, " the word, wealth, signifies that portion of the physical materials or means of enjoyment, which is afforded by the labor and knowledge of man turning to use the animate or inanimate materials or productions of nature " (6).

This formal definition, according to which " wealth is any object of desire produced by labor ", contains already a great and far-reaching material truth. It exposes the source of all values : this source is human exertion, and nothing else. " Without labor there is no wealth. Labor is its distinguishing attribute. The agency of nature constitutes nothing an object of wealth ", for where no men-made institutions intervene, " its energies are exerted altogether equally and in common ". This consideration leads Thompson to the basic tenet of his theoretical system and also furnishes the ultimate aim of his practical policy. It is expressed in one striking sentence : " Labor is the sole parent of wealth " (6 sq.).

This statement occupies in Thompson's thought the position of an axiom. It need not be proved, for it is self-evident. Can it be seriously questioned ? Certainly not. " Did there exist in nature any other means of producing or increasing wealth, but by labor superadded to raw materials, or to the productive powers of nature ? " (181). To pose this question is to answer it in the negative.

The sentence last quoted indicates that Thompson distinguished, as did Ricardo, three factors of production : " What is labor ", he exclaims (V), " but motion communicated to and in co-operation with the ever-active energies of nature ? " What is production, so we may translate his idea into the more technical language of orthodox theory, but labour applied to the soil and its treasures under the aid of machinery which is the embodiment of capital ? What divides Thompson from Ricardo is the fact that, starting as he does from a state of nature, a state in which land is not yet appropriated and capital not yet monopolized by a few, he regards only human exertion as an element of cost but not the offerings of nature. It is true, he admits, that men cannot " create any material thing : all that they can do is to find it out, and mould it or put it in a way of being operated upon by natural influences chemical, vegetative, and so forth ". But the material things, the raw materials, were there from the seventh day, and " labor superadded to the article, land, wood, cotton, etc. . . . is the only addition or change made in or to that article " since, and therefore the only source of its value to human society (96).

This argument implicitly assumes that, in the state of nature, land and capital goods are free commodities ; and this is, in fact, what Thompson explicitly asserts [1] : " Land, air, heat, light, the electric fluid, men, horses, water, as such, are equally unentitled

[1] He is aware of the fact that the labour theory of value is not applicable to those exceptional cases where scarcity obtains : " The price of pleasure grounds depends on the competition of the desires of the rich. . . . If labor . . . could create new sites equally suited to caprice for pleasure grounds ; the amount of this labor would stamp the value. But these favourite pleasure-grounds are in general limited in quantity, and such as cannot be imitated by labor. They have therefore a surplus value of their own, arising from the competition of desires, more or less reasonable, on a supply necessarily limited . . . If nature have limited the supply of the article so that labor cannot furnish the demands of desire, the artificial value of caprice commences : . . . whereas, in ordinary cases, the value of an article of wealth extends to the smallest quantity of labor that could produce it " (*Inquiry*, 14).

to the appellation of wealth . . . Why so ? . . . They exist in such quantities, and are used and enjoyed with so little exertion, some of them requiring—as air, light, and heat—a positive exertion for the exclusion of their operation upon us, that no sort of labor is necessary to gratify our desires for them. . . . There are more of them than are wanting for use : no human exertion has produced them : whoever will employ the labor necessary to appropriate any of them, becomes their owner : and the mere labor of acquisition makes that an object of wealth which before was merely an object of possible desire " (7). It is different with labour : labour is always scarce. " There are tribes, by whom neither corn, nor cottons, nor woollens, nor gold, nor rice, nor silver, would be esteemed articles of value, or wealth : but there are no tribes, there are no human beings, with whom human labor is not esteemed an article of value. Ignorant or enlightened, poor or rich, depraved or beneficent, labor is every where, to all men, an article of value : it is every where the price paid for the continuance of existence as well as for the means of enjoyment " (16). Thus if we consider, not the accidental institutions of a passing state of society, but the necessary conditions of the lasting frame of nature, we see that only one theory of value is true and possible : the labour theory. " Till directed by labor under the guidance of knowledge, the powers of nature, in point of useful production of articles denominated wealth, are beneath estimation " (8).

On the basis of this doctrine Thompson gives a convincing description of how land, originally valueless, comes in time to be valuable : " The first settler cleared the timber and erected a shed, and affixed the value of his labor to that part of the soil on which it had been expended, and to those contiguous spots rendered by it more convenient for use. A second settler, paying for the labor under the name of the land, still added to its value by expending more labor upon it, in clearing a larger space, cultivating useful crops, and improving the sheds, and perhaps rearing and domesticating some animals. A third settler pays an increased value for all these products of labor under the name of the soil to which they are attached, introduces stock and machines, all produced by labor, and leaving the former erections for subordinate or temporary purposes, erects houses and makes fences suited for permanence and convenience. Thus is a piece of rich land which was a few years ago an object of no value, now converted into an object of wealth. What has nature done towards this conversion ? Nothing. What has man, what has man's labor done ? Every thing. All that we call the work of nature, the mere existence of the land and its capabilities, were in as palpable existence before the land was converted into wealth as after it. . . . Labor was wanting to be superadded to mere desire, and in proportion as labor was bestowed upon them, they were transformed from mere objects of desire into objects of wealth " (11).

The case of capital is simpler still : capital goods receive their value in the same way as all other products. It is not their value but their duration which distinguishes production goods from consumption goods. For " what . . . is capital ? and how is it distinguished from the other yearly, or monthly, or daily, products of labor ? . . . All buildings, bridges, cities, inclosures, laying out and reclaiming of lands, ships, machinery, pictures, statues, and other desired works of art, though as much the products of labor as the apple, are distinguished as capital simply from their permanence, though in daily use and in the course of a more or less gradual consumption " (240). Therefore " capital is nothing mysterious : 'tis nothing else but that portion of the products of labor which is not immediately consumed " (239).

Yet, while it is true that the value of capital is determined by the amount of labour necessary, it is equally true that the amount of labour necessary is determined by capital. Thompson realized that capital must be considered not only as a product of, but also as a substitute for, labour. The illustration he employs is, like the language he uses, woefully inadequate, but the idea is nevertheless sufficiently clear : " In parched sandy countries, a well of water is a source of wealth ; while the land is the property of no one, not being worth the trouble of appropriation. Labor was not necessary to make the well, nature, we shall suppose, having produced it ; nor is the labor of drawing out the water to be alone estimated. But the existence of the well in that spot saves the labor that would be otherwise necessary to bring water there from its nearest supply ; and the value of the well is to be measured by the quantity of labor thus saved " (9). Thus the concept of capital has two aspects : a static and a dynamic one : capital is not only " the produce of labor " but " the produce of labor to facilitate its future progress " (203)— the value it possesses is determined on the one hand by the amount of labour it has made necessary, but on the other by the amount of labour it is making superfluous.

Thompson adroitly avoids the difficulty thus arising by restricting the validity of his labour theory of value to stationary states : " Though the [fundamental] proposition . . . asserts ", he says, " that labor is the sole measure of the value of an article of wealth, it does not assert that this sole measure is in all cases an accurate measure. As an article must be an object of desire to be an article of wealth, and as these desires and preferences are apt to vary with circumstances both physical and moral, particularly with the quantum of knowledge (of science and art) of the means of converting to use the materials and energies of nature ; it is evidently impossible that the absolute quantity of labor can be any accurate index to these. . . . What is asserted, is, that *in any given state of society*, with any given desires, at any particular time, *labor*, employed with ordinary judgment on objects of desire, *is the sole measure of their values* ; and, under such circumstances, an accurate measure. While the quantity of land and the supply of the materials of many articles remains stationary, population and knowledge at the same time increasing . . . no accurate measure of value, as applied to wealth, can be given. To seek it, is to hunt after a shadow. Nothing but labor or effort bears any relation to the converting of objects of desire into objects of wealth " (15).

However, one fundamental fact of the dynamical theory of value is obvious : the fact that the value of produced articles must sink when the capital employed in their production rises. For " the value of candles, oil, gas, etc., is only the value of the light extracted from them ; and as science improves and the modes of extracting are increased and facilitated, the value of light diminishes with the smaller quantities of labor necessary for its extraction " (8).

Hence, as labour is the source of value in the static state, so capital is the cause of its progressive diminution in the development of society. But unlike labour, capital is not an ultimate element. It is essentially a compound which must be further analysed. Capital goods are, as all other commodities, in the end reducible to two components : labour and raw material. To what ingredient, it must therefore be asked, is the power to be attributed which they give us, " of turning to use . . . the . . . energies of nature, making human labor more available in the production of the means of enjoyment ? " (157). The answer is plain : to the human ingredient. As their static value is due alone to the human element embodied in them, so is their dynamical effect. The value of capital as a dead thing, and the efficiency of capital as a living power, flow from the same source. The production of a machine is the moulding by man of passive matter spontaneously offered by nature ; its application is the direction by man of active energies, also spontaneously offered by nature : the parallel between the two cases, nay, their fundamental identity, is obvious. Thus the same factor which determines the dimension of values, governs even their diminution. The labour theory of value is not controverted by the fact of a dynamical development. The concrete thing which is called capital " is the mere creature of labor and materials, instead of being in any way their creator " (*Labor Rewarded*, 1827, 114), and it is only the living exertion of men, more exactly the knowledge they acquire, which " devises the means of constantly improving the arts, rendering labor more productive in quantity, or quality, of its productions, or in both, and thus indefinitely increasing wealth as a means of enjoyment " (*Inquiry*, 277 sq.).

Armed with this abstract theory of the natural state, Thompson approaches the concrete problem of actual society. He does so by advancing a shrewd comparison which leads straight to the fundamental issue : " Suppose a thousand individuals, healthy, willing to work, with acquired habits of industry in different departments, associated together for mutual support on the system of mutual co-operation and economy by all the aids of science, applied by art to useful purposes. Suppose them without tools, without a supply of clothes or food, till their labor could be made productive, without land to till, without materials to work upon. It is evident that these one thousand individuals are in many respects in a much more unfavourable situation for production than one thousand savages associating amidst the wilds of nature for a similar purpose. The civilized colony resembles the savage in being destitute of any supply of clothes but the immediate covering on their bodies ; they resemble each other in being destitute of tools ; they resemble each other in being destitute of a supply of food, till their labor can produce it : but in other respects the difference is extreme. The savage has all the materials of nature, unused around him, to work up. Are there minerals, plants, or animals within his reach, affording the materials for clothing, food, for tools, shelter, or other conveniences ? He has only to put out his hand and gather them, and transform them by labor into consumable or exchangeable wealth. Does he want land teeming with the powers of reproduction and inviting his arm to co-operate with and direct the sleeping energies of nature ? He is bewildered in the choice of rich land, claiming no owner, and ready to reward abundantly with its fruits and permanent possession the industry that will occupy and give it a value. How opposite, in these respects, the colony of civilized men, in a civilized community ! Against them, all the materials to work upon are appropriated by the previous labor, force, or fraud, of some of their compatriots, not a piece of stone containing any iron or any useful metal, not a branch of a tree, not a skin of any animal, no rude material that can be turned to any use for food, clothes, or covering, or any purpose subservient to convenience, that is not already obedient to an owner. Nature yields the civilized colony nothing in the way of rude materials. And as to land to work upon, which presents itself every where to the savage settlers, where shall the civilized colony find it ? Even the very mountain, bristling with rocks and repelling the tools and the toils of cultivation, is fenced round by the claims of ownership. Not a foot of land can the civilized colony procure to work upon without giving a full equivalent, according to the market value of the land. What equivalent have they to give for the land, any more than for the materials ? Nothing but their labor. The land itself to work upon, the materials [which furnish] the basis of furniture and clothing, as well as the tools to work with, must, as a preliminary step, be purchased by labor " (38 sq.).

This, then, is the characteristic feature of present society, the trait which distinguishes it from the original state of nature : that the goods which were once free are now monopolized : that the raw materials and the latent energies of the globe must now be bought : that a price, and at that a monopoly price, is set upon them. This fact finds its expression in the phenomena of rent and interest, the origin of which Thompson develops in spinning out his simile of the thousand settlers : "To accommodate matters to this striving colony, the owner of the land comes forward and says that he will not insist on an equivalent in labor for the purchase of his land ; but he will be satisfied with disposing of the yearly use of his land, getting in return every year so much labor, measured by its products, so much of the increase of the soil, as may be deemed an equivalent. The colony then undertakes to give the produce, every year, of a portion of its labor applied to the soil, in the way of rent for the use of the soil and its productive powers. The owners of the rude materials for manufactures make a similar claim on the labor of the colony for the use of the materials with which to work up the clothing and other comforts of the colony ; the productive laborers yielding a portion of the value of the articles they make to the suppliers of the materials, which portion constitutes their profit. Sometimes even the owner of the tools to work with, if they be very complicated and costly in their structure or require permanent fixtures or buildings, makes a similar demand on the unprovided laborers ; and even those that possess the food that the laborers must consume until the produce of this labor is in a state for consumption or exchange, demand a profit, a portion of the return of the labor, for their aid, with repayment of the whole of the food advanced. Will any one ask, Why should the laborer be burthened with payment of a part of his labor for the entire cost or the use of the tools, clothes, food, materials, or land, with or upon which he works ? Why not give him the whole absolute produce of his labor without any of these deductions ? Because other people who have appropriated this land, these materials, by labor or voluntary exchanges, who have made these tools or clothes, who have co-operated with nature in the production of this food . . . require the same security in the entire use of what their labor has produced, that is demanded for the unprovided laborer " (40).

In principle, therefore, rent and interest are justified : they are justified as the price to be paid for the labour of cultivating the soil and creating the capital goods. But they are justified only in so far as they represent such a price of human exertion, and they are not justifiable if they assume the character of monopoly prices to which no equivalent in human exertion corresponds. At present they are monopoly prices : their basis is not achievement, but force, their character not remuneration, but exploitation : " The rule of free and voluntary exchanges would appear, on a first view, to operate tremendously against the mere unprovided productive laborer with no other possession than his capability of producing : for all the physical materials on which, or by means of which, his productive powers can be made available, being in the hands of others with interests opposed to his, and their consent being a necessary preliminary to any exertion on his part, is he not, and must he not always remain, at the mercy of these capitalists for whatever portion of the fruits of his own labor they may think proper to leave at his disposal in compensation for his toils ? " (164 sq.).

Thus, in a capitalistic society, rent and interest are not prices which find their measure in the labour value of the commodity to which they refer, but monopoly prices which are put as high as it is possible to put them : and " so great is usually the proportion of his labor demanded, for the use or advance of these preparatory articles, by those who have appropriated them under the name of capitalists, that by far the greater part of the products of his labor are taken out of his disposal, and consumed by those who have no further share in the production than the accumulation and lending of such articles to the real operative producer. The idle possessor of these inanimate instruments of production, not only secures to himself by their possession as much of enjoyment as the most diligent and skilful of the real efficient producers, but in proportion to the amount of his accumulations, by whatever means acquired, he procures ten times, a hundred times, a thousand times, as much of the articles of wealth, the products of labor, and means of enjoyment as the utmost labor of such efficient producers can procure for them " (164).

This passage, it is true, is full of moral indignation. But it has an economic and not a sentimental basis. It is the anticipation of the result of a sober analysis which Thompson undertakes with reference to a simple example : " First the laborer, say the mechanic at woollens or cottons, earning about two shillings a day or about thirty pounds a year, pays for his house or lodging about five pounds a year. He has evidently no other fund out of which to pay this rent than the produce of his labor, whether deducted by the capitalist for whom he labors, or by labor paid to another. Next comes the claim of the employer who owns the buildings in which the mechanic works, the unwrought materials which he is to fabricate, and the machinery with which he must operate, as well as the wages to be advanced until the wrought article is exchanged. The amount of this capital, fixed and circulating, may be from thirty to a hundred pounds for every laborer employed, the average profit on which may be set down at ten pounds. There can be no other source of this profit than the value added to the unwrought material by the labor guided by skill expended upon it. . . . In the usual course of things, then, the productive laborer is deprived of at least half the products of his labor by the capitalist ; the amount of his labor being thirty pounds, and his rent and the profits on the stock that is said to employ him, being fifteen pounds " (166).

These are the facts of the case, and now we must ask : " What proportion of the products of their labor ought the laborers to pay for the use of the articles, called capital, to the possessors of them, called capitalists ? " (163).

In the present state of society it is clear that the antagonistic classes will give antagonistic answers to this question : " Two measures of the value of this use here present themselves ; the measure of the laborer, and the measure of the capitalist. The measure of the laborer consists in the contribution of such sums as would replace the waste and value of the capital by the time it would be consumed, with such added compensation to the owner and superintendant of it as would support him in equal comfort with the more actively employed productive laborers. The measure of the capitalist, on the contrary, would be the additional value produced by the same quantity of labor in consequence of the use of the machinery or other capital ; the whole of such surplus value to be enjoyed by the capitalist for his superior intelligence and skill in accumulating and advancing to the laborers his capital or the use of it " (167).

According to the point of view thus assumed, the practical result arrived at is vastly different : " The laborer pays five pounds a year for his house. The house cost fifty pounds, and is calculated to last fifty or one hundred years. By the laborer's measure of the use of this article of capital, he should pay one pound or ten shillings a year rent for the yearly loss in value, according to the time the house would be in consuming, with a trifling surplus to repay the trouble of the owner—say five shillings a year out of each of a hundred houses, or as many as it would employ one man to superintend, amounting to twenty-five pounds a year—to enable him to enjoy as much as any of the operative laborers. Fifteen to twenty-five shillings a year rent, instead of one hundred shillings, would be for this item the charge on the laborer. For the use of the capital of his employer, it would be in about the same proportion, or something more in consequence of the more perishable nature of the capital employed ; that part which consists in machinery not being liable to last as long as the house. If fifty pounds be the amount of the working capital, and if the average of its duration be twenty-five years [1], two pounds a year must be paid to replace this yearly waste, and for the trouble of the capitalist

[1] The original edition of 1824 as well as Pare's shortened reprint of 1850 (p. 129) have " thirty-five years ". This is, however, surely a simple *lapsus calami*.

—greater than that of the mere house-owner and requiring more skill and time—say ten shillings instead of five are to be added. Fifty shillings a year profit instead of two hundred shillings, would be for these remaining items, the charge on the laborer. Adding the rent and profits together, the laborer would have to pay sixty-five to seventy-five shillings per annum, for the use of one hundred pounds capital, instead of the three hundred shillings, or fifteen pounds, the half of the whole amount of the products of his labor, which he now pays " (167 sq.).

So enormous is in practice the difference between the two conceptions : while the laborers claim a share, and an equal share, in the increase of wealth which the utilization of the latent energies of nature has brought about, the capitalists aim at restricting their income to the minimum level, the level set by the miserable existence of primeval men, and appropriate all the blessings which the progress of the theoretical knowledge and the practical control of the elements has bestowed upon mankind.   For, in the last analysis, " what is the measure of that value as made by the capitalist ?   Before the invention of machinery, before the accommodation of work-houses in which to labor, what was the amount of produce which the unaided powers of the laborer produced ?   Whatever that was, let him still enjoy, with the additional ease and comfort in the production which the superiority of the tools and the protection of the buildings afford.   To the maker of the buildings or the machinery, or to him who by voluntary exchange acquired them, let all the surplus value of the manufactured article go. . . .   Let the whole capital for which the laborer pays, rent and profit, be regarded as one common instrument to add to the productive powers of his labor ; and let the several owners of this capital share between them, in proportion to its amount and perishableness, the additional value thus given to the labor of the ignorant producer " (168 sq.).

Thus characterized, which of the two principles is superior ? The labour theory of value, a theory built on an unprejudiced analysis of the state of nature, Thompson claims, gives a clear, a scientific, an incontrovertible answer to this question : " Property, rightful property, is the creature of labor. . . .   This is the great moral, or useful right of property ; which is above all [positive] laws, founded upon those universal rules of justice, to which all [human] laws, if just, must be subservient " (269). Surely, " the materials, the buildings, the machinery, the wages, can add nothing to their own value. The additional value proceeds from labor alone. The spade may as well be called the parent of the grain instead of the laborious arm that wields it, as any of these articles constituting capital, can be called the parents of the manufactured article. 'Twas labor that gave to all these their value as wealth, before they came into the hand of the mechanic ; and by his additional labor alone can their value be still further increased " (166). Therefore " the products of labor can in no case be considered but as the representatives of labor itself. The dead material is nothing : the active mind and hand are the sole objects of philosophical and moral regard ". They alone, we must conclude, can demand protection and preservation on the ground of the natural divine law : but what God has given to all in common, it is for no one to make his own. " The universal and paramount claim for security . . . can only apply to articles produced by labor " (90, 584).

This, then, is the practical result to which Thompson's theoretical investigation leads up : rent and interest, conceived, as they now are, not as the remuneration of certain necessary labours, the labours of soil-cultivation and machine-construction, but as the price for the use of definite physical elements, the elements below and above the surface of the earth—rent and interest are not eternal categories based on the lasting frame of nature, but time-bound institutions arising from the changeable constitution of society. They are monopoly prices, and their size varies with the degree the monopolization has attained : " The amount demanded for the use of capital depends more on the mode of its distribution than on the absolute quantity accumulated. Whatever may be the amount of the capital accumulated, whether large or small, if it all remain in the hands of the producers, the price demanded for the occasional use of any portion of it would necessarily be at the lowest, from the few persons unprovided with capital, and of course the feeble competition for the use of it. But where all the capital of the community is in the hands of men called capitalists, and scarcely any remains in the hands of the producers, there will the price of the use of it be very high, whether the absolute quantity of capital be large or small, from the multitudes, the great majority of the community unprovided with capital, and of course the immense competition to obtain the use of it " (171 sq.).

Thus the degree of exploitation obtaining in a certain society

is a function of the distribution of property obtaining in it :
under perfect equality of wealth there would be no exploitation
at all, because there could be no monopoly : but the wider
economic inequality becomes, the greater will be the exploitation
it engenders.   This fact leads to an essential question : how can
the uneven distribution of riches, now existing, be explained ?
—and, if explained in its causal foundations, how can it be
shown to operate as the instrument of its own renewal and
aggravation, of continual economic exploitation ?

Thompson's answer is simple and clear : " By means of mere
individual production, no fortune ever has been, ever could be,
accumulated.   So great is the love of enjoyment, being indeed
the only rational motive to production, that were one laborer
able to produce four times the quantity of another, almost the
whole of this increased production would be devoted to selfish
or social enjoyment, and not to accumulation. . . .   Forcible
seizure, fraudulent or voluntary exchanges, have always been
and still are, the only efficient means of acquiring large masses
of individual wealth."   Hence " it is not the differences of production of different laborers, but the complicated system of
exchanges of those productions when made, that gives rise to
that frightful inequality of wealth with all its train of physical and
social evils, which we every where behold " (*Lab. Rew.*, 10 sq.).

In itself, the practice of exchange is natural and beneficial :
" What does the simple introduction of exchanges tell to man,
capable of appreciating the truth ?   He sees that . . . the co-
operation of his fellow-creatures with him, and of him with them,
is necessary to their mutual happiness : he becomes interested
in the success of their joint labors ; he feels a sympathy in their
exertions ;   his feelings are carried out of himself in this first and
simplest exchange of labor. . . .   When in consequence he makes
an exchange, giving superfluity for superfluity, receiving an
object of desire for an object of desire . . . mutual satisfaction is
produced, mutual sympathy is excited, pleasure is felt at the same
time, from the same cause, by both, and thus a pleasurable
association is formed. . . .   The germs of genevolence and of
production are thus born, nursed, and expanded at the same
time : the same simple expedient, that of exchanges, has called
both into existence " (*Inquiry*, 50).   The sentiment of sympathy
thus brought forth, the social harmony thus created, has a sound
material basis : the fact that " in all free exchanges the interest
is reciprocal " (82).

However—and this is decisive—the exchanges must be really free in every respect to be truly advantageous to all concerned : " Free, or equal, competition implies the removal of all legal or moral impediments to the acquisition, by every human being, of equal chances for the production or accumulation of wealth. Amongst these equal chances should be equal means of knowledge and skill, equal freedom of action, equal materials for production and accumulation, equal rights and duties legal and moral. . . . Free competition should imply equal chances of success for all with equal organization at least at the outset of their career. . . . To give fair scope to the real, bona fide, freedom of competition of all with all, not only ought equal education, equal means of knowledge and skill, to be afforded to all ; but also, all ought at birth, or at setting out in life, in the race of competition, to be made equal in the means of success depending on capital " (*Lab. Rew.*, 53).

In all these regards, the real world falls short of the ideal. Indeed, " the whole system of human regulations hitherto, has been little more than a tissue of restraints and usurpations of one class over another " (*Inquiry*, 133). And of these restraints and usurpations, the restraint put upon the use of the free offerings of nature and its usurpation by a privileged group is the central and fundamental one : " The paramount mischief of all systems of insecurity . . . is, that by throwing into the hands of a few the dwellings of the whole community, the raw materials on which they must labor, the machinery and tools which they must use, and the very soil on which they live and from which their food must be extracted—these few . . . acquire the absolute regulation of the remuneration of all the productive laborers of the community, and possess the faculty of forcing that community or any portion of it to starve, whenever . . . the exercise of their industry does not . . . yield such a return as will not only give ordinary support to the laborers, but also that quantum of the products of the labor to themselves, under the name of profits on capital, which they have been accustomed . . . to look upon as their due " (422).

Thus, under capitalistic institutions, which are characterized by economic inequality, inequality in the distribution of national wealth, exchanges—and, above all, the exchanges which constitute the essence of production, the exchanges between the owners of the material means of production and the working men—are not free in this full sense of the word. In fact they are the very opposite : the conditions under which they take place are dictated by the propertied, and must be accepted by the property-less, classes : and it is thus that riches lead to further enrichment, and poverty to further exploitation. "By means of the possession of this fixed, permanent or slowly consumed, part of national wealth, of the land and materials to work upon, the tools to work with, the houses to shelter whilst working, the holders of these articles command for their own benefit the yearly productive powers of all the really efficient productive laborers of society, though these articles may bear ever so small a proportion to the recurring products of that labor " (587), while " the productive laborers stript of all capital, of tools, houses, and materials to make their labor productive, toil from want, from the necessity of existence, their remuneration being kept at the lowest compatible with the existence of industrious habits " (171).

Equality of wealth then secures freedom of exchanges, and thus creates social harmony ; inequality of property deteriorates the conditions of economic intercourse and thus poisons human society. For "what virtue is there left in these exchanges if they are not voluntary?—is not this circumstance the very essence of them ? Take away voluntariness from an exchange, take away from the laborer without his consent the produce of his labor, and what is the result, what is the operation but brute force and robbery ? As all voluntary exchanges confer happiness equally on both the parties concerned, and promote production and benevolence ; so do all involuntary exchanges annihilate industry and virtue " (51).

Yet the inequality of wealth which is the foundation, and the injustice of exchanges which is the form of exploitation, is detrimental only to the labouring many and highly advantageous to the possessing few. Therefore " the real interest of the capitalist, as such, is always and necessarily opposed to the interest of the laborer ; and he will . . . make use of all means in his power to make that interest available : the only personal check is his own calculation, always blinded by his interest, of the effect of his forced restraints on the spirit and thence on the productive powers of the laborer " (423). In fact, " a universal and always vigilant conspiracy of capitalists . . . exists every where, because founded on a universally existing interest, to cause the laborers to toil for the lowest possible, and to wrest as much as possible of the products of their labor to swell the accumulations and expenditure of capitalists " (171). This, then, is certain : " As long as that force-supported organization of things continues, by which one set of men possess the productive powers alone, and another possess the physical means of putting those productive powers into operation, so long will the latter, the capitalists, use the means in their power to render the labor and the happiness of all laborers subservient to their greatest interests. . . . Under the present system of things " which has developed the inequality of wealth and with it the deterioration of justice in exchanges to their highest pitch and perpetuates them, " the producer is, as to happiness, at the very lowest point of the scale at which he can be kept consistently with the continuance of his efforts " (176).

These considerations contain a conclusive critique of capitalist society : it has been judged by the laws of nature ; it has been tested by the standards of morality ; it has been weighed and found wanting. But, Thompson thought, *audiatur et altera pars !* Before the final verdict is pronounced, it is necessary to hear and ponder what the defenders of this system have to say. These defenders are the orthodox economists, and their approach to the problem is different from the approach of the utilitarian reformers in that it is narrower, concentrating only on one aspect, the material : " The ultimate object of political economy has been to increase the absolute mass of accumulated wealth in society, leaving it to moralists and politicians to divide the yearly produce and the permanent accumulation in whatever proportions their mysterious wisdom might think fit ; satisfied with the achievement of increasing the wealth (the productive powers of the labor) of the society, and confident that comfort and happiness must, somehow or other, or somewhere or other, be the necessary consequence of increased and increasing wealth " (36).

Hence the orthodox economists regard the maximization of material production as the essential task of any economic system and judge of its worth accordingly. Can it be claimed that capitalism, the order of inequality, is ideal in this respect ? Hardly : " The circumstances that really influence the abundance of the objects of wealth are these : abundance of materials to work upon, abundance of tools or machines to work with, and knowledge of the mind as well as skill of hand to elaborate out of these the objects desired. The natural course of things should seem to be, that every productive laborer should possess his own materials, his own supply of food while working, his own tools, his own dwelling, with appropriate skill and knowledge to guide these elements of production. It is hard to see how the seizure, or the possession, by any person out of these producers, of all the materials, food, tools, dwellings, and the monopoly of all the knowledge, leaving them the skill of hand or other organs, necessary for preparing these articles of wealth, should tend to render them cheaper, or produced in greater quantities : but it is very easy to see how such a circumstance should render them dearer. All these articles, knowledge excepted, constituting the capital, thrown into the hands of one, will enable him by the stimulus of immediate want to compel the others to work : but they must work for him, and of course at the lowest rate possible. Will such lowness of remuneration add to their alacrity of mind ?—will it increase their activity of exertion ?—will it increase their skill of workmanship ? " (241 sq.). Certainly not. Facts prove it. In the end " the employers are self-punished. Their calculation was, that whatever could be saved from the laborers would go to enrich themselves. This might be the case if man were a machine like the loom, uninfluenced by moral, and operated upon by mechanical, causes alone. . . . But this is not the case : man is liable to more, and more subtile, agencies, than the mere machine. Suppose him to be producing abundantly : deprive him . . . of half the produce of his labor, and the amount of the whole produce begins immediately to decrease. The motives of enjoyment and independence, which led him to improve his skill and sharpen all his faculties, have ceased to exist : he is dissatisfied, careless, hopeless ; he works no more with the usual alacrity, the produce is for another. . . . It becomes his fixed policy to give as little and as bad work, and to idle as much, as possible. Thus is the whole quantity produced always lessened by every increase of the short-sighted avarice of the employers " (257).

Hence, even if we accept the maximization of production as the ultimate and only ideal, we are led back to the problem of distribution : it is impossible to discuss them separately : justice of distribution is an indispensable condition of the maximization of production. " A review of the state or progress of all nations, whether industrious or indolent, will prove that industry has every where prevailed exactly in proportion to the motives held out in the form of rewards of industry, enjoying the product of its labor. . . . The great object is to supply sufficient voluntary

motives for production. . . . It would be quite superfluous to
hunt for motives to induce men to desire and aim at the appropriation and enjoyment of the materials of wealth after they are
produced. To appropriate and to enjoy without the labor of
producing, is too much the wish of mankind, and requires not
a spur but a curb. The motives to appropriation and enjoyment,
the constitution of man abundantly supplies, without any need
of external aid or arrangement of any sort ; the only difficulty
is to supply motives for production. . . . Any mode of distribution unfriendly to continued and increased production, is
like a child gnawing the entrails of the parent that produced it "
(33, 35). Surely " neither rude nor civilized engage in voluntary
laborious exertion for the mere sake of the pleasure of the exertion,
but for some advantage, some means of pleasure beyond, to be
derived from it. The greater the advantage, the more likely
is it that the exertion will ensue ; the less the advantage, the
less probable the exertion " (38). In other words : the nearer
the principle of distribution approaches the ideal of perfect
justice, the nearer the output of industry approaches the ideal
of absolute maximization. And, plainly, " the strongest stimulus
to production (and that which is necessary to the greatest production) that the nature of things will permit, is security in the
entire use of the products of labor, to those who produce them "
(35, 45).

This postulate of maximum production, however—security
in the entire use of the products of labour to those who produce
them—is nothing but the principle of freedom of exchanges
expressed in different words. If exchanges are truly free, everybody receives the full equivalent of what he gives—and the full
equivalent of what the workman gives is the whole produce of
his exertion. In other words : the maximum of production will
be reached only where exploitation is unknown ; but exploitation
is unknown only where property is equally distributed so that a
monopoly in the power of the elements cannot exist. Thus a
consistent critique of orthodox economics leads to the same result
as an unprejudiced analysis of nature : whether we start from
the original form of society or from its capitalistic state, it is
always an equal distribution of national wealth which emerges
as the ideal.

Thus strengthened, Thompson resumes and confirms his
critique of capitalism. " To perpetuate the results of force,
fraud, and chance, has been called security," he complains (589).

E

But this is to abuse the meaning of the word : " The security here spoken of, is the equal security of all, not the security of a few only. . . . It is the security . . . of the productive powers of every individual, not of the mere handful of accumulated products of those powers which some few have, by whatever means, accumulated " (584). In its true, in its natural sense, " security . . . means the exclusive possession by every man of all the advantages of his labor " (145), and " in proportion to the defect of the security [thus understood] will be the falling off in the production, till it shall ultimately cease " (584).

But wait a moment ! Has the argument here advanced not one decisive weakness ? Is it not a merely static theory, that is to say, a theory inapplicable to reality which is always dynamical ? Equality of wealth and distribution may be conducive to the maximum utilization of the productive potentialities given at a time, but is it not prejudicial to their further development and increase ? Thompson is ready to meet even this objection. Progress in production, he argues, is due to inventions. But " almost all useful discoveries have been made by persons in moderate or lowly circumstances ; the pressure even of want having been frequently the original impulse that launched genius on its wings.[1] Excessive wealth almost annihilates all motives to exertion " (159). Only " look . . . to the situation of the excessively rich. He is already supplied to repletion with those objects which are the mainsprings of human conduct, which serve as motives to human exertion. Every physical propensity has at hand the means of inordinate gratification. Does a wish arise ? it is gratified : volition is all that is required , exertion is superfluous. . . . Inequality of wealth . . . is on an immense probability of chances attended with this effect, that as it renders exertion unnecessary, so it renders it unpractised.

[1] This argument, it must be observed, cuts both ways. If it is true, if the needy alone are the promoters of progress, then its spring will be dried up if society is reformed in the sense of equality : then the advancement of wealth will, after all, be better secured and more quickly proceed in a capitalist than in an egalitarian order. Thompson was not blind to this truth : " Men ", he freely admits, " possessing the comforts and conveniences of life . . . would have little time or inclination to seek for knowledge out of their sphere, satisfied with that state of things, and not doubting its continuance, which secured them so many blessings. That great danger may arise to security, and consequently to production and happiness, from this over-confidence and contentment engendered by security itself, cannot be disputed " (Inquiry, 276). But he trusted that the unconscious urge of bettering one's position would, in his ideal society, be replaced by the conscious will to advance towards perfection : " Assuredly the community that is wise enough to establish, from a conviction of their utility, the natural laws of distribution, will also be wise enough to diffuse and perpetuate, through all its members, that knowledge, which is essential to its support " (ib., 277).

... Idleness ... becomes a sickly matter of pride and triumph " (182 sq.). In this way " excessive wealth begets excessive indolence " and nothing else, while " the desire of bettering their situation, of acquiring, by useful means, more of the comforts and conveniences of life "—a desire which is naturally weakest in those whose standard of life is highest above that of their fellow-men—" is the great stimulus to exertion to the mass of every community " (217 sq.).

But invention alone is not yet progress : it needs practical application, and this, in turn, presupposes the possession of capital. If the propertied classes do not bring forth the ideas of technical advancement, do they not at least furnish the indispensable means of its realization? Thompson is unwilling to admit even this : " The short-sighted vulgar amongst the rich ", he says, with more than usual pungency, " think that whatever is saved from the wages and enjoyments of the industrious mass of a community, is saved to capital ; forgetting that nine-tenths of these savings—admitting them to be effected by such means —are immediately consumed in unproductive and hollow show, or pampering sickly unenjoying appetites, by the rich, and that a very small part is converted into permanent capital " (255). Of course, he adds, " it is freely admitted that some portions of excessive incomes may by possibility be spared from immediate consumption, and devoted, by the rich, to accumulation, through the medium of the employment of productive labor. Such occurrences certainly are possible ; but as certainly they very seldom occur. As a class, the rich, particularly the very rich, are proverbially spendthrifts. . . . They annually consume what is annually produced for them, and the tendency of the whole of the very rich, as a body, is, in every country where they exist, rather to lessen the national wealth, or capital, by overexpenditure, by expending what does not belong to them, than, by abridging their expenditure in articles of enjoyment, to add to the capital for the employment of productive labor. It is not by means of these, but in spite of these, immense unproductive consumers, that the materials of national wealth, that a national capital, has been accumulated " (202).

Paradoxical though it may sound, Thompson contends, it is the poor to whom society must look for the formation of the capital needed to finance progress. " The niggardly parsimony which to the rich is a matter of contempt, is necessary for the poor man's existence. . . . So very small are the means of saving of the productive operative classes, that without a regularity and economy of which the more fortunate can scarcely form an idea, it is impossible that any savings can be made from their small earnings. Irregular habits are their greatest enemies " (214, 209). Indeed, Thompson goes so far as to suggest, that the contrast between bourgeoisie and proletariat is nowhere more strikingly expressed than in the contrast between prodigality and parsimony : " The tone of mind of the two classes is quite opposed to each other : the one serious and active, the other gay, or wearing the face of gaiety, and enjoying : the one accumulates, the other expends and consumes " (214 sq.).

Thus capitalism—the system of inequality, the system of forced exchanges, the system of insecurity : however we call it—is detrimental, not only to material production in its present state, but also to its further advance. Static contemplation and dynamic analysis lead to the same (negative) result : " It is plain, then ", we must conclude (209), " that . . . the ultimate consumption of the yearly income of excessive wealth [is] an annual loss to the community of a portion of the products of labor, most of which would be converted by a wiser distribution into an eternal accumulation of capital ", and hence that the reform of society in the sense of the egalitarian ideal, far from impeding economic progress, would be, in fact, an impulse to it, powerful and lasting.

Thus far the fact of inequality has been discussed in its economic effects : as a source of exploitation, as an impediment in production, as a check to progress. Now it is time to follow Thompson's train of thought one step further : to advance from his critique of inequality to his justification of equality—of equality as the fundamental principle of an ideal society. In so doing we shall speak less of material things and more of human sentiments : we shall concentrate our attention on the essential aim of social economy rather than on its external form. For, in the last analysis, its " ultimate object is not accumulation, is not capital, but enjoyment immediate or future. Herein differ the mere political and the moral economist. The accumulation of wealth or capital, and particularly in large masses, is the sole object of the mere political economist : happiness, health, particularly of the productive many, are with him secondary. Here they are primary ; and wealth and particularly accumulation, are only secondary. True it is that in a great number, perhaps in a majority of cases, the accumulation of capital, from labor, even under the restraints of insecurity, has produced more happiness than would have existed without such accumulation. Hence the proposition was generalized ; and from this most partial experience it was inferred, that to produce the happiness of society—as far as wealth was concerned—the one and only thing necessary was to increase production, accumulation, capital—which to be apparent must be in large masses and in a few hands. The moral economist, on the other hand, never loses sight of the great polar star happiness, from all sources, in the greatest quantity, consequently of the greatest number '.' (*Inquiry*, 413). Is it not obvious that this point of view alone is competent and correct ? " The increase of wealth, if it were not accompanied with an increase of happiness, would cease to be an object of rational desire " (37).

Yet, what is true of production, is equally true of distribution. Here and there we must apply the same standard of excellence : the felicific calculus. If " the only reason that can be given for the production of wealth at all, is, that it adds to the means of happiness : the only reason that it should be distributed in one way more than another, is, that it tends more to produce, to add to the stock of happiness, the object of its production, by one mode of distribution than by another " (19).

It is not, from the outset, evident that an equal distribution is most productive of social well-being. It has been shown, it is true, that inequality engenders exploitation, limits production, and retards accumulation : but these facts only establish a presumption in favour of equality and are not in themselves a perfect demonstration of its superiority in every respect. We must proceed without prejudice : " If it could be proved that more happiness on the whole would accrue to society by centring the whole sum of wealth in many or a few individuals, such should be the distribution of wealth. . . . Consistently with this principle, if the slavery of nine out of ten and the superlative happiness of the tenth increased the sum total of happiness, that distribution, of slavery, should be pursued " (20). Yet the facts do not point in this direction. Their careful analysis fully confirms the expectation which a study of the economic effects of inequality is apt to call forth. Its final result can be expressed in one simple sentence : " The more any given mass of wealth is diffused, the more happiness it produces " (125).

In order to prove the truth of this proposition, it is necessary to make one preliminary assumption : " All members of society (cases of mal-conformation excepted) being similarly constituted in their physical organization, are capable, by similar treatment, of enjoying equal portions of happiness " (21). The friends of inequality will be unwilling to accept this statement, but their arguments cannot but be inconclusive. How could they establish their contention ? " Such inequalities of capabilities of enjoyment . . . cannot enter into our moral and political calculations ; for they can no more than the galvanic fluid be seized and measured. We have no means of weighing or measuring them, even if their existence, and the inequality of their effects as to happiness, were as demonstrable as the light of the midday sun " (22 sq.).

Assuming then that—as far as joy and sorrow are concerned—all men are endowed with an equal sensibility, we can easily demonstrate that the maximum of happiness in a society will only be achieved if its wealth is evenly distributed among all members : " Of 1000 portions of the matter of wealth, the first 100, suppose, are necessary to repel hunger and thirst, and support life. The use of this first portion is as life to death : the value is the greatest of all human values, including the capacity for all other enjoyments, for which nature or education may have adapted the individual. What is the effect on the same individual of the application of a second mass, say of a second hundred, of these portions of wealth ? Nothing ecstatic, no change as from life to death ; simply the addition of some of the most obvious comforts of life demanded by real convenience. The effect of these second hundred in intensity of enjoyment, is so infinitely beneath that produced by the first 100, as to be incapable of any comparison. We proceed however, and to this second we add a third 100, and ask what is the effect of this third equal supply ? Does it produce an equal portion of happiness with either of the two former? With the first, it admits of no comparison ; with the second, of very little ; the first was existence, life or death ; the second, real comforts ; this third, what ? imaginary comforts, such as the opinions and customs around us render desirable. . . . To the three lots of 100 portions each, of the matter of wealth, we add a fourth lot of the same kind. The individual is already supplied in wants, in real comforts, in comforts of opinion the most approaching to utility : how shall he apply this additional, this fourth portion ? He necessarily looks out for those lighter sources of enjoyment, which hold the second rank in the opinion and customs of those around him. This process of seeking out lesser gratifications is unavoidable. . . . Utility having been long ago gratified, caprice begins now to display itself in the mere changes of form or quality of the articles used, or in the acquisition of the objects of mere pomp and exhibition. . . . Every hundred added is less and less productive of absolute increase of happiness to the possessor : but the difference of effect of each addition is less and less as we recede from the first portion and the first addition ; till at length an addition equal in amount to that which allayed hunger and secured existence and its capacities of enjoyment, becomes a matter of mere indifference. Such is the effect on happiness of the continued addition of successive portions containing equal quantities of the matter of wealth " (71-3). The social moral of this psychological investigation (the result of which has since come to great fame as the " law of the decreasing marginal utility of money ") is plain : " Successive portions of wealth diminish in their power of producing happiness when added to the same individual's share : but when divided amongst many individuals, the productive power of each portion is wonderfully increased, though the glitter of the effect may not be so apparent. The demand of justice would seem then to be, that the mass of wealth of the society should be divided in equal portions amongst its members " (91).

Now, the wealth of the society consists of raw materials on the one hand, and manufactured articles on the other. Of the former, the spontaneous offerings of nature, many are at our disposal in quantities outstripping the demand, and no principle of distribution need, happily, be applied to them. A problem arises only where scarcity obtains : " Suppose any article . . . were produced, by the mechanism of nature or by any other means, independent of human effort : suppose it to be produced, not like air or daylight, superabundant for the wants of all, but in such quantities as would give a limited supply to each individual in the community. . . . As long as the article is in such quantity as to be divisible into shares capable of giving palpable enjoyment, the whole sum of happiness will be increased by the equality of distribution . . . as every departure therefrom trenches immediately upon happiness, adding nothing to the gainer in comparison to what it takes away from him from whom the article is withheld. . . . Therefore in all cases, wherever labor has not been used in the production, equality must be observed in the distribution in order to produce the largest sum-total of happiness " (91-3). Will the same rule hold good with regard to manufactured commodities ? " Will an equal distribution of

. . . articles, obtained by means of labor, tend to produce the greatest possible quantity of happiness, as it would have done in the case of those same articles when obtained yearly without any labor of any individual ? . . . The industrious, whose time has been occupied, whose mental and corporeal powers have been respectively on the stretch, to produce these articles with the view of adding to their own comforts, stand forth and claim as their own, as their property, what their labor alone has made what it is, distinguishable from the unappropriated and unwrought articles around them. . . . The motive to their exertion was the use of the articles to be produced ; and the free use implies the power of free disposal. Is it useful to encourage this claim of right, this notion of exclusive property, on things appropriated and formed by labor ? " Indeed : " . . . without the acknowledgment of this right, it would be evidently folly to produce them at all. . . . Here then is a new rule of action, apparently antagonizing with the former rule of equality, counteracting it in all cases where labor is employed in producing an article of usefulness real or supposed " (94 sq.). Here, it seems, a new and stronger principle of distribution presents itself to our view : distribution not in equal shares, but unequal in correspondence with the different contributions made by men to the production of manufactured things. " That inequality in the distribution of wealth, and that alone, which arises from securing to every man the free use of his labor, and its products . . . should be upheld : because, without that extent of inequality, there would be no security, without security no production, without production no wealth to distribute " (144).

However, there is only an apparent, and by no means a real, contrast between the two principles. An equal distribution of the raw materials among all leads to the same result as guaranteeing the whole produce of labour to each. Equality of opportunity secures equality of happiness ; he who works less has less commodities to consume but more leisure to enjoy ; he who works more has more commodities to consume but less leisure to enjoy ; yet the choice is free, and so, in point of felicity, both are equal, because each in his independence so equilibrates toil and rest as to secure the greatest possible personal happiness. " By means of the voluntary exchanges of labor or its products, we have a rule of action which reconciles and brings into harmonious operation the two principles of equality and security, of procuring the greatest mass of the materials of enjoyment, and of producing by means of them the greatest sum of happiness " (97). Far from being antagonistic, " the genuine principle of equal security leads to an almost actual equality in the distribution of wealth, produced by impartial competition " (585).

Having arrived at this result, Thompson imagines that he has solved the riddle of the best society. " The only rational object of the production of wealth, as of all other human effort, being the increase of happiness to those . . . who produce it, equality of distribution tending the most efficiently to this end, except in as far as limited by equal and impartial security, and the freedom of voluntary exchanges (implied in security) leading directly to the utmost possible equality consistent with reproduction by individual competition ; what other conceivable means can there be of educing the greatest sum of happiness from wealth which it is capable of producing, than by maximizing the blessings of equality and security ?   So far from being irreconcilable with each other, it is only by an undeviating adherence to (real) equal security that any approach can be made to equality.   What has been hitherto worshipped under the false name of security, has been the security of a few at the expense of the plunder, the degradation of the many, particularly of the whole mass of the operative, the real, producers of wealth.   This spurious unequal security is as much opposed to equality of wealth, as equal security is friendly to it. Security as to wealth implies the free disposal of labor, the entire use of its products, and the faculty of voluntary exchanges. The maintenance of this real and equal security tending to the greatest production, leads also to the utmost possible equality " (97).

The last sentences contain the three great postulates which, Thompson believed, sum up the secret of social felicity.   He formulated them strikingly as follows : " First : All labor ought to be free and voluntary, as to its direction and continuance. Second : All the products of labor ought to be secured to the producers of them.   Third : All exchanges of these products ought to be free and voluntary " (178).   These rules represent the ultimate and decisive test for the worth or worthlessness of a social constitution.   " The Natural Laws of Distribution "— free labour, entire use of its products, and voluntary exchanges —" no law of any society can violate without detracting in a proportionate degree from the greatest mass of happiness which wealth is calculated to produce " (586).

It goes almost without saying that the capitalist order is throughout in sharp opposition to, and nowhere in agreement with, these postulates. " As long as two hostile masses of interest are suffered to·exist in society, the owners of labor on one side and the owners of the means of laboring on the other, as long as this unnatural distribution is forcibly maintained—so long will perhaps as much as nine-tenths of attainable human productions never be brought into existence, and so long will ninety-nine hundred-parts of attainable human happiness be sacrificed " (176). For " whatever view we take of human affairs, the forced and excessive inequality of wealth meets us as the nurse and the supporter of human imbecility and degradation ; equally pernicious in its moral, economical, and political effects. All this excessive, this injurious, inequality of wealth, has arisen from violating in a thousand ways, by force and by fraud—fraud always supported by force—the natural laws of distribution, free labor, entire use of its products, and voluntary exchanges. . . . Till all laws respecting wealth shall be formed on these principles, there will always exist in the bosom of society a focus of disorganization, of vice, and wretchedness " (222).

Hence Thompson has once more, and this time finally, demonstrated that " the radical defect in the constitution of society, that which must necessarily engender every other evil, is the excessive inequality of wealth " (221). He now sets out to find a practical remedy, and it is plain that he seeks it in the reunion, on an egalitarian basis, of property and labour. " As long as the laborer stands in society divested of every thing but the mere power of producing, as long as he possesses neither the tools nor machinery to work with, the land or materials to work upon, the house and clothes that shelter him, or even the food which he is consuming while in the act of producing ; as long as any institutions or expedients exist, by the open or unseen operation of which he stands dependant, day by day, for his very life on those who have accumulated these necessary means of his exertions ; so long will he remain deprived of almost all the products of his labor, instead of having the use of all of them " (590).

. However, is it really necessary to resort to a remedy so radical and indeed so revolutionary ? Cannot any monopoly be broken by a counter-monopoly ? If the possessing classes bar the workers from the material means of production through which alone their labour-power becomes useful, cannot the working people deny the capitalists the energies of their hands and brains without which machinery and land remain useless ? In other words : cannot trade unions establish a social equilibrium and therewith the freedom and equality of exchanges ? Thompson thought little of this possibility to which Hodgskin—at least for a time—had not been unsympathetic. Indeed, he wrote a little pamphlet—*Labor Rewarded*, the title of which already shows that it meant to be the counterpart of Hodgskin's *Labour Defended*—to curb the optimism which the spread of trade-unionism after 1824 was likely to kindle. " The highest price which Free Competition will enable Unions of the industrious to obtain for their labor ", he points out (78), " is not any thing like the products of their labor, but that rate of remuneration [only] which will permit the capitalists in their line of industry to reap the same profits that other capitalists in the same line, or in other equally hazardous lines, reap from their capital. Why so ? Because if any particular Union is imprudent enough to demand more of capitalists, they will transfer their capital to those other lines ; or if they [in fact] obtain higher wages than, as it is termed, ' the trade can afford,' the capitalists . . . will gradually lose their capital " in a hopeless struggle against competitors favoured by comparatively cheap labour. Thus trade unions can do very little : " Here then we have the limit of the benefits to the industrious which the union of those of any particular trade in any particular district can . . . effect. It will prevent wages from falling by individual competition amongst the workmen for any length of time, much beneath that remuneration which capitalists elsewhere give, retaining the usual rate of profits. Those of the industrious who are discharged by the avarice of individual capitalists for not underworking, being supported by the general fund of the union while out of employ, a very strong bar is thus raised by the industrious against any partial, unjustifiable reduction of wages, leading naturally to more extensive reductions, to privations, want, and misery. This is the utmost of the triumph to which such unions can look forward. They merely ward off a portion of the unavoidable evil " of capitalism (*Lab. Rew.*, 79). They are unable to effect more than " the keeping up of wages . . . to the highest point compatible with the exclusive possession of capital by one set of persons and of labor by the rest " (*Lab. Rew.*, 86 sq.). They are unable therefore to contribute to the establishment of an order in which the " natural laws of distribution " prevail.[1]

---

[1] It is only in a roundabout way, by securing higher wages and thus " promoting the acquisition of capital amongst the industrious themselves, that Unions [can and] must operate in order to make any real advance towards securing to the industrious the [full] products of their own labor " (*Lab. Rew.*, 87).

Hence the trade-unions hold no promise for the working classes. There is only one panacea for their ills : the radical reform of all existing property-relations. " If the productive laborers acquired knowledge, and could trace the immense abstractions made, under the name of profits, from the products of their labor, they must see the injustice of such an arrangement, and endeavour to become themselves possessed of all the articles under the name of capital, or of the means of commanding the use of such articles, necessary to make their labor productive " (*Inquiry*, 166 sq.).

In a social order conceived in the vein of these ideas " it is evident that every laborer would become a capitalist " (424). It would be, as it were, a capitalism without class distinctions. Yet is this not an unrealistic and unrealizable conception ? The orthodox economists, as protagonists of inequality, claim that only where there are rich and poor can enough capital be created to meet the needs of production and progress : hence, as antagonists of equality, they contend that where there are no rich and poor, production and progress will be starved and ultimately extinguished by the lack of capital. Their arguments, however, did not appeal to Thompson. " In such a community ", he asks, " would there be no accumulation of capital ? " And he answers : " Its accumulation would be immense, and greater than under any forced or fraudulent distribution ; so that there would be a profusion of capital without capitalists. How could these things be ? The great body of the productive laborers would be capitalists themselves, owners of the capitals (improvements, food, tools, seed), necessary for the cultivation of their small spots of land, of which they would be of course the entire owners : and the great body of the manufacturers would also be capitalists as well as laborers, each man owning his own little stock to enable him to work. . . . The increase of capital will, under all variations, be infinitely greater where the enjoyments and the skill of nearly the whole community are on the alert for its accumulation, than where the grandeur of a few capitalists only is interested to increase their display, at the expense of the comforts, and to the depression of the energies, of the rest of the community. Whatever may be the state as to knowledge, etc., the accumulation will be immeasurably greater, or where the capital is widely distributed, or where the productive laborers are capitalists, than where capital is confined to the hands of a few " (245). Surely, " all articles of permanent use, furniture, dwellings, tools and machines, materials for work, food or dress, permanent improvements in land or dwellings [which] constitute capital . . . may be accumulated or effected in a small way by each individual, giving independence and happiness to each individual ; as well as in a large way by capitalists, entailing dependence and misery on the industrious, and serving as the means of extorting from them the greater part of the products of their labor " (*Lab. Rew.*, 87). Indeed, the argument that the technical advantages of capital can only be reaped in a society infested with the social disadvantages of capitalism, seemed to Thompson almost childish : " To assert that laborers could not make houses for themselves, tools for themselves, machines for themselves, so as to make their labor more productive—i.e., could not produce and accumulate capital without the aid of some jugglers stepping in and appropriating to themselves these houses, tools, and machines, in order to exact the products of future labor for the use of them, is a proposition too absurd, when thus put in plain terms, to admit of refutation " (*Lab. Rew.*, 23).

Thus an economic order built on the principle of equality would not labour under the disadvantage of having too little capital : but it would also enjoy the advantage of never having too much. This is a valuable guarantee of its inner harmony which the capitalist system does not possess. " Men now accumulate capital for profits, because it is acquired, not at the expense of their own labor, but of the labor of others. Where the producers accumulate, the check of the inconvenience of production, is always sufficient to prevent injurious accumulation for profits, to prevent further accumulations than such as are necessary to increase the productive powers of their own labor " (*Inquiry*, 529).

Perhaps it could be said that a society of equality would be a society of mediocrity : that in it production would never advance beyond the stage of petty craftsmanship. But this argument overlooks the fact that economic independence is not inconsistent with voluntary association : " How then could great manufactures and great enterprises of commerce be carried on without great capitalists ? . . . Provided the capital is produced, it signifies not whether it comes out of one or fifty hands. Capital being every where diffused by security, a hundred or a thousand shares would be raised for any useful purpose, amongst shrewd and active men ; and . . . the joint-stock would buy the

machinery and erect the buildings " (253). The only difference
would be that " all those trades and manufactures . . . would
be undertaken, not as now by one great capitalist and hundreds
or thousands of ignorant, depraved, overworked slaves of law
or institutions, but by joint-stock companies of equals " (488).

Thus a capitalism without class distinctions—a capitalism
without capitalists—is conceivable. It would be a society of
justice : for " as long as the natural laws of distribution are
maintained, and wealth is acquired by labor and voluntary
exchanges alone . . . every increase of wealth is the reward of
an increase of labor, or of intelligence, or of both combined "
(229). It would be a society of culture : " Knowledge of the
mind would be in demand, as skill in the hand, and all other
useful faculties. Ease of circumstances would enable all to afford
an equivalent for the elements of knowledge by means of education. Knowledge would no longer be monopolized to support
the power and wealth of a few, but would be diffused, like cheap
cottons, as one of the means of happiness to all " (263). It
would be a society of high ethical value : " Morality . . .
requires adequate motives to set it into action. On the just or
unjust, the wise or unwise, the forcible or the voluntary distribution of wealth in a community, depend, much more than
upon any other or all other causes combined, the nature and the
energy of these motives to good or evil. . . . For what, in the
ultimate resort, on almost every occasion, is the great contest
between morality and immorality, between law and crime?
—for what, but for the possession of the objects of wealth?
Wealth at the same time supplies the motives to vice and virtue,
and is the object of pursuit, and the instrument of reward. Where
force is excluded . . . there will exist the maximum of motives
for the practice of the social and personal virtues. But just such
is the state of things under the natural distribution of equality
limited by security. . . . The unrestrained tendency of the
distribution of wealth, being so much towards equality, excessive
wealth and excessive poverty being removed, almost all the
temptations, all the motives, which now urge to the commission
of crime, would be also removed. From the wretchedness of the
poor, want, envy, indignation, or from the idleness and pampered
passions of the rich, almost all crimes proceed. Equality limited
by security, taking away the food of these desires and passions
both from the rich and poor, their effects would cease " (159 sq.,
230). In short, an egalitarian society would be a society of

universal harmony and happiness : " The industrious producers of a community . . . enjoying the full produce of their labor, nothing being taken from them without a fair equivalent, they would respect the acquisitions of others. Their wants satisfied, they would esteem it a wrong that others should be distressed, and would feel it soothing to their injured feelings to relieve them. . . . Beneficent conduct would expand. The sphere of enjoyment, like the heat of the sun, would be multiplied a hundred fold by the reflections from the cheerful hearts and smiling countenances of encircling happiness " (262).

We see : a society of liberty and equality, a community of producers free in their decisions and equal in their property, was the ideal of William Thompson as it was the ideal of Thomas Hodgskin. But while Hodgskin saw only one form in which it could be realized, Thompson conceived of two : as an egalitarian capitalism would reconcile the principles of harmony and happiness, he thought, so would a libertarian communism. " It is as inconsistent with human happiness in general, as with the greatest production of wealth, that capital should be possessed by one set of individuals, and labor by another," he says ; " utility demands that all productive laborers should become capitalists, that labor and capital should be in the same hands. But, under the protection of the natural laws of distribution, or of equal security, there are *two modes of production* which may be employed to attain this most essential object, to put all productive laborers into the possession of that portion of capital, and no more, which may be necessary to secure to them the products of their labor. . . . The two modes, under the shield of equal security, of effecting this union are,

"The mode of production by labor, with equal individual competition, [and]
The mode of production by labor, with mutual co-opera-tion " (*Inquiry*, 590, 592).

Between these two possibilities, a clear choice must be made. Thompson, setting about this difficult task, started from conceptions and convictions which were common to him and Hodgskin : above all the conception and conviction that no good can come from coercion. " The application of force, although it might rectify for a moment the evils of inequality, brought [wherever it was resorted to] in its train evils still more tremendous. . . .

That security in the use of the products of labor and in the free exchange of those products, which is necessary to insure reproduction, is annihilated by the exercise of force " (381). Forcible interference with the life of society would lead to its paralysation : a well-meaning attempt would end in a disastrous result. It cannot be doubted that " non-production is a greater evil than inequality of distribution " (ib.). The decisive question therefore is : " Can these deductions [from the rightful reward of the labourer, can rent and interest] be avoided without the production of preponderant evil in the employment of force ? " Only if this is the case, should a reform of society be undertaken. But " if the simple removal of restraints and the consequent diffusion of knowledge be not sufficient to abate these deductions, they ought not by any other means to be abated : for, no other means than those of force remaining, the employment of such an instrument would annihilate production " (172 sq.). Indeed, even " if nine-tenths of any society were persuaded that it would tend to the happiness of all . . . that all the existing accumulations of real wealth should be equally divided, so as to make all capitalist-laborers ; it would not be the interest of all to use compulsion towards the minority of one-tenth, being the possessors of the real wealth, to force this distribution " (598 sq.).

Fortunately, the introduction of an egalitarian order, be it of the individualist or of the collectivist variety, does not presuppose the use of force. " The means to bring about this desirable distribution [of property] are (1) Simple representative institutions ; (2) The entire abolition, under these, of all the restraints of insecurity (entail, primogeniture, combination local and general, wages-regulation direct or indirect, monopolies of knowledge of professions, of trades, bounties, game, privilege laws, public plunder [i.e., taxation], with all other expedients incompatible with equal security or the natural laws of distribution) with as little inconvenience as possible to any individual ; leaving untouched all past real accumulations, but guarding all future products of labor equally from all attacks of force or fraud, direct or indirect, public or private. (3) The progress and diffusion of knowledge, and the gradual perception of their real interests by all societies, would gradually effect the remainder ; that is to say, every thing useful as to wealth, as well as to every other means of producing happiness, in social arrangement " (600, cf. also 366).

Thus Thompson, like Hodgskin, believed that there was a spontaneous tendency towards equality which, if allowed freely to operate, would change society for the better. " In proportion as force and fraud have been removed in the progress of the development of wealth, the tendency has been towards the measure [of distribution demanded by] the laborer. . . . All institutions and expedients contravening the rules of distribution here laid down being removed, the producers being permitted to follow their real interests, and the acquisition as well as the enlargement of knowledge being facilitated to all, those deductions would soon be reduced to the lowest compatible with reproduction, and the producer would gradually recover the entire use of the products of his labor, or the nearest approach to it which the ultimate and extended interests of all producers would permit " (171, 173).

Here, however, the agreement between Thompson and Hodgskin is at an end. Both were convinced that evolution would lead to equality : but while Hodgskin was under the delusion that the end of the way was already in sight, Thompson contended that it was still far beyond the horizon : " The Competitive System ", he says against Hodgskin, " shall have worked out by the strife of good and evil this perfect freedom of labor and this equal diffusion of knowledge . . . at the distance of three or four centuries in the opinion of the most sanguine economists " (*Lab. Rew.*, 6).

But it was not only the fact that Hodgskin was more sanguine in his expectations than Thompson which divides the two : the contrast between them is much sharper [1] : for, in the depth of his heart, Thompson mistrusted the principle of *laissez-faire* altogether : he neither believed that it would within reasonable time lead to social equality, nor did he expect that it would guarantee universal harmony if equality was attained. " I think ", he confesses, " that the possession by Labor of the whole products of its exertions, is incompatible with individual competition ; though I [do] think that . . . slow advances may be

[1] In Graham Wallas' *Life of Francis Place* (1898, 268) we read : " Hodgskin's own style was too technical to have had much influence on popular political thought ; but William Thompson brought out *Labor Rewarded* (1827), in which Hodgskin's doctrine was expanded and put into rhetorical form." Halévy, too, represents Thompson as a disciple of Hodgskin (*Thomas Hodgskin*, 1903, 115, 194). In truth, however, Thompson's aim was to refute Hodgskin (cf. especially pp. 1–5, and 97). Moreover, Thompson wrote in the heavy and sometimes obscure style of the self-centred philosopher, while Hodgskin always expressed himself in the clear and lucid way of the professional journalist.

made towards it by rationally and fearlessly following . . . the Competitive System . . . in all its consequences " (*Lab. Rew.*, 97). Even if *laissez-faire* should in fact lead to a union of capital and labour on an individualistic basis—so runs Thompson's main argument against Hodgskin, the essential point in the discussion between *Labour Defended* and *Labor Rewarded*—society would not be free of all problems. For a new and insurmountable difficulty would at once present itself : the difficulty of imputation.

It had never occurred to Hodgskin that in an egalitarian society imputation could be problematic. Distribution, he thought, would present no difficulties where freedom prevailed : " If any question be raised, as to the share of any two or more workmen engaged in the same work ", he says, " I shall answer that this must be settled by the parties themselves " (*Right of Property*, 35). For " competition . . . is the soul of excellence and gives to every man his fair reward. Not, indeed, what he supposes himself to be worth, but what his services are worth to other men " (*Our Chief Crime : Cause and Cure*, 1857, 3 ; cf. *ib.*, 6–9). It is, therefore, according to his opinion, " the mutual action of men in society, what foolish people contemptuously call the ' higgling of the market ' ", it is " those friendly exchanges " which develop wherever the working of the social mechanism is not marred by wilful interference, " by which all the wealth of the world is always pretty fairly distributed " (*Ec.*, 1856, 1371).

Thompson took a different view. " The ' higgling of the market ' ", he contended, " will never effect a just remuneration to all, though equal laws and equal means of knowledge prevailed. . . . The springs of this higgling will be always kept in the hands of the adepts, and they will be so regulated, that prizes there will still be, and those prizes will fall into the hands of the most skilful in the higgling exchanges of competition ; and therefore, in nine cases out of ten, into the hands of the least benevolent " (*Lab. Rew.*, 33, 36). Indeed, the more highly developed a society, the greater the difficulty of imputation : " Almost every improvement [of production] renders more intricate the solution of the question, ' what portion of the product of general labor has any particular contributing laborer produced ? ' " (*Lab. Rew.*, 40). In any economically advanced society therefore " it is almost impossible to ascertain what portion of the produce of combined labor—and all labor to be economical must be combined out of the minute subdivisions of its various branches—has been the work of any individual laborer ", and so " it is impracticable to award to the individual, separately, the products of his labor ". Yet, he says—and here we perceive the foundation of his opposition to Hodgskin—" what cannot be done individually . . . may be done collectively " (*Lab. Rew.*, 37).

It is indeed the contrast between individualism and collectivism which is behind the opposition between Thompson and Hodgskin. Hodgskin was a confirmed individualist, an egalitarian liberal ; Thompson was a convinced co-operator, a libertarian communist. Egalitarian liberalism, he held, was better than liberal capitalism ; but libertarian communism was better still than either : " It is true that the undeviating adherence to free competition under equal security, would wonderfully increase useful activity, would almost banish pernicious activity, would extend and diffuse real knowledge, and with real knowledge benevolence would expand. But to this increase of useful activity, of knowledge, and benevolence, there are limits in the very nature of the principle of individual competition itself. These limits necessitate certain evils. . . . Free Competition . . . retains the principle of selfishness, necessarily warring with the principle of benevolence, as the leading motive to action, in all the ordinary affairs of life. . . . [Moreover] it occasionally leads to unprofitable and injudicious modes of individual exertion, from the limited field of judgment open to individual minds " (*Inquiry*, 368 sq.).

Unlike Hodgskin, then, Thompson identified individualism with selfishness, and competition with disharmony. " The object of all the exertions of individual competition as to wealth, is to acquire for immediate enjoyment or accumulation, individual property. Every individual, striving for self at the ultimate peril of want, destitution, and death, there is a constant motive operating to regard the interests of others as opposed to his own. There is therefore a constant temptation to sacrifice the interests of others to his own as often as it can be done, by whatever means may seem necessary to accomplish the end. . . . The interest of the individual, instead of being amalgamated with that of others, must still remain to a certain degree opposed to it. The very gathering together by every one of an individual heap of wealth, necessitates individual as opposed to general feelings, selfishness as opposed to benevolence " (*Inquiry*, 369 sq.). In fact, " such is the necessary result of competition, instigated under the pressure of want, and nourished at every step by the gratifications of antipathy—of which, pain or evil to others forms an

essential ingredient : it eradicates all feelings of benevolence "
(*Lab. Rew.*, 9).

However : the principle of free competition, if allowed to
operate in a classless society, would not only destroy its most
valuable effect, social harmony, but even endanger its very
foundation, universal equality. " By means of the spirit of
competition, and by means of the rewards of competition, all the
superior talents that may spring up amongst the industrious
classes, are [now] to be allured into the ranks of the mingled
aristocracy of force and chicane, the feudal, and the moneyed or
capitalist. Of what avail to the industrious classes though the
capitalist aristocracy were put down ; supposing for a moment
that such an operation were practicable under the system of
labor by individual competition ; what would be the gain to
the industrious classes if mental laborers, under the name of
men of merit, supplied their places, and reaped those prizes
which capitalists now enjoy, or rather possess? . . . A sorry
exchange the productive classes would make—an exchange of
masters only—pampering a new host of conceited swaggerers,
with their varied-coloured merits in their bonnets, instead of the
old stupid herd of capitalists " (*Lab. Rew.*, 9, 6).

Moreover, freedom of competition has not only social disadvantages, disadvantages of a moral and intellectual nature, but
labours even under economic difficulties, difficulties in the field
of material production : " While individual competition exists,
every man must judge for himself as to the probability of success
in the occupation which he adopts. And what are his means of
judging ? Every one, doing well in his calling, is interested in
concealing his success, lest competition should reduce his gains.
What individual can judge whether the market . . . is over-
stocked or likely to be so with the article which inclination may
lead him to fabricate ? He is evidently reduced to act on the
most general and vague probability. And should any error of
judgment . . . lead him into an uncalled-for and therefore
unprofitable line of exertion, what is the consequence ? A mere
error of judgment, though attended with the utmost energy of
activity and benevolence, may end in severe distress, if not in
ruin. Cases of this sort seem to be unavoidable under the scheme
of individual competition in its best form " (*Inquiry*, 374).

Thus it appears that " the mode of production by labor
with equal individual competition " is not the best arrangement
conceivable. " As long as individual competition lasts, the

interest of self must be the primary object of pursuit, the general good being necessarily subordinate thereto, and to be pursued only when conducive to the primary interest. . . . If the interest of self could be made to co-exist with that of others and to be mingled with it so as to form one homogeneous undistinguishable mass, this would surely be an improvement on the principle of individual competition " (379). We must ask then : " Is there no mode of human labor consistent with security but that of individual competition ? Will equal security permit no further approach to equality, and consequently to virtue and happiness, than that which individual competition can effect ? May not a mode of labor be found, consistent with security, and still more productive of happiness, than labor by individual competition ? . . . Such a mode of labor ", Thompson triumphantly declares, " has been proposed. It has been called the system of labor by mutual co-operation " (367). It has been proposed by Robert Owen, and its essence is the foundation of communist settlements on the basis of common ownership in the means of production and voluntary equality in the distribution of incomes.

The difference between the two principles is plain. " Every man for himself, is the basis of Individual Competition. Every man for every man (himself included) is the basis of Mutual Co-operation " (Lab. Rew., 18). It is equally plain which principle is superior : " The system of voluntary equality by mutual co-operation, not only professes to remove the evils of the institutions of insecurity, but also the evils of equal security arising from competition, allowed to exist but deemed unavoidable under the system of competition " (Inquiry, 392). It is true, " in the prima-facie benefits of equality, the two systems of social security (co-operation) and individual security (competition) are agreed. But the system of individual security requires a restraint on equality in order to ensure reproduction ; while the system of social security professes to require no restraint on the full enjoyments of equal distribution " (385).

It is, of course, a great and serious question whether such a scheme would really work : whether the colonists would in fact, for any length of time, be content with receiving an equal share of the common produce without regard to their individual exertion and contribution. Former experiments of this kind, Thompson knew, had miscarried—but he believed that the new scheme avoided the fundamental weakness which had wrecked all the old attempts. " All the schemes of equality hitherto proposed, have been found, on examination and from experience, productive of preponderant evil.   But they have all been founded on compulsion, or delusion, religious or otherwise.   Those founded on compulsion, are mere schemes of tyranny : if otherwise useful, the restraint would neutralize all their pretended benefits.   Those founded on delusion are the mere expedients of knaves . . . to gratify their love of power, gluttony, or wealth, at the expense of the dupes to whom their equality is preached. These two species of equality rejected, it never occurred that there remained a third species, which had never yet been tried . . . the system of voluntary equality, from a comprehensive view of the utility of mutual co-operation to increase individual comfort " (443 sq.).   Surely, " without security, equality could not subsist any more than any useful reproduction.   Forcible equality and fraudulent equality are inconsistent with security.   Voluntary equality [however] is dependent on it. . . .   The voluntary yielding the products of individual labor to a common fund, on condition of enjoying equally the products of all other associated labor, implies the most perfect security as far as that transaction is concerned " (391 sq.).   It secures the labourers in the possession and enjoyment of the full produce of their labour, not indeed individually, but collectively, as brother-co-operators.

This, then, is the way to a life of liberty and equality which Thompson called the working classes to go : " Unite in large numbers ; and by means of small previous savings out of the wages of your labor, or by borrowing in union, which you can never do disunited, small sums, about 20 *l.* for each individual, with your own future skill and exertions, form Communities of Mutual Co-operation, Joint Possession, and Equal Distribution. . . .   On land taken in a healthy situation, let some of you raise your own food, let others on that land erect your work-houses and dwellings, let others fabricate linen, woollen, and cotton articles for your clothing, let others make up those and other articles for use, and let others prepare out of the raw materials the most useful articles of furniture for the whole ; thus affording an unfailing market to each other " (*Lab. Rew.*, 114, 109).

Colonies of this kind would be communist societies within a capitalist world.   " All the co-operators must be productive laborers : all the productive laborers would be either directly or ultimately landlords and capitalists, landlords and capitalists of a joint benevolent stock for social universal happiness, not for selfish individual distinction " (*Inquiry*, 394).   And yet : though antagonistic to their environment, they would not disrupt it. " Whatever number of individuals from the different isolated occupations of life associate together for common benefit, the rest of society is left unmolested, its previous accumulations of capital untouched. . . . The associated communities produce and consume like large families, of such numbers as to supply conveniently the whole of each other's wants and comforts of all sorts worthy of the trouble of supplying them by labor, without in any way interfering with those who labor by competition. The associated communities, for all important articles, are a demand and supply to themselves " (592 sq.).

The last words already indicate the first great advantage which the communist societies would have in advance of the capitalist world around them : they would be free from crises : " Under the new arrangements, an excess of industrious producers, an excess of supply, can never be complained of, the whole community and all the individuals in it, and all newly-admitted increase of numbers being always consumers and producers to each other. . . . Thus would supply and demand be strictly and eternally commensurate " (399, 425).

Yet further advantages would soon appear : " Under the proposed arrangements of mutual co-operation, it would be the interest of every member that the knowledge and the skill of every one of his associates should be as great as possible, as much greater [as] possible even than his own, as his interest depends incalculably more on the skilful co-operation of his associates than on his own individual exertions. Under these new circumstances every one would be interested in removing the ignorance and awkwardness, and infusing and adding to the knowledge and skill, of his associates, to increase the common produce, as much as he is now interested to perpetuate the one and obstruct the other, for fear of educating a rival to his own gain " (*Inquiry*, 397 sq.). Thus would the equality of distribution increase the efficiency of production : " Unequal remuneration renders it the interest of those possessed of skill in any department of industry to conceal from all others the mode of acquiring the peculiar manner of operating, which, improved by habit, becomes skill. . . . Were the skill diffused, the unequal remuneration would cease. . . . But remuneration being equal, and the laborers possessing the whole products of their exertions, what motive can prevent the skilful from diffusing their tact by instructing their companions ? " (*Lab. Rew.*, 25).

However, is it not so that the increase of production due to an improvement in the general level of knowledge and skill would be counterbalanced and indeed outweighed by a still stronger decline in the individual willingness to work ? The same motive which would induce every co-operator to augment the productive contribution of the others, would induce him to restrict his own : the greater efficiency of the others would benefit him, the greater exertion on his own part would not do so. Obvious though the fact is, Thompson brushed it aside with all the optimism characteristic of idealists : " All enjoyment implies action. Without mental or muscular activity, to keep up a constant succession of pleasing ideas or emotions—all modifications of feeling—in the mind or brain, there can be no happiness. . . . Absolute idleness, then, or a love of idleness, under free labor, implying the entire use of the products thereof and of exchanges of them, is not to be apprehended " (Lab. Rew., 21 sq.).

Yet, Thompson thought, not only need a decrease of industry and application not be apprehended, emulation and diligence may confidently be expected to increase. The dissocial incentive of personal greed may be somewhat weakened by the voluntary equality of income-distribution, but the social stimulant of ambition, the desire to gain the respect of one's fellows, will be greatly strengthened by it. " The mere praise of being the best workman, is sufficient to keep alive the superior efforts of the superior men " (Inquiry, 470), and this spur to action will be an unfailing spring to progress because " the influence of the public opinion of large numbers voluntarily associated together, when that opinion is founded on reason, and can have no other object but the interest of the associated, is irresistible " (Lab. Rew., 85).

May we not see its strength even to-day ? " It is doubtful whether in almost any well-authenticated case, the mere love of wealth, for its palpable pleasures or distinctions, or both, has been the sole motive to any really useful exertions of genius, in writing or actions. . . . It is a fact as certain and as pleasing as it is important, that almost all the useful of the higher attainments and discoveries of men, in science and action, have been produced by the operation of the better motives. . . . To gain renown, that is to say, the sympathy and the consenting judgment of their fellow-creatures now living, or even to anticipate the sympathies of future generations, is at this present hour, in general society, a sufficient motive with numbers to devote, not only their whole time and exertions, but also their wealth . . . to intellectual and other pursuits connected with human improvement : the love of activity animates others ; the desire of increasing and diffusing happiness many more. These three motives, in various ways compounded and modified, have actually produced, and are now producing, the greater part of the higher useful intellectual and moral exertions amongst men " (*Inquiry*, 516 sq.). But to-day, " in general society, 'tis only a few, the rich, that are above the reach of want, and permitted to come under the possible influence of these higher motives. . . . In the co-operating communities . . . all are raised above the reach of want : there, all have leisure for intellectual pursuits. . . . There are no constantly operating sources for distraction to bribe or force all exalted talent and exertion into the eternal career of competition for endless heaps of individual wealth. . . . There will operate most strongly the desire . . . of benefiting all of the family of mankind " (*ib.*). And so, Thompson concludes, " the motives which produce useful energy of thought and action, exist in greater force in the associated communities than in general society " (*ib.*).

Still, this is not more than an unproved assertion. It might happen that the willingness to work would be weaker in the communist colonies than in the capitalist world. But is this an argument against them ? Indeed not. It is the maximum of happiness, and not the maximum of production, which they endeavour to realize. " If the pleasures of sense and intellect, to be derived from the entire use of the articles produced by labor, joined to the pleasures of useful activity, of sympathy, benevolence and public opinion, should, on trial, be found inoperative to induce rational men and women to produce many things which are now produced at great cost of time, repulsive toil, health, and even life itself—should we regret that such articles would cease, under equal remuneration, to be produced ? No : but we should rejoice at it. Our object being human happiness, activity is only desirable in as far as it tends to promote that object " (*Lab Rew.*, 31).

However (Thompson knew), not even the most perfect proof that the co-operative colonies would lead to the greatest possible felicity of their members would convince his arch-adversaries, the orthodox economists. Indeed, he realized that exactly such proof would provoke their most dangerous argument : the argument of Malthus. But he did not fear it. Perhaps over-population would wreck the Utopia : but over-population is not an unavoidable evil. It can be prevented : " In the physical constitution of man ", he says, " there is [indeed] a possibility of increasing the numbers of his kind at a quicker rate than the quantity of food. [Yet] there is also a physical possibility of increasing the number of sheep or of silkworms beyond the quantity of food necessary for their support. . . . Why should not the same principles of prudence be used in regulating the increase of men as in regulating the increase of sheep or silkworms ? " (*Inquiry*, 535 sq.). In fact, there is a strong and rational motive to use them : " Increased comforts beget, under varying circumstances, an equal desire to retain those comforts, and consequent disinclination to part with them, through the expenses of marriage, as much as through any other means " (542). Malthus's argument against all attempts consciously to promote human happiness [1] cannot apply to a society provident enough to subject its population to forethought and planning. " Every advance made in the career of industry and comfort has a tendency to engender habits of prudence, and instead of producing a superfluous population greater in proportion to food and comforts than the previous numbers under a smaller share of industry and comforts ; their uniform tendency on the contrary is to produce a lesser proportion. A greater absolute population always follows increased industry and comforts ; but as certainly a smaller relative population, a smaller population in proportion to the increased comforts and necessaries of life " (538 sq.).

Thus, if " the mode of production by labor with equal individual competition " is a better society than the capitalist order of to-day, " the mode of production by labor with mutual co-operation " is best. " As to all the vices and crimes arising from the mere pursuit of individual gain, by the competition of individual with individual, or with all other individuals, nothing is more plain, than that such vices and crimes could not have place in a society where no such thing as individual gain, as individual possession, was known. . . . The passions of envy, jealousy, hatred, pride, vanity, etc., and the crimes against person

[1] The proof that the tendency towards over-population which arises from physical factors, is considerably modified by social circumstances, is perhaps the best part of Thompson's work. It suffers, however, from one great defect : the problem of diminishing returns is not seriously discussed in this connection. In a later context, Thompson does his best to minimize the effects of this law, and advocates in the end an expedient which virtually abandons the principle of non-coercion : " The will of the majority decrees a tax in the shape of rent, in lieu of all other taxes, to be levied on the rich lands in proportion to their surplus fertility over the poorest generally cultivated lands " (*Inquiry*, 578).

or property, to which they sometimes give rise, are almost always connected with property ; and will therefore cease with the altered circumstances of joint and social possession and enjoyment. . . . No sane animal will contend for that which can be got without contention. Contention is a forced unpleasant state surrounded with mistrust and apprehension, and therefore not entered on but with a view to some countervailing benefit : here the countervailing benefit is withdrawn, and therefore the contention can have no cause. . . . It will therefore cease . . . as a lamp ceases to burn, when the oil or gas that supplied it is withdrawn " (*Inquiry*, 415 sq.).

With mutual hate, an old source of unhappiness will be closed ; with mutual love, a new source of felicity will be opened up : " The pleasure of seeing others happy is as much an individual pleasure, as the pleasure of eating a pine-apple " (514). Indeed, it is a pleasure pregnant with still greater pleasures : " Nothing [is] so contagious as happiness. . . . By an association of our nature, from which there is no escape, dependant partly on organization and partly on early inevitable habit, the usual indications, by means of the countenance and otherwise, of happiness in those around us, excite a glow more or less lively of kindred feelings in ourselves, whenever some real or supposed counteracting interest does not mar the effect. . . . Scarcely any bounds can be assigned to the increase which individual happiness is capable of receiving from the associations of reflected happiness " (421). Therefore, " to the enlightened moralist, what a field would these associated communities afford ! With what a development of human motives, whose very existence the infancy of his science had hardly suspected, would they supply him !—motives gentle and all-pervading like the descending dews, unappreciated till the leafy forest and the bending crops of gladness attest their universal operation " (429).

Desirous to see the social organization so full of promise realized, Thompson undertook in his last book—*Practical Directions for the Speedy and Economical Establishment of Communities on the Principles of Mutual Co-operation, United Possessions, Equality of Exertions and of the Means of Enjoyments*—to show how a colony of this kind could best be built up. But the more he advanced from theory to practice, the more he was forced to sacrifice the principle of liberty to the ideal of equality. He still envisaged voluntary associations, it is true, but the freedom to be granted consisted in fact only in a freedom to join and leave at will : as long as a co-operator belonged to his colony, Thompson thought, he should be obliged to undertake the work which the chosen leaders, acting under the control of the community, allotted to him. Would such a society still have been a society of liberty as well as of equality? Would it not rather have been a state which Thompson himself once characterized as the " slavery of mankind to vexatious laws, the collective will or caprice of many masters united, differing only in degree and modification from the old subjection to the individual will and the lash of one master "? (*Lab. Rew.*, 35). The experiment has not been tried : but it seems hardly doubtful that reality, which forced Hodgskin to abandon the principle of equality, would have forced Thompson to forsake the ideal of liberty, however near and dear it was to his heart.

The heirs and disciples of John Locke had exalted liberty and equality as the fundamental postulates of an ideal world, but they had also endeavoured to demonstrate that they were, in the last analysis, the principles underlying actual society. Thomas Hodgskin, re-examining reality after the industrial revolution, found economic liberty in fact rampant, but he felt that the same could not be said of social equality. Nevertheless, even to him equality was a piece of reality, reality in the making, and he believed that it would soon be fully developed. William Thompson did not share this delusion : he was convinced that men, if they wished to live in an egalitarian order, would have consciously to create it.

To the disciples of John Locke, liberty and equality had been ideas never to be divorced. The industrial revolution made them incompatible with each other : establishing the ascendancy of large-scale enterprise, it destroyed the social democracy of independent artisans and subjected the impoverished masses to the dictate of capital. Confronted with this evolution, Thomas Hodgskin in the end gave liberty precedence of equality. In him realism was stronger than idealism. William Thompson made the opposite choice. In him idealism was stronger than realism.

Yet the union of liberty and equality remained the day-dream of mankind. It reappeared, though somewhat altered, in Karl Marx, whose system of thought was a synthesis of Hodgskin's theory of development and Thompson's collectivist Utopia. Thus the old ideal was taken over by the critic of political economy, and political economy lost its ideal.

THE SCIENTIFIC FOUNDATIONS OF MODERN ECONOMICS

By the middle of the nineteenth century, the industrial revolution had done its work. Society, which a hundred years before had seemed to develop into a peaceful community of independent peasants and artisans who, serving each other, served themselves, was now torn by violent class struggles. Instead of the hoped-for harmony, a terrible antagonism had sprung up : the antagonism between factory-owners and factory-hands, between the lucky heirs and the unlucky disinherited, between capital and labour which John Locke had fondly hoped to see for ever united.

This, surely, was not the best of all possible worlds, annunciated by Gottfried Leibniz, which the classical economists had believed to be in the making ! Their doctrine was disproved by the hard facts of reality : a new philosophy of economics was needed. Yet the real and the ideal were no longer near to each other, and there seemed to be only one alternative : either to take up the sordid task of capitalist apologetics, or to embrace the dangerous cause of socialist revolution. Faced with this decision, the majority of modern economists resolved to shirk the issue. It became fashionable to insist that political economy was not concerned with the happiness of human kind : that it is not a social philosophy, but a physical science.

Yet before this comfortable doctrine became universal, two thinkers tried to solve the old problem by new ways and means : Hermann Gossen and Richard Jennings. The result of their endeavours was negative : and so, unwillingly and unwittingly, they confirmed the fundamental thesis on which John Locke and Gottfried Wilhelm Leibniz had built the sublime social philosophy of classical economics : the great truth that society can only realize its worldly aim if liberty and equality are alike the guiding principles of human co-existence and co-operation, ideals never to be divided and divorced.

I. The Disappearance of the Old Social Philosophy

The deistic creed had been the inspiration of Locke and Leibniz, Thompson and Hodgskin : a deep trust in the goodness of God was also the foundation of Gossen's thought. He, too, was firmly convinced that the Creation was perfect (186), and that all reasoning, philosophical and scientific, must start from, and strive towards, this great truth. Indeed, his praise of the Maker is more fervent even than that of his predecessors : Man, he exclaims [1] (277), if you have fully comprehended the beauty of creation, sink down in adoration before the Being Who, in His incomprehensible wisdom, power, and goodness, has been able and willing to give you, by apparently insignificant means, happiness so great that it passes all understanding !

These words, however, similar though they are to the language used by the philosophers of classical economics, hide a spirit in essence very different : a world-view not transcendental but positivistic, a trust not in revelation but in science. The foundation of the " true religion of the Creator ", Gossen contends (187 sq.), is given by the truths which we find set forth in our scientific literature to which economic writings (like his own *Exposition of the Laws of Human Intercourse, and of the Principles of Human Action arising from Them*) must also be reckoned ; the dogmas of this religion are the laws of nature which need no faith based on human authorities because they carry with them a proof of their correctness so irresistible, that no man who has ever grasped them, can call up in himself a doubt of their truth ; the sacraments of this religion are the physical and chemical experiments which can be undertaken to demonstrate and confirm the laws of nature enunciated by science : the doctrine that the Creator is really present in the sacraments here becomes true ; the priests of this religion are the men who succeed in discovering a new law of nature, or in defining more strikingly a truth already known, and with every piece of knowledge gained " they proclaim the power, the wisdom, and the goodness of the Creator with a call of trumpets stronger than that which brought down the walls of Jericho ". Lastly, the moral principle of this religion demands that man should shape his actions, according to the laws of nature, in a way which is likely to render the sum

---

[1] It is obvious that the fairest way of discussing the ideas of a thinker of the past is to discuss them on the basis of his own words ; this practice has so far been followed in the present investigation. But in the case of Gossen, it is impossible to proceed in the same way. Gossen wrote in the unattractive style of the Prussian bureaucracy to which he belonged, and his mode of expression is by no means improved by his rather clumsy endeavour to clothe his ideas into high-sounding pathetic sentences which he regarded as particularly convincing and compelling. His work cannot be translated literally. I have therefore attempted to summarize his theses in a way which does justice to their ideal content, not, however, without in every instance faithfully indicating on which page the passage referred to and discussed may be found. The quotations refer to any edition of the work ; the first was published in 1853.

of happiness on earth a maximum : a precept which needs neither heaven nor hell to enforce it but will be followed spontaneously, once the knowledge has become universal that every infringement of this ethical rule by a man will infallibly reduce the sum of his own enjoyments, and reduce it the more, the more serious the infringement has been, the more grievous the sin which he has committed.

A deep and decisive change from the old doctrine of social harmony to a new theory of individual happiness corresponds to the transition from the philosophical deism of the eighteenth to the scientific deism of the nineteenth century which is mirrored in these words. Gossen never saw the body politic as a unit. "The measure of the physical welfare of a nation ", he said in a definition which fully reveals his a-social turn of mind,[1] " is the degree of the enjoyment of life which every individual, belonging to that nation, can procure himself." The classical economists, following Locke, had taught that the faithful fulfilment of the divine laws would lead to the greatest possible well-being of society as a whole ; the modern economists, following Gossen, were to teach that the free operation of the laws of nature must lead to the greatest possible well-being of each individual man. The difference might seem trifling : it is in fact immense. It is immense, because classical economics included a normative doctrine of distribution which is, from the outset, excluded from modern economics.

Excluded from the outset : for the starting-point of Gossen's argument is the individual—the isolated individual. This fact is characteristic of the deep gulf which divides the old economics and the new. Locke had set forth a sublime social philosophy : convinced that God has willed the common happiness of all, he sought to show how the supreme command of the Creator ought to be realized by the establishment of a certain social order, the organization of society on the basis of equality. Gossen expounded a sober physical science : assuming that God has willed the self-sufficient happiness of each, he undertakes to demonstrate that this purpose is realized by the operation of a certain

[1] This significant sentence occurs not in Gossen's well-known book, but in an unknown paper written for the higher examination demanded of candidates with academic education in the Prussian Civil Service (the so-called Assessor-Examen) which Gossen took in 1843. It is partly reproduced in an (as yet unpublished) investigation by an undergraduate of Giessen University : Karl Robert Blum, " Hermann Heinrich Gossen. Eine Untersuchung ueber die Entstehung seiner Lehre. n.d." (cf. p. 99). I am grateful to Prof. F. A. von Hayek, who possesses a typewritten copy of the little treatise, for having made this interesting material accessible to me.

individual instinct, the inborn tendency of self-assertion. For this is the agreement, the only agreement, between reality and ideal which he brings to view : the low and sordid agreement between the elementary selfishness of the human beast and the untutored urges of his physical nature.

Man, Gossen points out (1 sq.), wishes to enjoy his life ; he regards the increase of his well-being to the highest pitch as the purpose of his existence. All men, without exception, act according to this principle, from the cradle to the tomb : the king as well as the beggar, and the penitent monk not less than the frivolous man of society. If men's mode of action, as we observe it in real life, shows many and material differences, this has its cause merely in differing estimates of the magnitude of the various gratifications between which we can choose, and in differing opinions about the obstacles which the present gratification of one desire might oppose to the enjoyment of other gratifications in the future. All men, however, agree that every human being strives to maximize his pleasures—to maximize the enjoyment of his life.

But not only is it undeniable that this maximization of happiness is regarded as the purpose of existence by all men without exception : it is, Gossen asserts, even the true purpose of human existence, the one which the Creator has willed. For, he argues, the fact that the urge towards this aim operates in every breast uneradicably and incessantly, can only be explained if we assume that God has planted in us a power whose operation becomes apparent in this desire, just as we endeavour to explain other tendencies in nature by supposing the existence of corresponding forces which operate according to definite laws. The purpose of the Creator in giving rise to this power, this powerful egoism, in making it part and parcel of human nature, can only have been the wish that it should operate, that it should dominate and direct man. To counter and destroy it—the avowed intention of many systems of morals —is to thwart the designs of the Maker : and how can a creature carry its presumption so far ? (2 sq.).

Not to weaken but to cultivate the selfish instinct, given to us by God—not to oppose but to further its operation, is, therefore, the proper end of all ethical action, and, in particular, of all scientific work. It is the task also of political economy, as Hermann Gossen sees it. In his hands, the science becomes a science of individual prudence. Human life, he explains, lasts a considerable time, and there are a great many enjoyments which the individual can procure himself at any instant, but which, by their consequences, force upon him privations (if not positive sufferings) at a later stage that are out of proportion to the pleasure experienced before. Man would therefore be badly deceived if he should assume that he could realize the purpose of his existence in the most perfect way by procuring himself at any moment that particular pleasure which happens to appear greatest at the time : to find the true magnitude of a gratification, a broader view must be taken : it is not enough correctly to estimate the present enjoyment arising from it, but it is indispensable to deduct all those pains and privations which the realization of the pleasure in question is fit to call forth in the future. Here we have the fundamental problem of economic science : to show the way to the attainment of the true maximum of happiness for the whole life—to the absolute maximum which really deserves this name and which no cleverness and cunning can further augment (1). Political economy—the " science of enjoyment ", as Gossen wished to designate it (34)—is thus a truly ethical science, a science based on the religion of the Creator, teaching as it does, how the supreme precept of the Deity, the highest commandment of the moral code—make yourself happy —can be most fully realized.

It is plain that economic science can only fulfil the task thus allotted to it if it first achieves a thorough understanding of the way in which pleasure is felt and pain experienced by the individual : it is to psychology therefore, and especially to self-observation and self-analysis, that Gossen turns for enlightenment. In doing so, he meets two laws of pleasure which possess outstanding importance. They run as follows : 1. The magnitude of a pleasure continually decreases, until in the end satiety supervenes, if we continue to apply the pleasure-giving object without cessation to our senses. 2. A similar diminution of enjoyment occurs when we repeat the conditions of a pleasure experienced before : the initial magnitude of the gratification is smaller the second time, and the period of enjoyment up to the moment of satiety is shorter ; both the initial magnitude and the duration of the pleasurable experience diminish the more, the more rapidly the repetition is brought about (4 sq.).

In these physical laws of our sentient nature we possess fundamental truths from which valuable inferences can and must be drawn. Three of them have an important bearing on

F

the subject-matter of economic science, enjoyment and happiness : 1. For every individual gratification, there exists a mode of enjoying it—dependent mainly upon the more or less frequent repetition of that gratification—by which the sum of enjoyment is maximized. If this maximum is reached, the sum of enjoyment is diminished both by a more, and by a less, frequent repetition. 2. A man who is free to choose between different gratifications but whose time does not suffice to enjoy all to the full, must, in order to maximize the sum total of his pleasure, procure himself the partial enjoyment of all of them, however different their absolute magnitude may be, before he procures himself the total enjoyment of any one, be it even the one that is greatest. He must procure himself the partial enjoyment of all of them in such a relation that the magnitude of each gratification in the moment when the enjoyment is broken off is the same for all of them. 3. A possibility of augmenting the sum of enjoyments is afforded, not only when we learn to increase a gratification already known, be it by refining the pleasure-giving object, or by improving the mode of its application, but also whenever a new gratification is discovered, be it ever so small in itself (11, 12, 21).

These propositions follow with cogent necessity from the fundamental fact from which Gossen deduces his whole doctrine : the fact that all pleasures diminish in magnitude when we persevere in them for any length of time. Monotony therefore keeps human happiness low, while it is increased by variation, and increased the more, the greater the variety of enjoyments which are within the individual's reach. Man can for this reason only succeed in realizing the purpose of his life in the utmost degree when the whole of creation, with all the forces operative in it, is known to him : for only then will he be aware of all the enjoyments, actual and possible, which are offered to him. The first rule of his action is therefore to strive with all his strength for the attainment of this knowledge. Here we see already, Gossen declares, how the Creator, by the character which He gave to the laws of enjoyment, made it an absolute certainty that the human race will not rest, but progress in art and science, until they have reached the goal of supreme felicity which He, in His incomprehensible wisdom, saw fit to hold out to them (23).

But the way towards this goal is beset with difficulties. At the very first steps already the fact is brought home to man that even a thorough comprehension of the laws of creation does not suffice to secure him the full attainment of the purpose of his life : the fact that, if he wishes to enjoy, he must act upon the external world, to give it that shape in which alone it is capable of ministering to his desires. And this, in turn, leads to the following question, which is of greater practical importance than any other : how do we know, and how can we state, whether an external object has been given a better shape in relation to the purpose of man's life, by an individual or collective action upon it ? In other words : where is a measure by means of which different states of the external world can be compared with each other ? (23 sq.).

It is the theory of value which has to solve this problem. The property of a material thing by which it is fitted to assist us in the attainment of the purpose of our life is commonly expressed in the phrase : the thing has value for us. It plainly follows that the value of an external object for us rises and sinks in exactly the same degree as the assistance which it affords us to this attainment of the purpose of our life : that is to say : that the magnitude of its value is measured exactly by the magnitude of the enjoyment which it procures (24). Value and pleasure are ideas never to be divorced. The laws of the one are at the same time the laws of the other.

It is interesting to observe how the social problem with which the classical economists had grappled so courageously, the problem of equality, makes its appearance even in this rigidly individualistic doctrine of value. To the fundamental law of decreasing utility corresponds, of course, an equally fundamental law of decreasing value. That is to say : the first specimen of a certain species which a man acquires has for him the highest value, just as its application affords him the greatest satisfaction, each succeeding specimen of the same order has, however, less and less value, until, in the end, all value is lost (33). The individual atoms of a particular means of enjoyment possess therefore a very different value. If we observe such a means of enjoyment under the assumption that the mass of atoms in the hands of a man is continually increased, we see, that with the increase of the mass, the value of every new atom added to it will continually decrease, until it has sunk to zero. Hence only a definite, a definitely limited, number of such atoms, i.e., a definite mass, has value for a concrete individual, and an increase of the mass possessed beyond that amount is completely valueless for him (31)—though it may be extremely valuable for his neighbour.

This observation, though it applies equally to all commodities, is particularly true of durable goods, among which all capital goods must be reckoned.   Gossen is quite aware of this fact : if the decrease of value which runs parallel to the increase of the mass at an individual's disposal occurs even in the instance of articles whose matter is consumed as the enjoyment proceeds —he points out—the fall in value must naturally be a quicker one in the instance of commodities which can be used repeatedly, and so much the quicker, the more often the repetition of use can take place.   For the possibility of repeated use implies that so much less matter is consumed as repetitions occur, and therefore that the owner achieves complete satisfaction with a correspondingly smaller stock of that particular means of enjoyment (31).

On a later occasion Gossen comes still nearer to the egalitarian doctrine of the classical economists, implied as it obviously is in his own laws of enjoyment and value.   Speaking of a metallistic monetary system, a system in which every coin has its value not only as money but also as matter, he points out that, under such circumstances, a man will use an article given to him as money by another man, only in its monetary capacity, if the things he can buy with it have a higher value for him than the article itself, considered as a means not of exchange but of enjoyment : and he draws the conclusion that everybody values money as such exactly as he does his marginal enjoyments, i.e., his enjoyments at the time of their breaking off (199 sq.).   From this statement follows with the greatest cogency that the last shilling of a rich man has less value—i.e., creates less happiness —than the last shilling of a poor man because the one has been able to descend much deeper on the scale of his desires, to ascend much higher in the satisfaction of his needs, than the other, and consequently that the transfer of it from the richer to the poorer would decidedly increase the aggregate well-being of both.

Yet, however self-apparent these inferences may be, Gossen closes his eyes to them.   All that he gains from the law of the diminution of value is a piece of good advice to the pleasure-seeking individual : if your forces do not suffice for procuring yourself all possible means of enjoyment to the full, you do best to procure yourself each of them to such an amount that the last atoms of any one represent for you the same value (33).

However, as the true magnitude of a pleasure can only be found if we deduct the pains connected with it, so the true value of a commodity can only be stated with exactness if we take into account the pain-costs of its production. The value of things produced by labour, Gossen explains (35), is diminished precisely by so much as the pain of exertion is to be estimated which is involved in the bringing it forth. This pain of production is, like the pleasure of consumption, uniform in quality. For if we analyse the way in which values are created by labour, we find that all human action is exclusively motion—the bringing the different materials existing in nature into such spacial relation and physical connection that the desired result is achieved by dint of the elementary forces inherent in them : if the cook does his work, what he does is to move the meat, the salt, the butter, and the other ingredients needed, into a pot, move the pot thus filled to the fire, and trust for the rest to the spontaneous agency of the forces inherent in matter. It is the same with all production : labour is motion, and nothing but motion. Indeed, it is physically impossible for us to exert influence on the external world in any other way. Our body holds only one power by which we are enabled to produce changes in material things, the muscular power, and this is a power which is, by its very essence, limited to producing movement in and around us (35).

It is in the motion to be effected, then, that we have to seek the cause of the pain experienced in, and bound up with, the creation of value. As the pleasure of consumption is connected with the gratification of our senses, so the pain of production is connected with the exertion of our muscles. A quantitative analysis leads in both cases to similar, not to say parallel, results. Movement—all movement—is in its first stages a pleasurable experience. But this pleasure, the pleasure of activity, is, like all gratifications, subject to the law of continuous decrease. If it has sunk to zero, not only does the enjoyment cease, as is the case in the instance of gratifications which the external world affords without exertion on our part, but the necessity of an expense of energy for the continuation of the motion immediately begins to cause us pain. This pain is the negative counterpart, as it were, to the positive pleasure experienced before. While the pleasure, starting from a maximum, continually decreased and tended towards zero, the pain, starting from zero, continually increases and tends towards a maximum—the absolute exhaustion of all muscular power (36).

If we now consider this muscular exertion in its bearing on the purpose of human life, it is at once obvious that man will have to procure himself this gratification according to the same principles as any other, because motion belongs, as we have seen, within certain limits to the sources of enjoyment.   To maximize his happiness, he will have to walk and to talk—indeed, he will have to work—as long as the pleasure of activity is still positive. But not even when it has sunk to zero and become negative, will it be advisable, and indeed reasonable, to call a halt, provided that by the exertion a pleasure-giving object is brought into existence.   For in this case two items will have to be taken into the account : the pleasure or pain connected with the production, and the pleasure, the always positive pleasure, connected with the consumption, of the means of enjoyment thus procured.   The net result alone will decide.   In other words : in this case man is able further to augment the sum of his enjoyments by continuing his labour, i.e., by persevering in motion, beyond the point up to which it is pleasurable in itself, as long as the pain involved in production does not outweigh the pleasure afforded by the thing produced (38).

These considerations lead Gossen to a statement of the greatest importance for theory and practice : the statement that, to maximize the happiness of a man—to bring about the most perfect realization of his purpose of existence—the magnitude of his enjoyments at the point where they are broken off, must keep the balance to the pain experienced by him in the last· moment of his work (43).   The absolute maximum of value attainable is reached if work is continued until (marginal) pain and (marginal) value become equal (39).   The final result of Gossen's investigation—the " main principle of the science of enjoyment "—can therefore be expressed in the following words : " To achieve a maximum of enjoyment, man must divide his time and his energies between the pursuit of the different gratifications in such a way that the value of the atom last created of any pleasure-giving object is equal to the magnitude of the pain which he would experience if he should create this atom in the last moment of his exertion " (45).

According to Gossen's firm conviction, this proposition contains the ultimate solution of the fundamental problem of economic science. It reveals, so he contends, both how the individual has to value the objects of the external world which enter his sphere of life, and what rule of action follows from this valuation. The results thus gained, he asserts, tally " most exactly " with experience. Nothing can be more characteristic of his general outlook—of the individualistic philosophy which he bequeathed to the following generations—than the proof which he offers for this assertion. " In order to reach the most perfect certainty in this respect," he says to his reader (45 sq.), " only read Campe's tale for children, *Robinson Crusoe*,[1] up to the point where he finds his man Friday." There you have the proof : for Robinson's mode of action will find general approval exactly in proportion to its agreement with the principle enunciated above.

Edgeworth has called this theory a " theory of economic equilibrium " (Palgrave's *Dictionary*, II, 232). But its subject and object is only the economic equilibrium of the individual, not the economic equilibrium of society. The " conclusions tolerably obvious to common sense " (*ib.*) which Gossen draws from it, and which are set forth with tiring exhaustiveness in the language of symbols (48–80), confirm this indictment. The final result of the careful mathematical investigation, which is summed up in the following passage, again exposes his extreme individualism which regards the isolated individual as the only object both of scientific interest and of ethical action : " In order to increase the enjoyment of his life to the highest pitch, man must endeavour

" 1. to augment as far as possible the number of pleasures open to him and their absolute magnitude,

" 2. to augment as far as possible his labour power and his efficiency in applying it,

" 3. to diminish as far as possible the exertion necessary for the total satisfaction of his desires, and

" 4. to use his energy in the pursuit of the different pleasures in the way which is indicated as reasonable by the foregoing computations "—i.e., practically so that the magnitude of enjoyment at the point where it is broken off, is equal for each of them taken separately, and a maximum for all of them taken together (81).

However, even the greatest individualist cannot overlook the fact that individual happiness is conditioned by, and indeed dependent upon, social co-operation. Therefore Gossen introduces the social bond, by way of an appendix as it were, into his argument and doctrine. The four conditions for the attain-

[1] This is a short version of Defoe's novel, very popular in Germany.

ment of supreme individual happiness, which is the purpose of human life, he points out, are to a certain degree self-contradictory. On the one hand, man must endeavour to procure himself as many different gratifications as possible : and this endeavour leads to a splitting-up of his time and energy between a great many operations. On the other hand, he must strive to increase his productivity as far as possible : and this demands that he should concentrate his activity on one object only, for only so can he acquire perfection in his work. Social intercourse obviously offers a way out of this dilemma : by exchange, the two contradictory demands can be complied with at the same time. Division of labour increases both the efficiency of production and the variety of consumption. The laws of enjoyment teach us, how and why : if only one commodity be produced by a man, the great mass at his disposal is at first, in spite of his productive efficiency, of comparatively little value to him : but an extraordinary increase of value can swiftly be effected by exchanging any one unit of it against any one unit of some other means of enjoyment which he did not possess before. Now, the same advantage is obviously gained by the individual with whom he barters : and so it is that life in society ministers to individual happiness (81 sq.).

Yet the laws of enjoyment not only disclose why exchange with others is advantageous to isolated man, they also indicate where the advantage comes to an end. Clearly, exchange remains favourable for an individual, and should be continued, until an equalization of values has taken place—until the quantities in the man's possession have so changed that the value of the last atoms of the two (or more) articles which are involved in the transaction has become equal for him (84).

This formula indeed demonstrates how each of the contracting parties can increase and maximize his happiness by the exchange. But this is not enough : to every act of barter belong at least two individuals. We need therefore an ampler formula : a formula which covers both. In other words : we must find and expose the conditions of the social maximization of happiness in this little trading community. How is the exchange to be performed if a maximum of value in this sense is to be achieved ? Gossen does not shirk this question : he gives a plain and convincing answer. Each of the two articles involved must be distributed after the exchange between A and B in such a way that the last atom which either of them retains or receives, has equal value for both. This truth is found by the simple consideration that, if any other distribution should prevail, the transfer of the atom which has less value for the one into the hands of the other would add to his happiness more than it would detract from the happiness of his partner, and thus an increase in the aggregate sum-total of well-being would be brought about. Here Gossen at last faces the social problem and solves it in the only spirit in which it is capable of solution —the spirit of equality : " In order to create, by means of exchange, a maximum of value, every single article must be so distributed among all men that the last atom which each receives of any commodity represents for him the same value as the last atom of this commodity for any other " (85).

Thus Gossen solves the problem of social felicity in the same sense as the problem of individual happiness : to the personal must correspond an interpersonal equalization of values and enjoyments. But it is simple to find a theoretical formula, and difficult to reach a practical solution. Strictly speaking, even the application of the principles according to which the individual can secure his personal maximum of happiness, is impossible, because such application would presuppose an exact measurement of the pleasures experienced in consumption as well as of the toil undergone in production. Here the difficulties are still graver and greater. In the case of the isolated individual, a rough estimate based on self-knowledge may enable us to dispense with an exact measurement ; but in the case of society as a whole, even this substitute fails us, because we have not, and cannot have, any direct experience of other people's sensations which we must know in order to carry out the interpersonal comparison of values and enjoyments on which the realization of the social maximum of happiness depends (91).

Gossen's disciples have declared this problem theoretically insoluble : Gossen regarded it as practically solved. In consequence of their common nature, he points out, all individuals have, in a given country, the same needs to satisfy, and their scales of preference are also more or less identical since they, too, are fixed by man's physical constitution. Yet even if there should be originally some differences of inclination, they would be compensated by the rise of social habits which bring about and uphold a definite uniformity in the satisfaction of human wants (Blum, l. c., 50 sq.). Thus there is, from the outset, a firm basis for interpersonal comparisons. And, indeed, the everyday economic intercourse in a civilized community could not take place without them : the social division of labour which we see so firmly established, presupposes the existence of certain relations in which all pleasure-giving objects can be mutually exchanged. For the individual can only restrict his economic activities to the production of one or a few articles if he knows that he will be able to exchange his products for other things vitally needed, and exchange them in a more or less predetermined relation. How these exchange-relations are formed, we learn from experience. They are formed by means of the monetary system, and the monetary system arises little by little through the habitual expression of all values in terms of one commodity which thus becomes the general measure and medium of exchange (91 sq.).

Once money has been invented and introduced, Gossen declares, it becomes easy to realize the maximum of happiness both personal and interpersonal. With the help of this index, the individual can, without difficulty, choose the branch of production which promises the highest reward : he need only discover by what type of work he will be enabled to gain the largest sum of money, in order to obtain the most perfect certainty that it is this activity which will procure him the greatest possible sum of enjoyment. And as money makes it easy to choose the best branch of production, so it helps to find the best division of consumption : in spending a given amount of purchasing power, the individual need only estimate what concrete means of enjoyment that is within his reach, will procure him the greatest gratification, in order to make absolutely sure that he uses his income in the way which leads to the highest possible degree of satisfaction (93 sq.).

Now, it is clear that the happiness of society as a whole is truly maximized, if the well-being of all its individual members is increased to the highest pitch. And it is in every instance increased to the highest pitch, if all can freely follow the laws of enjoyment, practically applicable as they have been made by the establishment of a monetary system, which makes incomes and prices mutually comparable. It is therefore freedom, and freedom alone, which represents the fundamental condition of a maximization of social felicity. As the laws of enjoyment are constituted, Gossen asserts, the endeavour of every individual to augment his enjoyment of life leads, after the introduction of money, to the result that each receives a share in the social product according to the pain which he has taken upon himself in its production, as soon as it is possible to remove all obstacles which prevent the individual from using his money in the most reasonable way, and from engaging in that line of production which is most favourable for him in the given circumstances (99). If only this condition is fulfilled, if only perfect liberty is granted, Gossen declares, men—all men—will be as happy as they can possibly be. For by the construction of the laws of enjoyment, the Creator has contrived that the human race incessantly use their intellectual and material powers in such a way as always to procure themselves the maximum of enjoyment, *as soon as all obstacles are removed which hinder the individual to use his money in the most appropriate way and to embark in that line of production which offers the highest reward* (101).

This result of his investigation seems to Gossen fully to confirm the optimistic trust in the goodness of God from which his argument started.   Economic science, he contends, convincingly demonstrates how the Creator has achieved His benevolent design : He has granted man the freest self-determination, but by the law of decreasing utility He has ensured that the individual will use this freedom only in the way which is most conducive to the well-being of the whole (277). Indeed, by this means God has made the fairy-tale of paradise a reality. Even more : He has surpassed the old legend, because, in the real world, the material gratification of our desires is accompanied by the moral conviction that whatever we enjoy we deserve to enjoy, and whatever we contribute to the enjoyment of our fellows under the system of divided labour and mutual exchanges greatly surpasses the exertion which they have to undergo in order to contribute to our enjoyment. The full realization of this true paradise, however, of this paradise on earth created by our own hands, entirely depends upon the removal of the obstacles to free choice in production and consumption, which alone, as we have seen, stand in the way of supreme happiness for every one and all (102).

The fundamental opposition of this theory to the classical doctrine is obvious at once : while Locke and his disciples had declared that both liberty and equality are indispensable conditions of universal felicity, Gossen's train of thought ends in one postulate only—the postulate of *laissez-faire.* Yet we must be careful not to be deceived by words. It is not difficult to see that Gossen's claim is only true if the term liberty is taken in its

widest sense—the sense in which it includes full liberty of ascent :
that is to say—equality of opportunity.   He is unwilling to speak
about this point, and he never speaks about it explicitly : but
implicitly he cannot but admit that the absolute maximum of
social happiness can never be reached unless the society in
question is built, not only on the principle of liberty, but also on
the principle of equality.

The very next steps of his argument already indicate the
great and decisive difficulties of his doctrine which arise from the
fact that it is based on a pure, and not on an egalitarian, liberalism.   For now he comes to discuss the phenomenon of rent
which he has so far left out of account.   He reluctantly admits
that, even in this best of all possible worlds, there is a natural
source of social injustice : the different productivity of different
portions of the soil.   Equal labour is rewarded by unequal
results, according to the place where it is performed : one plot
of land may favour human exertion much, the other little.   The
possession of the better ground spontaneously increases the sum
of enjoyments of him who holds it.   Under a legal system of
absolute property, the ownership of qualitatively superior pieces
of the soil can therefore be made a source of income, and, indeed,
a source of income without labour (102).   For what is a rent ?
" The effect of the receipt of a rent ", Gossen himself states,
" is, that—as far as it will go—its owner can procure himself all
gratifications without exertion " (105).   But the land-rent is
only one special case among a great variety of unearned incomes,
just as the productive power of the ground is only one instance
of the many forces of nature which have been made the object
of private appropriation, and thence the instrument of un-
deserved enjoyments (Blum, *l. c.*, 54, sq.).

Here Gossen is—in spite of his purely individualistic approach
to, and purely libertarian solution of, the problem of social
felicity—confronted with the fact of exploitation.   It glares at
him even through his lifeless mathematical symbols.   For what
is the true meaning of the statement that one and the same formula
expresses the magnitude of the rent paid and of the rent received,
only that in the one case its sign is positive, in the other negative ?
What can it mean but this : that the same amount of purchasing
power which is surrendered by him who pays the rent, accrues
to him who receives it : that the loss of the one is the other's
gain : that the happiness of the property-less is diminished so
that the well-being of the man of property may be increased ?

By a defalcation from the rent to be paid, so Gossen's algebra and geometry teach us, the same result is achieved as by an addition to the rent received : by both the sum-total of happiness is augmented (114). But—alas !—the two things can never happen at the same time : if the rent to be paid is reduced, the rent received must fall with it : if the welfare of the debtor is to be increased, the income of the creditor must be curtailed. Here then we behold a serious conflict of interests which liberty alone can never settle : a problem of social felicity which only an egalitarian arrangement can overcome.

Thus the postulate of equality, which seemed excluded from Gossen's scientific system of thought, reappears and demands its due. In his theory of action, Gossen endeavoured to demonstrate how the perfect realization of unlimited freedom in production and consumption would multiply the well-being of the community. But in his earnest quest for supreme social felicity, he found himself in the end confronted with an inevitable decision : either to abandon his ideal, or to accept the postulate of equality. In this respect, he is the true representative of the modern economists who came after him ; and, therefore, it is expedient, before we try his practical suggestions, to make ourselves acquainted with the theoretical teachings of Richard Jennings, who, together with Hermann Gossen, showed the coming generations the way to a new economics.

Gossen's book, considered as a link in the chain of intellectual development, is characteristic of the deep change which all thought underwent in the first half of the nineteenth century. He occupied, as it were, an intermediate position between the old and the new : on the one hand, he had not yet parted with the deistic creed of the age of Smith, but, on the other, he was already imbued with the scientific spirit of the Spencerian age. In Jennings,[1] we see the transition perfected. He was a scientist and nothing else. This is already apparent in the definition of society which he advanced. " A civilized nation is evidently an organic body, that has arrived at a certain stage of maturity at which it has become susceptible of common feeling, capable

[1] Since Jennings' name does not appear in the *Dictionary of National Biography*, the following details concerning his career, which I owe to the kindness of Mr. Walter Roberts, may not be without interest : Jennings was born in 1814 and received his education at Eton and Trinity College, Cambridge. Called to the bar in 1838, he was connected with Lincoln's Inn. He was a Justice of the Peace both for Middlesex and Carmarthenshire and held in 1859 the office of High Sheriff in the latter county, where he seems to have possessed landed property of some size.´ Jennings died in 1891.

of joint action, and competent to entertain a public opinion "
(*Natural Elements of Political Economy*, 1855, 218).

The great change, however, which affected political economy
like all other branches of knowledge, consisted not only in a
transition from a transcendental to a positivist world-view, but
also in a transition from a social to an individualist philosophy
of life. To define society as a living whole, may seem at first
to involve a rejection of individualism. Yet Jennings was as
modern in this respect as in the other. The following passage
clearly shows how swiftly he abandoned his social definition for
a purely atomistic approach to the problems of economic reality :
" Human communities are living organisms. This appellation
would probably be considered just, even if nations were to be
regarded as consisting merely of an aggregate of unconnected
human beings, but much more justly may it be applied to them
when they are understood to be connected by the ties of marital
and filial affection, of friendship, patriotism, love of society, love
of display, and by all the other sentiments and passions which
bind us, directly or indirectly, to our fellow-men, and the
operation of which is most strikingly visible in such of our actions
as are concerned with the realization and the fruition of wealth.
Now, it has been well observed, in reference to physiology, that
no living organism can be fully characterized but by a description
comprising all the particulars, not merely of the organized body
itself, but also of the medium in which it exists, not merely of its
organs, but also of their functions—not merely of the agent, but
also of the thing acted on." So far, so good. But the next
words bring a quite unmotivated change. " If this observation
be applied to the subject of Political-economy, it is evident that
every comprehensive description of this branch of philosophy must point expressly both to man and to exchangeable
objects ; to man, the organism, and to exchangeable objects,
the medium by which civilized man is surrounded, on which
his organs act, and from which they derive the means of his
support, his satisfaction, and his gratification. The subject,
therefore, which Political-economy undertakes to investigate may
be described as the relations of human nature and exchangeable
objects—as the effects which human nature produces on exchangeable objects, and the effects which exchangeable objects
produce on human nature " (61-3).

Thus it is, in effect, not the relation of the human family to
the physical universe, but the relation of individual man to the

concrete objects surrounding him, which must be regarded as the subject-matter of economic science.   "When we reflect upon the series of events which, in the popular acceptance of the terms, without reference to any school of Political-economy, constitute the production, the distribution, and the consumption of wealth, as they are known to each of us by daily experience, it becomes at once evident, that whatever may be the natural laws which govern each of these phenomena, the thing governed is the mutual relation, direct or indirect, of two simultaneous events, one occurring in the province of human nature, and the other in the external world.   When nations produce, laborious efforts are made and felt by men, whilst matter receives improvement ; when they exchange, quantities and qualities are mentally compared, and actions are decided on and executed, whilst forms of matter are transferred ; when they consume, satisfaction is felt, whilst material objects are absorbed, or resolved into other elements : on each of these occasions there occur simultaneously mental phenomena and physical phenomena, mutually connected by laws, to determine which is the chief object of abstract Political-economy."   Indeed, " all the phenomena of Political-economy are of two kinds, caused severally by the action of matter on man, and of man on matter " (9 sq., 21 sq.).

This starting-point is at once curiously similar, and strikingly opposed, to the starting-point of John Locke.   It is similar in form and opposite in fact.   It is similar because it is also concerned with the inter-relation of matter and man, but different because the word man does not mean here the representative of the collective whole, but the independent and self-centred unit.   For it is in the mind of the individual that Jennings looks for the laws of the market : " A very little consideration ", he says (12), " will probably make it manifest, that in order to conduct this investigation according to the system, and in the order which alone can be successful, we must commence, in the present state of psychology, with discussing questions which properly appertain to that branch of philosophical inquiry."

But is this not a totally inappropriate approach ?   Political economy is a science of the body politic ; it should seem therefore that it has to begin with, and, indeed, to limit itself to, the analysis of inter-human—that is to say, super-individual—relations. Jennings, in deciding this question, is again openly inconsistent : he accepts the premiss, but he rejects the conclusion : " Political-economy, indeed, like every other portion of political philosophy,

ought, in justice, to be required to investigate those principles
only which are peculiar to social and political conditions of life,
or which are never seen in operation except when men are
observed in the form and under the condition of aggregated
masses, connected by social ties and bound by civil institutions "
(12), he admits ; but, he goes on to say, it is "imperatively
necessary . . . that the student, before he investigates the superadded mental laws, which influence the actions of aggregated
men, should acquire a knowledge of the primary mental laws
which guide the actions of each isolated individual " (13).
Therefore, he asserts, "this branch of philosophy cannot be
thoroughly understood until the subordinate principles of psychology have been adequately investigated " by "an inquiry
into the elementary nature of individual man " (16) ; and, he
concludes, " in pursuing the course indicated by these and similar
considerations, we shall be led to examine, in the first instance,
certain elementary principles of human susceptibility " (21).

Yet, if we thus base our analysis of the economic system upon
an investigation of the isolated individual, shall we ever reach
our scientific aim ? We want to build a science of economic
life, to formulate the natural laws of social intercourse : but
the individual is endowed with a free will, and this freedom
frustrates all attempts to bring his actions under universal rules
of absolute regularity. We have therefore seriously to consider,
" whether any analogy can be reasonably deemed to exist between
the movements of purely material substances and the actions of
animated beings, or whether there be not something in the
mystery of life incompatible with the supposition, that any of
the actions of a living creature are guided by invariable laws of
Nature " (44). However, Jennings thinks, we need not be dis-
couraged ; for, in the last analysis, man is but a somewhat more
highly developed animal, and this fact helps us out of our difficulty. " To resolve this question by the simplest and the most
incontrovertible evidence, recourse would, in such a case,
naturally be had to that field of observation in which the laws
of mere animal life are paramount, and in which also their effect
can be observed in large numbers of instances ; such as is offered
by the actions of several gregarious families of the brute creation,
which live in a state of nature, and carry on their respective
modes of production and of consumption in harmonious co-
operation. Without referring to natural history for an account
of such works of the animal kingdom as the houses of beavers,

the accumulation of ants, the migration of birds, and the like, if the personal attention of the inquirer were to be directed to the labours of a few hives of bees, and he were to register the amount of their industrious population and the quantity of honey accumulated and consumed during several successive years, he would find it impossible to resist the conviction that these actions are governed by fixed natural laws . . ." (44 sq.). Now, " Political-economy treats only of those human suscepti- bilities and appetences which are similar or analogous to those which . . . [can be] witnessed in the brute creation ; . . . it examines only those motives which are derived, more or less remotely, from the attraction of pleasure or the repulsion of pain . . ." (45). It is therefore, in spite of its individualist starting-point, and in spite of the freedom of the individual, a science in the true sense of the term, a physical science. For, after all, " the involuntary movements of certain parts of the body, as the pulsation of the heart, and the inflation of the lungs, are known to be subject to fixed and invariable physical laws, no less in the case of the human subject than in the case of the lower members of the animal kingdom " and so " can be examined independently of, and without reference to, those predominant, intellectual and moral and religious aspirations to which, in common with all the other functions of the human body, they subserve " (46). Thus we may confidently assume that " when human nature should be examined abstractedly, and the human masses should be regarded as entirely occupied in collecting the sweets which lie hid in the wilds of the creation . . . the in- dustrial and fruitional actions of nations would be found to be governed by definite and invariable laws of Nature " [1] (48).

In this way, Jennings not only abandons his social definition of the body politic for a purely individualist approach to its economic problems, but even discards the idea of man as a spiritual being for a purely physical conception in the vein of

[1] Jennings' materialism was so great that he did not confine this conviction to the " industrial and fruitional actions of nations ". He was not disinclined to embrace a radical determinism, in the sense of a necessary dependence of the higher spiritual phenomena upon the lower physical facts and tendencies. " A wider view ", he says, " may possibly show that this law of the uniform continuance of the great actions of Political-economy is subject to the influence of other laws of still wider jurisdiction. It may appear, as some have thought, that the energy of human action moves in a slow revolution round our globe,—that the natural course of human activity may be traced, advancing from East to West, and from South to North, over a path deter- mined by the position of the magnetic pole, and that there may thus be witnessed, in the vast fields of History and of Physical Geography, that co-existence of the phenomena of human action and of electromagnetic currents which are apparent to every observer of the nervous system " (151).

the most consistent materialism.   In fact, already his attempt
at a division of the subject matter of economic science leads him
from psychology on to physiology : " Matter ", he says, " comes
in contact with human organs externally, as in consumption, or
laborious efforts are originated internally, as in production and
distribution ; from these causes there arise sensations, which are
more or less satisfactory,. or the reverse ; these sensations, when
remembered together with the objects, or together with the
actions in which they originated, give rise to complex conceptions, in which the objects and the actions are regarded as more
or less valuable : thus, briefly described, is constituted the chain
of causation which leads inwards from matter to the seat of our
ideas. Again, that which leads outwards from the seat of our
ideas to matter may be indicated thus : the conception of an
object of preponderating value, and known to be within the
possibility of attainment, is formed and entertained ; a desire
to possess the object ensues ; the gratification of this desire is
determined on by the will ; the intellectual faculties, or the
bodily parts, are exerted ;   their efforts tend directly, or indirectly, to affect external matter. If these phenomena be
considered consecutively, it is evident that the principal motive
by which the performance of these actions is to be regarded as
instigated, and on the conditions of which the manner and degree
of their performance chiefly depend, is the conception of value
mentally entertained.   It is obvious, therefore, that it is to this
mental conception . . . that we must look for the classificatory
distinctions of Political-economy.   Bearing in mind these considerations, we shall conclude, that the field in which the classificatory marks best adapted for our purpose exist, is not that of
external material Wealth, but that intermediate field betwixt
mind and external matter which is offered by the organization
of the human body, as exhibited by the researches of anatomy
and of physiology " (22–4 ; 27).

Nothing can be more characteristic than this abrupt but
conscious transition from " the conception of value mentally
entertained " to " the organization of the human body ".
Jennings does not rest until he has reduced all his fundamental
conceptions to physical categories.   " It is quite evident that in
both Consumption and Production there occur a simultaneous
action and reaction of external objects upon man, and of man
upon external objects : when the operations of Consumption are
performed, food may give support, comfort, gratification to men,

whilst men masticate, swallow, digest, and assimilate food ;
raiment may give decency, protection, or decoration to men,
while men expose raiment to friction, or to the influences of the
sun and the atmosphere ; but it is manifest that the *purpose
contemplated* is not the destruction of food, or of raiment, but
certain benefits accruing to the consumer with which this destruction is by nature indissolubly connected : and when the
operations of Production are performed, whilst the labourer
moves the soil, the weaver plies the shuttle, the carpenter con-
structs with wood or the mason with stone, resistance, difficulty,
fatigue, are felt ; but these are the inseparable adjuncts of labour,
and not the *end proposed* or the object immediately contemplated
by the producer. It is clear; therefore, that these two great
classes of actions will be rightly described, Consumption, as
comprising actions of which the *motive* is the contemplated effect
of external objects upon man, and Production, as comprising
actions of which the motive is the contemplated effect of man
upon external objects " (79 sq.). Yet motives are but shadows :
" To refer to motives as marks of classification, is to employ for
this purpose metaphysical abstractions " (80). Sensations, as
phenomena of the body, seem to offer a ground of division which
is more in agreement with the demands of scientific exactness.
" The sensations which are paramount in Consumption being
usually attended with pleasure, and the sensations which are
paramount in Production being usually of an opposite character,
it might at first appear easy to denote our classes . . . by a
reference to this circumstance " (86 sq.). But not even this
procedure seems to Jennings scientific enough. Sensations may
be bodily phenomena, but they are not tangible. What we
need are classificatory marks that can be seen. Such, however,
can only be furnished by anatomy and physiology : " In order
to substitute for these abstractions, objects cognizable by the
external senses, we may have recourse to Physiology, and consider the processes of the human organism . . ." (80 sq.). Only
if we take this course shall we arrive at a satisfactory—that is to
say, " scientific "—distinction between the economic categories
of consumption and production : " When external matter
produces sensible effects upon man, impressions are always made,
in the first instance, upon certain trunks of nerve-fibres, which
lead *to* the sensorium. . . . When man acts upon external
matter, impressions are always made upon similar but distinct
trunks of nerve-fibres, leading *from* the sensorium . . . these two

classes of fibrous trunks being never convertible, but each being used invariably, as the parallel lines of a railway are commonly, for distinctive communication, in opposite directions. . . . There appears to be no reason why these two several channels of sensational influence, and of motor force, thus distinctly marked out by Nature, may not be employed to denote the two classes of human actions in which they invariably take a part " (81 sq.).

These considerations—considerations which may appeal to the scientist, but must seem strange to the social philosopher— lead Jennings to his fundamental definitions. Consumption he describes as " that action and reaction of matter and man, by which matter supplies the means of gratification to man, while man diminishes or annihilates the valuable properties of matter. The former of these processes is the object of consumption, which is therefore denoted, physiologically, by the fact that, during its continuance, the operation of the afferent trunks of nerve-fibre prevails ". Production, on the other hand, is " that action and reaction of man and matter, by which valuable properties are imparted to matter, whilst reflex impressions of resistance are felt and sustained by man. The former of these processes is the object of production, which is therefore denoted, physiologically, by the fact that, during its continuance, the operation of the efferent trunks of nerve-fibre prevails " (73). Between production and consumption, however, the field of economic science is divided. They are " the two great branches of the subject of Political-economy " (82 sq.).

This classification of economic phenomena, and the whole body of doctrine based on it, is characterized by the obvious fact that it excludes from the discussion the social problem—distribution. In the case of Jennings, the consequence and purpose of the purely individualistic approach to economics is still more obvious than in the case of Gossen : the building up of an economic theory which can disregard the conflict of classes and discard the ideal of equality, no longer to be realized but by a social revolution. To Jennings, distribution is merely " an intermediate process, that determines how valuable objects, which have been produced, shall be consumed " (73), and no more.

Now, the principles of production and consumption which Jennings developed on the basis of this physical anthropology, are closely akin to those enunciated not long before by Gossen.

He, too, formulates a law of diminishing utility : " With respect to all Commodities, our feelings show that the degrees of satisfaction do not proceed *pari passu* with the quantities consumed, —they do not advance equally with each instalment of the Commodity offered to the senses, and then suddenly stop,—but diminish gradually, until they ultimately disappear, and further instalments can produce no further satisfaction. In this progressive scale the increments of sensation resulting from equal increments of the Commodity are obviously less and less at each step,—each degree of sensation is less than the preceding degree. Placing ourselves at that middle point of sensation . . . which . . . is the best position that can be chosen for measuring deviations from the usual amount, we may say that the law which expresses the relation of degrees of sensation to quantities of Commodities is of this character,—if the average or temperate quantity of Commodities be increased, the satisfaction derived is increased in a less degree, and ultimately ceases to be increased at all ; if the average or temperate quantity be diminished, the loss of more and more satisfaction will continually ensue, and the detriment thence arising will ultimately become exceedingly great.   From this law of the variation of sensations consequences will be found to ensue, affecting more or less all the problems of Price and of Production " (98–100).

Confirmed individualist though he was, Jennings did not fail to see, and was unprejudiced enough to state, the social implications of this important observation : the social relativity of values in a class-society : " It is but too well known to every condition of men, that the degree of each sensation which is produced, is by no means commensurate with the quantity of the Commodity applied to the senses,—to the rich, that much more than enough is incapable of affording much more satisfaction, that when the cup of pleasure has been filled it is to no purpose that the stream of Wealth remains unexhausted,—to the poor, that much less than enough produces feelings very different from mere loss of satisfaction " (96 sq.).

With Jennings, as with Gossen, a law of increasing exertion corresponds to the law of decreasing enjoyment : " Let any muscular effort be made, as, for example, let the arm be extended in a horizontal direction, and be held there, counteracting the force of gravitation : the first sensations may be the indifferent, or perhaps agreeable sensations of activity and of power, arising from the exercise of the muscular sense ; but the sensations

which succeed assume a different complexion, and progressively
merge into sensations of resistance, of a necessity for effort . . .
and ultimately of a painful reluctance to persist : such are the
class of sensations which may be distinguished as the sensations
of Physical Labour.   Again, let the brain be exerted to perform
any mental work, as, for example, to cast up long and complicated accounts ; the feeling first experienced may be the pleasure
of occupation, of the employment of previously acquired knowledge, of surmounting difficulties ; but if the undertaking be
persevered in, and we attempt continuously to overcome the
feeling of resistance (if this word may be used to indicate a
sensation which we all feel to be very similar to the resistance
felt during Physical Labour, and which Physiology sanctions by
the observation that cerebral movements accompany efforts of
thought), sensations will arise which, if it were possible, we should
willingly shake off.   These accompaniments of our toilsome
thoughts . . . we may distinguish as the sensations of Mental
Labour " (116 sq.).   As long as exertion is pleasure, it underlies
the law of diminishing utility ;   as soon as it becomes work, it
falls under the law of increasing disutility : " If we turn our
attention, in the first instance, to the point at which action
becomes labour, when the feeling of pleasure, consequent upon
the exercise of our faculties, becomes merged in a feeling to which
we are averse, it will be quite evident that this state of feeling
would not continue if the work should be continued, but that,
on the contrary, the degree of the toilsome sensation would
increase, and would become insupportable, if the work should
be protracted indefinitely . . .   Between these two points, the
point of incipient effort and the point of painful suffering, it is
quite evident that the degree of toilsome sensations endured does
not vary directly as the quantity of work performed, but increases
much more rapidly, like the resistance offered by an opposing
medium to the velocity of a moving body . . .   Thus, if the
quantity produced . . . were to be divided into any number of
parts of equal magnitude, the amount of toilsome sensation
attending each succeeding increment would be found greater
than that which would attend the increment preceding, and the
amount of toilsome sensation attending each succeeding decrement would be found less than that which would attend the
decrement preceding " (118–20).

Like the law of decreasing pleasure in consumption, the law
of increasing pain in production has important bearings on the

practical problem of social policy, which Jennings openly admits :
" When this observation comes to be applied to the toilsome
sensations endured by the working classes ", he states, " it will
be found convenient to fix on a middle point, the average amount
of toilsome sensation attending the average amount of labour,
and to measure from this point the degrees of variation. If,
for the sake of illustration, this average amount be assumed to
be of ten hours' duration, it would follow that, if at any period
the amount were to be supposed to be reduced to five hours, the
sensations of Labour would be found, at least by the majority of
mankind, to be almost merged in the pleasures of occupation
and exercise, whilst the amount of work performed would [at
most] only be diminished by one half ; if, on the contrary, the
amount were to be supposed to be increased to twenty hours,
the quantity of work produced would [at best] only be doubled,
whilst the amount of toilsome suffering would become insupportable " (119 sq.). Therefore, " if Nature rightly teaches us that
the last fractions of protracted Toil are attended with ever-
increasing suffering . . . a purely scientific Political-economy
cannot rightly hold that the tenth hour of the artificer's time
must still be inexorably devoted to the purposes of Production "
(215).

From the feelings of satisfaction and dissatisfaction thus
experienced arises, by dint of the principle of association, the
phenomenon of value which governs all economic life : " The
sensations which we have examined are remembered in their
various degrees of intensity, and in their opposite qualities, as
satisfactory or toilsome, in conjunction with the objects and with
the actions which they have invariably accompanied, and,
becoming thus mentally combined with them, invest them
ultimately in the mind with that attribute of Value in respect
of which they are balanced by the judgment, and are selected
by the will, and become the efficient motives of the actions of
Consumption, of Distribution, and of Production " (124 sq.).

This subjective theory of value indicates the point where
Gossen and Jennings meet : it is the starting-point of modern
economics. And it is here that we most clearly see how the
physiological doctrine of the one naturally combines with the
mathematical approach of the other : " Why . . . are air, light,
and water of no value ?   In this question there is an ambiguity ;
as a whole, light and water are of extreme Value, but if it be
asked why any definite quantity of light or of water is of no Value,

the answer is obvious—because it can generally be spared, on account of the indefinite quantity that exists. . . . Under peculiar circumstances a small quantity of water, as in the mid-passage of the desert, and of light, as ancient lights in a city, are valuable " (210 sq.). Thus a functional relation exists between the mental and the material magnitude, between the stock of the commodity valued and the value bestowed on the commodity : " The organs of the human body . . . are capable of conveying to the senses satisfaction or gratification only within certain definite limits ; hence . . . no Value can be attached to a limited amount of such objects as exist in unlimited quantities, for the obvious reason that if such an amount were to be withheld, others of equal magnitude could be substituted for it, and this until all the wants of human nature should be satiated. . . . When a moderate quantity of a Commodity has reached the senses of the consumer, each successive addition of the Commodity produces sensations progressively less and less satisfactory, and vice versa ; hence . . . in proportion as objects are less abundant, any limited quantity must be held more valuable, and in proportion as they are more abundant, it must be held less valuable, the Value of every Commodity being dissipated as it increases in quantity, like a circle in the water . . ." (208 sq.).

From the concept of subjective value thus defined, Jennings then advances to the concept of objective value. " The fisher-man . . . extends to his estimation of the finny tribes, of his nets, his boat, his hut, not only a ray of the satisfaction which is derived from appeasing hunger and gratifying the palate,—the miner extends to his estimation of his coal, his shafts, and tram-road, and ropes, and pickaxes, not only a grateful remembrance of the uses of fuel,—the husbandman extends to his estimation of his flour and his grain, his agricultural implements and his farm, not only a sense of the benefits which the staff of life affords, —but each of these, and all other members of a civilized community, in their several vocations, extend to their estimation of every Commodity a consciousness of the benefits that may be derived from all those for which it can be exchanged, and thus affix to it the highly complex attribute of Exchangeable Value " (176 sq.).

This exchangeable value becomes measurable through the medium of money. It is true, " to measure a complex *mental* conception by means of an instrument formed of *material* substances, might at first be thought almost paradoxical. . ... If, however, it be borne in mind that human actions are the exponents of human thoughts, and that by these human actions are caused the indications of the physical instrument to which we are about to advert, it may in some degree be anticipated what functions such an instrument will be found to discharge, when universally employed in the numberless operations of Interchange. Money, the great material instrument of commerce, discharges two principal functions : primarily, it is a representative of Value, in discharging which function it becomes, secondarily, a measure of Value " (178 sq.). In this sense it may be said that " Price is commonly used as a measure of Value " (*Social Delusions concerning Wealth and Want*, 1856, 68).

Yet while subjective value may be conceived as a purely internal, i.e., individual category, objective value and price are obviously external, i.e., social phenomena. Where is the bridge between them ? An analysis of barter provides the answer to this question : with regard to the prices at which the commodities involved change hands, " it will be remarked that the degrees of Value thus indicated would not exactly coincide with the conception entertained by either of the parties to the Exchanges, but would represent the medium of the amounts of Value attached by them severally to the Commodities ; if it were otherwise, neither of the exchangers would have any inducement to exchange, their only reason for exchanging being, that they mentally attach different degrees of Value to each Commodity. The amount of Value therefore which would be thus indicated is precisely that average amount which we require to be informed of when dealing, not with an individual, but with a community " (*Natural Elements*, 233 sq.).

It is in the direction of this subjective theory of prices, that Jennings endeavours to find a competent solution of the problems of interest and wages. " As Value is attached to the possession of Property ", he points out, " a proportion of that Value is naturally attached to the temporary use of Property, whenever it is in its nature durable. . . . Enduring objects may be said to have several temporary Values, as many in number as the several successive occasions on which they are capable of being used. . . . Moreover, whilst it is thus the nature of some objects to render their services throughout a length of time, it is also the nature of many others to increase and multiply : in time, vegetation grows—in time, animal life is multiplied—in time, men labour, and accumulate the fruits of their labour. . . . We may feel assured that in every country, as soon as the Exchange of articles of equal Value came to be practised . . . the act of lending for a valuable consideration, or of parting with the temporary use for hire, would also be performed ; and since in the great majority of cases Commodities would be so let on account of their availability to assist human Labour, or of their natural powers of Production, it is evident that the amount of hire would be principally determined by their instrumentality in realizing Products. . . . If the object hired produced much fruit, the owner would receive much , if less, he would receive a less amount " (245–8).

This explanation of interest is undoubtedly very primitive, based as it is on the physical productivity of the capital goods ; in his theory of wages, which is reminiscent of Gossen's leading concept, the economic equilibrium of the individual, Jennings showed a somewhat more fortunate hand : " The determination of the amount of Wages must be commenced by regarding the labourer abstractedly as exhibiting two functions, capabilities and susceptibilities. In the former of these characters the labourer appears as an organic machine, void of the sense of toil, contributing to the progress of productive industry by means of the efferent nerves . . . and commanding, therefore, like any commodity that bears a money price, the Exchangeable Value of these services. . . . In the second of these characters the labourer appears as a sentient endurer of toil, felt through the afferent nerves in its different degrees of dissatisfaction . . . and only endured in contemplation of preponderating amounts of satisfaction " (184 sq.). Now, " whilst the laborious action is regarded as possessing a positive Value on account of its pecuniary reward, it is regarded as possessing also a negative Value, on account of the toilsome feelings which are its inseparable accompaniments. When Labour is regarded as an exchangeable Commodity . . . this negative and this positive Value affect conjointly the Price that is paid, or the amount of Wages " (187).

Thus every page of Jennings' book exhibits the same spirit : the spirit of the physical sciences. There is no problem of social intercourse which he does not try to solve by a study of the isolated individual. How different had been the spirit of the classical economists ! A critical review of Jennings' *Natural Elements of Political Economy*, written by Thomas Hodgskin, reveals the whole depth of the contrast between the old economics and the new. Not that Hodgskin was averse to individualism : "According to the most accurate and profound philosophy ", he wrote in one connection, " material objects . . . are to be considered only as signs, or occasions, for calling into existence some particular states of consciousness " (*The Word Belief Defined and Explained*, 1827, 24). But his intellectual approach was individualistic only where the individual was concerned, as in epistemology, and not in his analysis of social life. Therefore he strongly resented and rejected Jennings' attempt to introduce subjectivism into economics. " It never has been doubted that value is a mental conception, the result of the desires, labours, and interests of individuals," he says ; " but the fathers of the science no more thought of going into a physiological and psychological investigation of the conception than legislators have thought of going into an investigation of conceptions and actions before they formed conclusions as to morality, and enforced them by criminal jurisprudence. It was for them to recognize the familiar conception, and trace some of its influential causes, such as labour and the relation of supply and demand, and its consequences, such as the stimulus which high or low value or price gives to or withholds from the production of different commodities. The investigation proposed by Mr. Jennings was no more necessary for their purposes, or the purposes of the science, than an investigation into psychological and physiological causes of the conceptions of shelter and warmth were necessary before building houses and making clothing " (*The Economist*, 1855, 681 sq.). This, obviously, is true : but if Hodgskin meant to imply that there was no way from Jennings' theoretical speculations to any practical ideal, he was mistaken. Like Gossen, Jennings deduced from his abstract principles concrete proposals which, he was convinced, would lead society to greater and greater felicity.

II. THE DISSOLUTION OF THE OLD SOCIAL IDEAL

Since it is, according to Gossen, not only the spontaneous desire, but at the same time the moral duty, of every man to enjoy his life to the full, the task of political economy is not only to develop the rules according to which the provision of the human race with material goods is taking place, but also to find the means by which it can be augmented to the highest possible pitch. It is the mission of the science to assist man in his endeavour to maximize his happiness, and it is this task which constitutes its true importance (34).

As we have seen, all Gossen's theoretical considerations end in one practical conclusion : the thesis that perfect freedom is the condition, the only condition, of perfect felicity. This fundamental postulate is expressed in two concrete demands : freedom in consumption, and freedom in production : the individual must be at liberty to spend his income in the way which secures the maximum satisfaction of his wants, and to embark in that line of production which promises the maximum reward for his labour. Given this double freedom of choice, the road to supreme happiness is open.

Not much is said by Gossen concerning the first of these two points. The elaboration of scientific principles for the best distribution of a given amount of purchasing power among the various means of consumption would presuppose the possibility of an exact measurement of the various enjoyments involved : it is not feasible as long as mental magnitudes elude our grasp. Yet practice provides a sufficient substitute : custom, the result of social experience, is, and ought to be, the guide of the individual. By a slow but persistent process of approximation, men have come near to the most reasonable method of catering for their needs, and by accepting the standards of his fellows, every man can be certain of making the best use of his money, at least in the given state of human knowledge and experience (126 sq.).

It is the second point, the postulate of freedom in production, which constitutes the real problem of social felicity. Here things are not what they ought to be : indeed, they are changing from bad to worse. For it is " an undeniable fact that the situation of most factory workers has become more deplorable from year to year " (162).

The first indication of the fact that the existing system of production is not sound, must be seen in the regularly recurring crises which are a terrible source of human suffering. The true cause of temporary unemployment which is the scourge of the working classes, Gossen points out, is the circumstance that of all valuable commodities only a certain limited supply is really in demand and can be sold, and that this quantity is subject to fluctuations. If the state of the market makes it necessary to reduce the output, the number of hands hitherto employed in this line of production must be diminished accordingly, but not all the workmen rendered superfluous succeed at once in exchanging the branch of industry which has become unfavourable under the new conditions, for a more favourable one (151). From this diagnosis of the evil follows the remedy : the only means of relieving the temporary distress of the labourers who are out of employment, Gossen asserts, is to afford them sufficient help in their spontaneous endeavour to go over, as soon as possible, to other types of work (152). The Government, he concludes, should do everything to facilitate the transition from one branch of production to another, but not more (158). The spectre of a universal crisis by which all industries are equally hit, did not haunt Gossen : he lived at a time and in a country which had as yet had no experience of this gravest of all social maladies.

Thus it is freedom, and freedom alone, by which the temporary diseases of the body politic must be healed. But freedom, and freedom alone, is also the answer to its more chronic ills. Gossen profoundly believed in the self-healing forces of social life. The removal of the obstacles that prevent the individual from engaging in the most promising branch of production, which he recommends as the panacea, is, according to his own opinion, nothing but a means of strengthening the natural forces which spontaneously regulate human intercourse (168).

Now, the first of these obstacles consists in the fact that man is born without knowledge and abilities, and cannot therefore take up any productive work without having been systematically prepared for it. It is education, by which this difficulty can be overcome. If the maximization of happiness is the end to be pursued, the training of the younger generation must be made subservient to the purposes of useful industry. In other words : education must be thoroughly practical. According to the dictates of nature, the first fifteen years of life should be devoted to it : then it should be brought to a close, because, before that age, man is physically weak and thus fitted only for learning, while, after that age, he is strong enough to start in production (193). The pædagogical ideal should be to render every individual a modern man in the full sense of the word. The modern age is the age of positivism and progress, the age of science and technique. The most important subjects of teaching are therefore the physical sciences and the technological disciplines. Special care should be taken to make every child a master of mathematics. For the operation of the various forces of nature can only be clearly brought to view if the mathematical formula is found and understood which expresses in every instance the causal connection between the determining power in all its possible degrees, and the magnitude of the effect produced. From this point of view, mathematics appears simply as a part of language, that part which is called upon more clearly and correctly to describe quantitative ideas than is possible by ordinary words, and consequently the study of mathematics to the point of comprehending the truths laid down in such formulæ as those of economics is just as necessary as the learning of the mother-tongue itself. The subjects on which unreasonably most weight has been laid in the past, notably the dead languages, are, on the other hand, at least comparatively speaking, only of little use to modern man, and therefore not much time and work should be sacrificed to, or rather wasted on, them (191 sq.).

In these suggestions Gossen exposes his true character : he was a thorough capitalist utilitarian, hostile to all values which are not material. Yet he had not only the bad but also the good characteristics of his kind. If he conceived the ideal man as an efficient producer, he also envisaged him as an enjoying consumer. He had not yet discarded the conviction that a fair relationship should exist between exertion and reward. Although he did not stress the point, it is clear that he wished to see education so organized as to guarantee some equality of opportunity. In particular, he demanded that no difference should be suffered to exist between the instruction given to boys and to girls : since the laws of enjoyment are the same for both, no discrimination can be justifiable (195).

Indeed, in this connection Gossen even takes up the defence of the egalitarian ideal. The more general diffusion of a high education in the sense of modern scientific principles, he points out, will appear dangerous to, and be opposed by, those who fear that this better training of the broad masses will ultimately deprive them of their privileged position. They argue that most labours necessary for the preservation of human society on the present level of civilization are, by their very nature, so repulsive that they would not be willingly performed by men so highly educated and refined. The intended reform of education in the vein of equality would therefore result in a backward development of material culture, if not in still more serious difficulties. Against this argument, Gossen sets the assertion that the Creator has made no kind of work indispensable for His creatures which would be unduly exacting or morally harmful. Only man has invented professions of which he need feel ashamed when he called into being soldiers and hangmen, slave-drivers and harem-guards. Yet, if a doubt should still remain, the following consideration would destroy it : of all necessary labours which men have to undertake, those are usually regarded as most repulsive to human nature which are performed by knackers : it is, for this reason, their function which nobody would take upon himself in an egalitarian society, if the fears which the enemies of equality entertain were true. But we see that free men who undoubtedly belong to the most highly educated class constantly perform such labours and, indeed, in a form which is still more repulsive : for the work of the anatomist in dissecting dead bodies differs from that of the knacker only in this, that its objects are not animals but men (196 sq.).

This incredibly clumsy attempt to defend the egalitarian principle—the principle of freedom of ascent—is in its way characteristic of Gossen's thought and Gossen's time. Whenever he speaks on the subject of liberty, he is a realist : as soon as he touches upon the theme of equality, he turns utopian. Equality was to him still an ideal, but only a platonic one—an ideal more to be worshipped than pursued. Liberty alone was to him a practical proposition, a concrete political postulate within easy reach. His tone changes as he turns back to it : for after this short excursion into the realm of fancy, he comes to discuss a topic of the day : the problem of monetary reform, the reform of the monetary system in the spirit of *laissez-faire*.

When man has been enabled by an appropriate education to provide for his own needs, he is confronted with the important question which branch of production he would do best to choose in order to maximize the sum of his enjoyments. The decision is not difficult where incomes are expressed in terms of money, for it is obvious that the highest wages are the best. Unfortunately, there is no natural standard by which real incomes can be compared with each other : there is nothing that the Creator Himself has singled out and destined to perform the functions of money. It is for man to supply this deficiency, and thus economic science has to investigate what institutions would provide the most adequate and desirable monetary system (198).

To fulfil its mission as a measure of value and means of exchange, the commodity used as money must be as stable in its proper value as possible : it must be either above all change, or, if it be subject to changes, the variations that occur must be not fortuitous but regular and easy to foresee. It is further essential that it should be a thing that can be amassed and stored without difficulty, and that its physical properties be such that the value of a stock rises and falls exactly in proportion to the quantity held. Lastly, it is desirable that it should not be bulky in comparison to its value, for only if a small particle represents a relatively high amount of purchasing power can market operations smoothly develop and payments be promptly performed (198 sq.). Yet of all these conditions, stability is the most essential, and the estimation of the monetary unit will reach almost perfect stability if an object is chosen whose qualitative character is not influenced by time, and whose quantitative relation to the other goods [1] can be constantly kept more or less steady. Such an object has been chosen. Practice has decided long ago that of the precious metals gold and silver unite the necessary requirements in such perfection that, as a means of exchange, they leave nothing to be desired (203 sq.).

Thus metallic money, though not a spontaneous institution of creation, is almost as ideal as if it were one. To interfere with a monetary system of this kind must therefore be evil. The introduction of paper money is such an interference, and, indeed, an interference of the gravest order. For by the issue of certificates representing gold and silver, the precious metals are deprived of the quality which so perfectly fits them to serve as a measure of value and mediator of the market—quantitative stability. To bring the monetary system back to its natural state, it is therefore absolutely necessary to abolish all paper money, including those securities which, not bearing interest, may be used as money, whether created by government or by private companies, whether issued at home or abroad (208).

In the view of this extreme metallism, Gossen conceived and suggested several concrete mint reforms which, he was convinced, would make the monetary system really fit to perform its important functions in the economic life of the community (209–28). He was a confirmed adversary of monometallism. Silver coins, he argued, are indispensable for smaller payments, yet to degrade them to a mere fractional currency without full intrinsic value would take from the monetary system too much of its automatism (216 sq.). On the other hand he rejected the legal fixation of a rigid exchange-relation between gold and silver, demanding that it should be left entirely to the free market to determine their

---

[1] " zu den thatsaechlichen Umstaenden ".   Gossen's mode of expression is somewhat hazy.

relative values (213–15).   It goes without saying that he strongly advocated full freedom of coinage.   The government, he thought, should state as exactly as possible how much the minting of each particular species of coin really costs, taking into account the salary of the functionaries entrusted with this work, and the interest and replacement of the capital invested in the mint, and declare itself ready to mint metal for every private individual who hands in the bullion and pays the minimum costs actually arising (221 sq.).   Under such arrangements the standard of value, subject only to the spontaneous tendencies of economic development, would clearly indicate the line of production which, at the time, enjoys the maximum return and thus safely guide the individual in his search for the profession which yields the highest income and with it the greatest happiness, attainable under the given circumstances.

The next proposal put forward by Gossen as necessary for, and conducive to, the realization of the laws of nature is the postulate of effective arrangements to guarantee that every individual will receive and retain the full produce of his labour without deductions.   This demand is strongly reminiscent of the formula which occupied the central position in the programme of the early socialists, but the parallel between men like Thompson on the one, and Gossen on the other hand, is verbal rather than real.   They thought that the practical solution of the problem could only consist in a radical reform of all existing property-relations.   Gossen's conclusion was the opposite one : he held that only the strong protection and full preservation of private property in its established form would promote the well-being of the community.   Individual ownership of the means of production did not seem to him to constitute a major problem ; if it was a problem at all, it was a problem happily conquered by practice.   Existing legislation concerning the defence of the material as well as immaterial goods of the individual, he points out, corresponds on the whole to the needs of society.   By the safeguards afforded, everybody may rely on receiving without defalcation the benefits flowing from the fruits of his exertion (228).

Indeed, it is in this connection that Gossen most strongly emphasizes his staunch adherence to the capitalist system and genuine abhorrence of the communist ideal.   Apart from all theory, he exclaims, history proves on every page that the nations have progressed in well-being almost in proportion as they have

G

improved the protection of private property. Only after Roman ideas and institutions, based as they were on the sanctity of all property-relations, had found entrance into the forests of Central Europe, do we see the German, clad as yet only in raw animal skins, transforming himself into a civilized peasant provided with a fixed habitation and enjoying the primitive comfort connected with it. Unfortunately, not all submitted to the law and respected their neighbours' goods : single individuals succeeded in subjecting to themselves the broad masses of the people and reducing them to the state of bondmen—bondmen who were not permitted to retain the full produce of their labour. This is the reason why material welfare remained stable through so many centuries. As soon as private property was again universally acknowledged and adequately protected, first in the case of the free townsmen, and later quite generally, the unbroken advance of humanity in its career of progress and happiness, which is still continuing, began (229).

Thus a capitalist society will for ever be more productive than a communist one. It is a fact confirmed by the broadest experience that, as soon as any labour is to be performed by common exertion, every individual seeks at once to reduce the toil which falls to his share as much as he possibly can, even if all have the same interest in the success of the undertaking (230). Yet not only the growing wealth but even the bare existence of civilized society depends upon the institution of private property. The social division and integration of labour which is the material basis of all higher culture, would be technically impossible without it. The formation of prices and the preservation of property are mutually conditioned by, and indissolubly connected with, each other. Only a capitalist system possesses a competent measure for stating the quantities in which the various articles are needed by the community and must be produced (231).

The postulate that every man should be guaranteed the full possession of the proceeds of his labour cannot therefore mean that the state should reform the given property-relations : it means, on the contrary, that it should respect them. This, Gossen complains, has not hitherto been fully the case. The institutions of entail and of legitimate portions, the laws against luxury and against usurious contracts, protective tariffs and other measures of the same description, infringe upon the principle of free and unlimited private property. The same must be said of all legal prescriptions which bar the access to any profession :

examinations for admission, licenses and the like.[1] Guilds, and
particularly closed guilds, fall, of course, into the same category
(232 sq.). Only when these obstacles to the unhampered operation of the laws of nature will have fallen—only when the
programme of uncompromising capitalist liberalism will have
been fulfilled to the last—will society be able to achieve that state
of earthly bliss which the Creator has promised to, and made the
aim of, each and all.

These considerations, no doubt, contain Gossen's creed. Yet
an unconditional rejection of the communist ideal is not in itself
necessarily an unconditional acceptance of the capitalist reality.
A decision for the principle of private property is not yet a
decision against its wide and equal distribution. The next links
in Gossen's chain of thought make it perfectly clear how in-
escapable the problem of equality is for him who proclaims the
principle of liberty as the key to universal happiness.

The increased and still increasing utilization of the forces of
nature for the process of production, Gossen points out in taking
another step forward, has brought it about that a man can only
engage in certain branches of industry if he disposes of capital
sufficient to buy the often costly tools and machines. But the
necessary means are not always at hand. This fact has serious
consequences : it is apt to prevent many individuals from actually
embracing the profession which holds, according to their view,
the highest promise of gain and happiness (239). The difficulty,
in the present state of society, is great. Yet Gossen is confident
that it can be overcome without a redistribution of accumulated
wealth.

On one point, Gossen is perfectly clear in his own mind : to
guarantee every one the attainment of full felicity, society must
afford to all equal opportunities. Freedom includes freedom of

[1] It is a point of detail too interesting to be missed that Gossen expresses himself
in this connection most decidedly against all endowments of scientific and artistic
institutions. Together with "examinations, concessions, and laws of settlement",
he attacks "the fiction of so-called legal persons which were, in the past, given permission to buy perpetual rents in order to support some branches of production (sic !)
which were regarded as worthy of support in the interest of the community". Thus
arose not only churches and monasteries, but also universities and schools. The
foundations created to give these institutions material help are, according to Gossen,
not only superfluous, but even pernicious—pernicious to a high degree. "All that
exists must itself create the means of its further existence, otherwise it does not deserve
further to exist. Even church, art, and science only deserve to exist if the achievements of the persons belonging to these professions are so highly paid on the free
market that they yield incomes of adequate size without additions out of funds held
by a legal person" (234 sq.). Hardly ever has a man been more candid than
Hermann Gossen : hardly ever has the spirit of capitalism found a more striking
expression, and at the same time a more telling condemnation, than at his hands.

G*

ascent : freedom of ascent is equality. No social organization can claim to be called ideal which knows unearned and un-deserved privileges. The daughter of a beggar woman, Gossen says, appears on earth with the same rights as the daughter of a king (234). And his argument is by no means merely political : it is economic in the true sense of the word. If the gain of a monopolist is decreased by competition and a more even distribu-tion of income is brought about, he states, " the augmentation of happiness in the increased number " of traders " by far outweighs the loss incurred by the monopolists " (153). It is, we may add, the decreasing utility of money which leads to this result. But if this be true, it follows with absolute cogency that only full equality of opportunity will engender the highest sum-total of happiness conceivable.

Gossen did not expressly admit this conclusion ; at heart he could not but accept it as correct. This is apparent in his anxiety to prove that a more even distribution of riches would not neces-sarily diminish the well-being of the rich. A slave-owner, he points out, may indeed believe that his happiness is increased to the highest pitch if he pushes the exploitation of his human cattle to the utmost limits, but when we compare his sum of enjoyments with that of a highly educated man who, without any inherited rent, perceives his mission in the creation of values for others, even a superficial estimate of the respective lots of pleasure will not leave it in doubt that the scales decide in favour of the latter. The abolition of all privileges, down to the very last license, would therefore, at least in the long run, by no means be connected with a lasting disadvantage for the privileged themselves (197 sq.).

Equality was therefore, even to Gossen, an important condi-tion of social felicity. A difficult problem, if not an insurmount-able difficulty, he had no relish for this topic. Yet he faced it, if unwillingly, and his serious endeavour to find a satisfactory solution that was not socialist—to present a plan for re-establish-ing equality without re-distributing property—shows the futility of all attempts to build an ideal society on the foundations of the capitalist system as it had emerged from the great transformative process of the industrial revolution.

Already Gossen's account of the rise of class-distinctions (or, rather, the account of it which can be constructed from various remarks widely scattered throughout his book) exhibits a curious flaw. Landed and commercial property are not treated alike :

the latter is represented as the result of a blunder, the former as the spoil of a crime. When, in the middle ages, the division of labour first developed and various branches of industrial production grew up beside agriculture, the fact could not long remain unnoticed that competition cuts down prices and thus diminishes traders' incomes. Narrow-minded as they were, the townsmen strongly resisted this tendency, not understanding that freedom would benefit them more in their capacity as consumers than it could possibly harm them in their capacity as producers. Thus arose corporations and guilds, prohibitions to carry on this trade or that beyond the city-gates, to introduce foreign products for the home market, and the like. It was the inevitable result of these restrictions that the quantities produced remained small and the prices demanded and incomes earned high. The privileged traders were essentially monopolists who exploited the community. Their gains were out of all proportion to their achievements and enabled them to amass vast fortunes. Thus the present inequality of commercial wealth was due to an incomplete comprehension of, and wilful interference with, the beneficent laws of liberty (163 sq.).

Entirely different was the development that took place in agriculture. According to the testimony of history, single individuals succeeded in usurping the dominion over vast stretches of the soil, and, with it, over the men living there, forcing their bond-folk to surrender the rents to which the bounty of nature gave rise. Without exertion, they secured incomes so rich that not even the greatest prodigality could possibly dissipate them. Thus the landlords in the country assembled (willy-nilly as it were) vast funds which added to their great political privileges the still greater power of economic wealth (174).

Thus two infringements of freedom, one forcible and one peaceful, gave rise to that inequality under which society is now suffering. Still, even so, some equality of opportunity and liberty of ascent would have been granted, had not a further act of interference supervened. By borrowing capital, enterprising individuals among the poor could have secured the means of future success. But the legislation of the day made borrowing difficult, if not, indeed, impossible. Guided by misconceived, though excusable, humanitarian considerations, the Church prohibited, and the State restricted, the taking of interest, despite the fact that free economic intercourse offers the debtor better protection against exploitation than any legal commandment can ever achieve (*ib.*).   Without free bargaining, however, bargains cannot freely develop.

If, then, a monopoly of capitals came into existence, the usury laws must be blamed.   They counteracted the spontaneous tendency towards a continuous redistribution of wealth in favour of the enterprising and successful, and if the old proverb, " Money makes money ", is still true, it is due to them (177 sq.).

However, the usury-laws-have fallen into disuse long ago, and still no appreciable progress has been made towards an equality of wealth and opportunity.   What hinders the process of self-healing which we should trust the natural forces of the body social to develop ?   There is one great obstacle, Gossen explains, which must be removed before a change for the better can come about : to lend a man who has no other guarantee to offer for the fulfilment of his liabilities than his personal qualification and his enterprising spirit large sums of money, is all too risky.   The .capitalist must be given better security before a free movement of money can be started which will procure the capable among the property-less with the means to ascend on the social scale. This can be done by the foundation of a common bank with the purpose of concentrating and redistributing all idle capitals available, based on the principle adopted long ago by the great insurance companies—the principle of solidarity among creditors and debtors with regard to the losses inevitably occurring (239).

This, then, is Gossen's concrete suggestion : the state should found under its authority a loan-society, without, however, accepting any guarantee other than the responsibility for its correct administration, i.e., for losses arising out of neglect or embezzlement on the part of employees.   This institution should be empowered to grant loans [1] at any rate of interest to all applicants capable of giving either material pledges or personal guarantees, and allowed to procure itself the funds for these loans by the issue of bonds yielding interest and payable to the bearer.   The society would lend its facilities to all grown-up individuals who are independent and reside within its territory, thus affording a fair chance of ascent to every man, however indigent (239 sq.).

[1] Even poor and unemployment relief, Gossen held, should be given in the form of loans, for which interest must be paid.   Only where exceptional misfortunes have taken place is charity permissible.   But this charity should not be organized, neither by the state nor by private associations.   Beware, he says, of creating a magistracy. In the case of such an institution it cannot but happen—since some binding instruction must be given to the functionaries—that the individual receives, as it were, a sort of legal claim which would bring back all the faults of a public system of relief payments. The help has to come from private persons exclusively, not even from standing societies (237).

In this way, equality of opportunity would be established, not by visionary communist experiments, but by practical capitalist business methods. The bank would be a self-supporting, perhaps even a flourishing, commercial enterprise. Is it possible to envisage a better plan of social reform?

The scheme, it is true, sounds very sober. But it is a different question whether it is likely to fulfil the high expectations which Gossen set on it. He realized that loans against pledges would not occur very often. A man who possesses an article valuable enough to serve as a pledge is, by the supposition, not without property. He can procure himself the sum wanted simply by selling the pledge, and need not look for any outside help. Thus only loans on the basis of personal guarantees would be of major importance : only they would be conducive to the purpose contemplated, the affording of economic opportunities to the poor (246).

In view of this fact, Gossen was anxious to draw the circle of eligible guarantors as wide as possible. As a guarantor, every citizen should be admitted who was a householder, resident within the district during a stated period, perhaps five years, who had during this time faithfully fulfilled his obligations towards state and borough, and was not himself in need of relief or indebted to the bank (240). Yet, alas !—it is a very different thing to make people entitled to act as guarantors, and to make them willing to do so. It is very easy to give the right—it is very difficult to create the inclination. Where can a proletarian, however gifted, find a capitalist, however benevolent, to stand security for him? Gossen's plan is absurd. It is the product of a petty bourgeois environment and of a petty bourgeois brain. It cannot answer the needs of an industrialized society, where ninety-nine are indigent and one alone out of a hundred rich. It cannot bridge the gulf that yawns between the classes—it cannot guarantee the ascent of the gifted. Its futility is too obvious to require detailed demonstration. Gossen himself was aware of its narrowness. As a rule, he says (249), loans will only be sought by young men when they first desire to set themselves up in the world, and their guarantors will be their parents or other relatives, sometimes, perhaps, the masters under whose guidance they have received their training. Yet a proletarian's parents and friends are always proletarians, and how can a lame man stand on the shoulders of the lame?

After this truly feeble scheme for the abolition of the inequality of commercial fortunes, it is surprising to find that Gossen advances a radical plan for the equalization of landed property.[1] Indeed, what he advocates is a consistent agrarian socialism. The moral difference between the two types of material wealth noted above here bears its political fruit. When everybody has been given an appropriate education ; when a rational choice of profession has been made possible by the establishment of a sound system of money ; when the capitals needed for the carrying-on of highly mechanized industrial enterprises have been made available by the general loan society, there is only one obstacle left to prevent the individual from realizing his personal maximum of happiness : the fact that, under the present circumstances, man cannot freely choose and occupy the locality most favourable for his branch of production. By the introduction of private property in the soil, human institutions have made the removal of this obstacle very difficult : where it prevails, it is entirely left to the caprice of the owner whether or not he will devote a plot of ground in his possession to the use for which it has been destined by nature. Therefore the individual appropriation of the land is evil. This bar to happiness, it is plain, could best be removed by the transfer of all property in immovables to the community (250). Were the state to hold all landed estates, every particular locality could be leased to the highest bidder, and thus the most fair and favourable distribution of the soil would be secured (251).

The main question then is this : how can the present private property in immovables be replaced by public ownership ? This, Gossen declares, is a serious and subtle problem. The attempt of the communists to cut the Gordian knot and resort to simple expropriation is to be rejected. Private property is sacred. It is true that the original appropriation of the soil was not a strictly legal act. But the present owners have all acquired possession under the guarantee of the community, be it by purchase or by inheritance (257). Their rights, therefore, demand full protection.

Fortunately, it is not necessary to apply revolutionary means in order to procure the state full control of all landed property. For the government is free to enter into competition with private persons in every instance where an estate is offered for sale, and several circumstances co-operate in making it the more potent

---

[1] Set forth for the first time in the examination paper mentioned above where mines and houses are expressly included in the scheme. Cf. Blum, *l. c.*, 72–86.

bidder, especially the fact that the state can borrow money at a cheaper rate, and therefore grant a higher price, than any individual (258).

For the acquisition of all land, the treasury would of course require vast sums. But there is a most fortunate fact which makes this painless socialization through free purchases possible without increasing the burden of taxation : the fact that rents are steadily and progressively increasing. The state, as landlord, would make ever-greater gains year after year and thus accumulate a fund which would enable him slowly but surely to pay off any debt that would have been incurred in the buying-in of the landed estates.

This continuous augmentation of rents is not a fond expectation but a natural and necessary development. Gossen argues along Malthusian and Ricardian lines [1] : population is for ever increasing, and the new soil that must be taken into use in order to meet the increasing demand, can only be worked under higher costs. Therefore the rent paid from the superior stretches of land already in cultivation must constantly and continually rise. Gossen estimates that the yearly advance can, at a minimum, be set down at 1% (255 sq.).

Since in Prussia the value of the $3\frac{1}{2}$% Government Securities oscillates around 94, the creditors of the state appear to be content with a yield of something less than $3\frac{3}{4}$% from their capitals. Bonds bearing interest at this nominal rate would, therefore, be estimated and accepted at full value. If the government should decide systematically to buy land and finance this policy by the issue of such securities, it could offer a price equalling $26\frac{2}{3}$ times the amount of the actual rent. Experience proves that on terms like these large estates can easily be bought in many parts of Prussia (261).

Now, if we suppose that all rents grow annually only by 1%, and at the same time cautiously assume that the interest of the public debt is as high as 4%, the income of the state from the land would suffice, not only to defray the current interest-payments, but also (as Gossen demonstrates mathematically) to redeem the principal within forty-seven years. The steady fall of the debt and the no less steadily proceeding rise of the revenue would combine to secure this favourable result. From the forty-eighth year onward, the whole amount of all rents due would remain at the free disposal of the treasury (263, 265). Taxes

[1] For his dependence upon Ricardo, cf. Blum, *l. c.*, 60 sq.

would then be unnecessary (273 ; cf. Blum, *l. c.*, 72 sq., 85).
Yet such a rapid paying-off of the debt would be unfair to the
living generation, which would thus be excluded from the benefit
of the measure. It is obviously desirable not to use the whole
difference between the increasing rent-income of the state and the
decreasing interest-payments connected with the debt for the
paying-off of the principal, but to divide the amount coming in
between the paying-off of the debt and the defraying of public
expenditure in general, thus progressively easing the tax-burden
borne by the community. If the income of the state from rents,
after payment of the interest of the debt, is divided between the
two purposes in the same relation in which this net-income
stands to the remainder of the purchase-money yet to be re-
deemed, the whole debt would disappear after seventy-four years.
Under an arrangement of this sort, more and more money would
flow from this source into the public purse, enabling the government gradually to decrease taxation, until in the seventy-fifth
year all the rents accruing to the land-owning state could be
used for its current expenditure and taxation would cease altogether (265 sq., 271). Thus the last obstacle to the free operation
of the laws of nature, the last obstacle to the attainment of
supreme happiness by all, would be painlessly overcome.

Once the inequality in the distribution of landed property
was radically removed, Gossen thought, perfect equality would
arise of itself. It is difficult to see on what grounds this optimistic
belief is founded, since the abolition of the right of inheritance
is not contemplated. Gossen's argument is twofold, but in both
aspects it is equally utopian. The endeavour to leave to one's
offspring an estate as large as possible, he asserts, will disappear
when the true religion of the Creator will be more widely understood and more generally entertained. For it is a fundamental
teaching of this religion that it is the duty of every individual
to earn his enjoyments by his exertions. But not only social, even
selfish motives will lead to a spontaneous disappearance of the
custom of inheritance. A man who really wishes to maximize his
earthly happiness must provide for his old age. Therefore it is
rational to invest the bulk of one's savings in life-annuities. In
a society in which egoism is not decried but acknowledged, not
suppressed but fostered, this will become the universal practice.
Then, however, the estates inherited will be of such moderate
size, that a perfect equality of opportunity will be practically
achieved. Everybody will depend upon himself alone, and the

good things of the earth will be distributed according to merit. The laws of nature will freely operate and fully realize what socialists and communists desire : a just reward for each, and the greatest happiness of all. Indeed, the earth will be a perfect paradise (275 sq.).

In its grand consistency, this argument is certainly imposing. Of all thinkers Gossen alone followed the principle of capitalist philosophy to its logical conclusions : it is the consummate selfishness of each, of which he expects impartial justice for all. Yet his view of human nature was mistaken. In a world as we know it, self-regard will never sink so low as to give way to an altruism based on purely religious sentiments : nor will self-regard ever rise so high as to destroy the love to one's children which nature herself has implanted in the human heart. The way to equality which Gossen envisaged would not lead to its goal. The scientific economics which he developed cannot combine with an idealist view of the world ; the principle of individualism which he confessed cannot engender a truly social philosophy. Those who came after him abandoned the non-realistic appendix to Gossen's realist analysis of the capitalistic system. Jennings' work marks a further step in the progressive degeneration and dissolution of the old social ideal. For although it starts with a formal denunciation of economic liberalism, it ends, as we shall see, in a real acceptance of capitalist society.

Richard Jennings was not only more advanced than Hermann Gossen because he abandoned the deistic creed of the eighteenth century to which the other firmly clung ; his more modern attitude is also expressed in the fact that he did not retain the concept of ideal society which had still been the inspiration of his kindred contemporary beyond the Rhine. Yet he shared Gossen's conviction that economic science has the task of reforming the world. " Is it merely a barren tract of knowledge ", he asks (*Natural Elements*, 51), " or is it available for improving the physical condition of mankind ? " It would be valueless, Jennings seems to answer, if it did not minister to the needs of society. Indeed, he goes so far as to suggest that a scientific basis for economic theory is desirable mainly because it is conducive to social reform. " The skilled metaphysician ", he says, meaning the confirmed adherent of utilitarian eudæmonism, " will probably regard the adoption of these means as unnecessary, if not ridiculous ; he, indeed, will not require them—*nabit sine cortice*—but it must be borne in mind that of the very numerous politicians who are interested in our social condition, very few, comparatively, are skilled metaphysicians ; on the contrary, a familiar recognition of the laws of Psychology is by no means a common occurrence in this country—by many of those who have examined them they are regarded as vague, indefinite, and unsatisfactory. . . . On the other hand, no one is incredulous respecting Physiology ; there are, indeed, few who do not admire its discoveries, and feel an interest in its expositions. To raise, therefore, through its means, a scaffolding that may afford a footing whilst a higher edifice is being reared, is a device which, although possessing no claim to be considered a manifestation of taste or of talent, is nevertheless useful, if not absolutely necessary, at the present moment, in order to constitute a system of Political-economy that shall be competent to deal with our great social problems " (*Social Delusions*, 92 sq.).

But, of course, science was much more to him than a cheap cloak with which to cover practical ends. He was convinced that " the effect of applying Physiology and Psychology to Political-economy will . . . remove this branch of learning from the condition of a political to the condition of a physical and a metaphysical science " (110), and, according to his view, this applies both to pure and to applied economics. For " the more closely we examine the subject, the closer do we find the analogy existing between the treatment of organized living bodies and the treatment of political bodies ; if the health of either be good in all its parts, to interfere, and to disturb it, is doubtless foolish ; if not, remedies are in the one case in the hands of the physician, in the other they are in the hands of the citizen and of the states-man " (109 sq.). Yet not only has political economy to teach how to restore a diseased body politic to health ; it must also find the means for improving its strength and increasing its welfare when nothing is amiss. It is true, " it has been always found that Nature's laws are so constituted as to produce effects which are usually beneficial to mankind to a certain extent, but ", he says, nevertheless, they " are capable of being rendered more beneficial by the application of human art ". This art, the " art of Political-economy may be deduced from the principles of the science, and can be practised " (*Natural Elements*, 52 sq.), just as the art of medicine is deduced from the principles of the science belonging to it, and is being practised. Therefore " the object of our consideration is not the observance of religious or moral duties, but simply the determination of some of the conditions of national prosperity. . . . Changes, such as these, are pointed out by the unbiased advice of natural philosophy " (*Social Delusions*, 154, 127).

This belief in the possibility and, indeed, necessity of a scientific welfare-policy determined Jennings' attitude towards the doctrine of *laissez-faire*. In the style of his time, he, too, confessed liberalism, but only in a detached and somewhat doubtful way : " In the advanced stage of civilization, to which our observations are here directed, each individual among the People acts, as has been very frequently remarked, instinctively for the good of all. The often-cited example of the corn-factor, who, regarding only his own interest, follows in pursuit of it precisely the same course that a disinterested public officer would pursue, is but a single instance of the operation of that law of Nature which generally causes each individual to promote, to a certain degree, the public weal, although occupied solely in the pursuit of his own advantage " (*Nat. El.* 221). To a certain degree, then, the free operation of the spontaneous forces of economic intercourse realizes social harmony : but only to a certain, and not to a very high, degree. " Experience unhappily proves that in a civilized community the interest of highly influential individuals is not unfrequently opposed to the public interests." To quote but one example : " Factories have been suddenly closed, leaving the owners with large fortunes, and their work-people destitute." Surely, " these and many similar occurrences incontestably prove that human art is now required to administer to the necessities of a fully developed organism " (222). Now, the highly influential individuals whose selfish desire is at variance with the common interest, are not only the public functionaries but also private entrepreneurs : " Notwithstanding our authorized tenets respecting this question, it is evident that the interest of every proprietor and of every class of proprietors, whatever course of conduct circumstances compel them to pursue, is opposed to the welfare of the public regarded as a whole. It is the interest, for example, of the possessors of corn that corn should become scarce, because their stock would then command a higher price ; of the possessors of wine that wine should become scarce, for the same reason ; of the possessors, in short, of every kind of commodity that that commodity should become scarce ; but it is the interest of the whole nation that corn, wine, and every other kind of commodity should be abundant. It is no refutation of this argument to insist, that the actions of each trade, and of each individual, are generally so guided by the conditions of society as to promote the good of the whole community ; our proposition still remains intact, that the separate interest of each part is generally opposed to the interest of the whole.   It is clear, therefore, that they who observe any interest apart from the others, and endeavour solely to promote its prosperity, run a great risk of militating against the public welfare " (*Social Delusions*, 52-4). In spite of the spontaneous tendency towards social harmony, it is, therefore, impossible to leave things to their natural course : the counter-tendency towards social conflict is too strong. *Laissez-faire* would favour the one as much as the other, and possibly, or probably, the latter more than the former.   Hence, " in whatever country this tenet should continue to be in the ascendant, expenditure would continue to be a bane, and . . . whilst the rich might become richer, the poor must inevitably become poorer, to such a degree as would ultimately . . . perhaps endanger the stability of Government and the institutions of the country, however such consequences might be for a time averted by the passing circumstances of the day " (15).

Conscious interference, conscious reform, Jennings concludes, is therefore necessary.[1]   Nowhere is its necessity more strikingly obvious than in the continually recurring crises which even the most perfect freedom does not seem able to overcome.   Here we behold an instructive example of the inner connection between economic theory and social policy : " Money not only supplies a natural measure of the rate of industrial operations, it also supplies the means of controlling them, to those who have large sums at their disposal.   In consequence of the practice of lending, there exist in all civilized countries a certain number amongst the most active and enterprising of the leaders of industry, whose operations are . . . dependent on the terms on which they can obtain loans of Money ; if Money is lent at a low rate of Interest, old operations are pushed forward, new and often hazardous enterprises are commenced, and the industrial world glows with lively and sometimes with superabundant energy ; if Money can be procured only at a high rate of Interest some works cease to be remunerative, and are abandoned, speculative projects are

---

[1] In a short article on Jennings, published in Palgrave's *Dictionary of Political Economy* (ed. Higgs, 1923, II, 473 sq.), Edgeworth says : " The proposal that we should select our statesmen by a sort of examination in the theory of value shows a certain want of humour."   This criticism, which tends to make Jennings ridiculous, is very unfair.   It may find some justification in his awkward words, but it has none in his clear ideas.   What Jennings wished was that legislation should not be entrusted to men who were, on principle, hostile to all social reform.   Cf. especially *Social Delusions*, 61-3, 65, 88, and 98-100.

discontinued, and operatives find it difficult or even impossible to obtain employment " (*Natural Elements,* 248 sq.). The practical implication of this theoretical observation is plain : " The healthy progress of Industry depends very much on those who have the power to lend for higher objects than mere gain, or who can stipulate for or refuse a certain rate of Interest principally, or solely, for the purpose of securing the public welfare —in other words, the rate at which the wheel revolves can be regulated by those who have the power to regulate the supplies. This power, if it be not already possessed, might evidently be secured without difficulty by the executive branch of every Government. In the case of many States there are already in the Exchequer large sums invested in floating securities, or the revenues of the State are partly derived from Crown Lands which might be converted into Money, and be used under proper control for the purposes here indicated. . . . If a Board of Public Economy were to be entrusted with the administration of these funds, and loans were to be issued after each month's interval at such rates of Interest as public policy might indicate . . . the ebb and flow of speculation and panic would certainly subside in the stream of regular enterprise " (249 sq.). Thus, from what actually is, we may logically deduce what ought to be done : " Were a Board of Public Economy to be established, for the purpose of debating publicly on the Dynamical condition of Industry, and of fixing by its decisions the rate of Interest at which loans should be granted, it is difficult to conceive how great might be its influence in directing to right conclusions a public opinion constituted like that of England. Small facilities afforded, or small difficulties interposed, at the right time and in the proper direction, might prevent on the one hand the overwork of the labouring classes, ever accompanied by the exhaustion of their best energies, and frequently by the pollution and the annihilation of their better nature, and on the other hand that stagnation of trade which is the dead sea of the workman's existence, and the fruitful mother of such social pests as combinations, and strikes, and lock-outs—the cankerworms of Productive Industry " (258).

But the trade-cycle with its sufferings is not the only evil result of free capitalism. There are others, more serious because they are more lasting : evils connected with the very nature of our social constitution : " A great disproportion of classes exists in every country ; undesirable habits and practices are everywhere visible " (241). These, too, Jennings declared, must be scientifically fought, and, if possible, radically removed.

However—why should it be taken for granted that a disproportion of classes is bad ? Can science, the great impartial and incorruptible umpire, pronounce a judgment like this ? Jennings, unprejudiced as he was, saw the basis of equality—the foundation of the demand that the means of enjoyment should be evenly distributed—in the common nature of all men, exactly as Gossen had done before him : " As the human body is universally found to be framed after the same type, by its conformity with which all its parts are known to belong to man, whatever their varieties of feature or of complexion, of stature or of strength, so the human mind, whatever idiosyncrasies it may exhibit in particular instances, is universally found to offer to the philosophical observer the same general class of natural phenomena ; among the most general of these . . . are comprised those phenomena the consideration of which has hitherto occupied our attention—whether the sensations of Pleasure that are derived from the possession of objects which constitute Property, and which are greater than, and prevail over, the sensations of toil that accompany the efforts by which alone they are commonly produced, or the consequent conception of Value set upon these objects, or the will to labour for the purpose of producing, and to exercise self-denial for the purpose of accumulating them " (195 sq.). The fact that one man cannot directly experience the sensations of another did not seem to Jennings to raise a difficult problem. In social science, as in social life, it is sufficient for all practical purposes that we can safely conclude from the outward deportment of our fellow-men their inward feelings : " It is familiar to all that, imperceptible as the thoughts of other men are to the observer so long as their effects are limited to the mind within, when they cause external actions they can usually be deciphered without difficulty, and that, on the other hand, intangible as the human mind is to the hand of the operator, emotions may be roused, and exertions may be stimulated through the intervention of external objects ; in applying these general laws of mind to the subject before us, we have had occasion to enlarge upon the fact that the actions of Exchange mark the value which men set upon objects, and that changes of Value cause changes of Production, of Distribution, and of Consumption. It must be sufficiently manifest that whenever the Political-economist is able to observe, and to control, the course of these actions, he can regulate the conditions of Valuable Commodities, and whenever he can observe and control the conditions of Valuable Commodities, he can regulate the course of these actions " (230 sq.).

What we must find, then, is a practical and efficacious way to " regulate the conditions of valuable commodities ". Jennings undertook to search for it, and he came to the conclusion " that to whatever hands is committed the duty of raising, and expending, the revenues of a State, in the same hands rest the means of regulating the whole subject-matter of its Political-economy " (231). Indeed, taxation was to him the answer to all social problems, including the problem of social equality : " It is certainly not beyond the power of Taxation to raise the condition of the poorer classes, and that probably without subtracting from the real welfare of the rich. If, for example, a Legislature were to be sufficiently independent of private considerations to enact that, in the case of proprietors dying without leaving near relations, a considerable share of their property should revert to the funds of the State, these lamentable evils might cease, and it is not impossible that . . . the State might once more be regarded as *parens patriæ* " (242 sq.).

Thus the quest, not for the best, but for a better society, became for Jennings the quest for a better, and, indeed, the best system of taxation. It is his second book, written to combat *Social Delusions concerning Wealth and Want*, that gives a full exposition of the welfare-policy which he envisaged. But his programme is bitterly disappointing : his denunciation of *laissez-faire* and his plea for equality had been purely academical. Confronted with reality, all that he suggests are miserable reformlets—measures which indeed point in the direction of the egalitarian ideal, but are far too weak ever to reach it.

The concrete problem he tackles first is characteristic of him : the only form of inequality whose abolition would leave, and has left, capitalist society unimpaired. " Were a Statesman, thoroughly imbued with a knowledge of all the natural elements of Political-economy, and mindful both of the wants and the tastes of human nature, and the properties and the quantities of valuable commodities, to regard the state of our nation as a patriarchal Economist would regard the state of his community, rising far above personal and party interests, and affectionately considering whether its present condition is such as ought to satisfy his knowledge of the provisions of nature, and his means of action, it is probable that the first object that would arrest his attention would be the unnatural and often unhappy condition of nearly one half of our population—the female half " (*Social Delusions*, 110 sq.). Great are the sufferings of the weaker sex in a world where the stronger is allowed to win in the struggle for existence : and " all, or nearly all, of these evils are caused . . . by want of the proper avocations of women and suitable remuneration, by a dearth of the employments that are demanded by their natural capacities " (112). Here *laissez-faire* will not do : help is necessary. " Why . . . is so large a portion of the sex devoid of these occupations, in states that are highly civilized, and governed with the best intentions, under the guidance of our present tenets of Political-economy ? For the same reason that they would be robbed of their property . . . if Jurists were to adopt the maxims and to practise the system of non-interference ; because man is strong, and woman is weak ; because the property of the poor is their employment, and the proper employments of one sex are forestalled and preoccupied by the other. Were Political-economists to apply to the natural avocations of women . . . the fostering care of that subtle, and winning, and almost imperceptible influence which is placed in their hands, and which they cannot but administer with some effect, whilst determining the incidence of taxation . . . these frightful evils might in a great measure be averted. . . . Suppose, for instance, the tax on in-door men-servants, which is at present raised solely for fiscal purposes, were to be largely increased for the express purpose of encouraging the employment of women in feminine occupations, what would be . . . the consequent change in the condition of women ? " (113 sq., 116). The change would be immediate and radical ; should it be found insufficient, " there would probably be little difficulty in applying the same indirect influences to those branches of trade and of manufactures in the prosecution of which women ought to be employed. . . . A small tax levied on the employment of men in shops would, doubtless, in a short time, provide suitable occupations for a large number of intelligent and skilful shop-women. . . . Should circumstances require a further use of this means of action, it would be found that a large proportion of the work of copying clerks, compositors, watchmakers, tailors, and many other classes of operatives, might be placed in the hands of women . . ." (119 sq.).

This example exposes the ways and means of social reform.

They can and must be applied to other problems as well. " Let us take another view, and again look upon the state of our nation as a patriarchal Economist would look upon the state of his community. We see children under ten years of age everywhere set to work, attending or watching in the fields, sweeping, hawking, or stealing in the streets, if not surreptitiously employed in mills and mines. Every one knows that this is very bad economy. . . ." Something should be done : it can best be done by taxation. " Were . . . an assessment to be levied on the employers of every child under ten years of age in the event of their paying wages, directly or indirectly, for such child-labour " it would soon dwindle into insignificance and ultimately disappear (122, 125).

Thus working conditions would be gently but surely improved : and in the same way a steady reform in the mode of life could be brought about among the broad masses : " Gin-palaces, divans, and shops dedicated to the consumption of stimulants injurious alike to the physical and the mental energies of the consumers, can scarcely be regarded as fitting substitutes for convenient dwellings, wholesome food, good education ; yet a judicious tax avowedly designed for moral ends, if it could be imposed, would powerfully divert Labour from the Production of the former to the Production of the latter class of Commodities " (*Natural Elements*, 243).

It goes without saying that the reforming power of taxation does not end here. Jennings himself had proclaimed that it could be used for the mitigation, if not for the abolition, of social inequality. But now, thinking of political measures in concrete terms, his courage fails him. Slyly he abandons coercion for persuasion : from a scientific economist he turns into a moralizing preacher. " Money is power ", he exclaims, " and . . . power cannot be exercised without responsibility." Therefore " patriotic and philanthropic principles . . . ought to actuate, in purchasing, those who have the means and the opportunity of regarding something beyond the gratification of their own wants and wishes ". To be sure, society must be transformed : yet the " Crusade " should be directed not only " against the lethargic doctrines of State policy " but also against " the noxious ordering of private expenditure " (*Social Delusions*, 133, 164, 208).

Thus, before having even faced the social problem, Jennings retraces his steps and makes, as it were, a fresh start—a start which leads him into a different direction. " Let us recur ", he

says (140 sq.), " to the case of our Patriarchal Economist. . . .
Suppose . . . a part of his community to be insufficiently fed,
ill clothed, badly housed, and moreover to be in want of employment." What would he do and what should he do ? He would
" order the number of persons employed in manufacturing the
materials necessary for producing such commodities as food,
clothes, and houses to be increased, the manufacture of articles of
superfluity being partially superseded or suspended ". Jennings'
programmatical pronouncements would lead us to expect that
he recommended a strict tax upon luxuries as the appropriate
way to bring about this desirable change in the direction of
national production. But he argues otherwise. " An order to
make a commodity differs very little, except in point of time,
from a purchase of that commodity. If money is spent habitually
on any one class of commodities, instead of the effects of a special
order, the effects of a general order are produced, and they who
thus spend their money, determine, though unseen, the purposes
to which the effects of a corresponding number of labourers shall
be directed through long periods of time " (141). Thus " a little
consideration of surrounding circumstances, and a little firmness
in practising what is felt to be right, are alone necessary to
enable every purchaser to exercise some influence on the welfare
of our working classes. . . . There are, it is evident, many cases
in which a right of option may be beneficially exercised by a
considerate purchaser for the purpose of avoiding that disturbance
of comfort, or perhaps sacrifice of health and abridgment of life,
which are the consequences of certain occupations. . . . It may
be frequently a matter of indifference, and sometimes a subject of
embarrassment, to decide which of several materials, or fabrics,
or colours, it is best to select ; yet on this choice may depend
the alternative whether working men and women shall devote
many hours, perhaps weeks or months, to a healthy and engaging,
or to a repulsive and deleterious, employment " (177 sq., 176).

It is obvious that no attempt at a reform of society can be
more feeble than this appeal to the good heart of the public.
And yet—even this mildest of all means Jennings did not wish to
see carried very far : he was anxious to make it clear that he
did not want to touch in any way upon the foundations of the
capitalist order. " One of the most obvious methods of promoting social prosperity ", he says, " is to establish such thriving
and healthy occupations as command a remunerative return, and
naturally make those who are engaged in them prosperous and

contented, in the place of occupations which, stagnating, or having become effete, cause those who are engaged in them to be inadequately remunerated and consequently ill-supported, if they do not also become either discontented or servile ; one of the first of our cares, accordingly, should be to encourage occupations of the former, in preference to occupations of the latter class. . . . To purchase from charitable motives is to hang out false lights to trade, and to induce those who are sailing in a wrong direction, instead of abandoning it before it is too late, to continue in a course which must be difficult and dangerous, if it does not lead to certain ruin " (164 sq., 167).

These words prove beyond all doubt that the changes which Jennings intended to bring about were meant, not to weaken, but rather to strengthen, the working of the existing system of society. He desired social reforms, it is true, reforms in the sense of a humanitarian ideal, but still only reforms in the sense of a humanitarian capitalism. The drift, the decided and conscious drift, of the following considerations exposes his leading idea : beginning with a call for a more humanitarian attitude towards spending, they end with a call for a more capitalistic attitude towards saving : " Were considerable sums of money to be steadily withdrawn from the purchase of a certain class of commodities, the capital employed in this branch of production would soon become unprofitable, and these commodities would be produced in smaller quantities. Were the same sums of money to be steadily invested in the purchase of other commodities, their production would become profitable, and their quantity would be continually increased. Were there to be a reduced market for articles which only serve to gratify vanity or to foster luxury, these would be produced in less quantities ; were there to be an extended market for the objects requisite to support industry and the means of multiple production, these would be produced in larger quantities : laces, silks, cambrics, velvets, perfumes, would be produced in smaller quantities ; axes, spades, ploughs, threshing machines, steam-engines, crops of corn, would be produced in larger quantities. . . . How would this affect the condition of the community at large ? . . . It may be sufficient to reply, that the physical condition of every industrial society depends principally on the proportion between the amount of its population and the amount of its capital, and that the condition of every such society may be as much improved by an increase in its capital, of which we hear so little, as by a repression

of the increase of population, of which we hear so much "
(139 sq.).

Thus Jennings, who had set out from the thesis that the outstanding evil of the modern world was the great disproportion
of classes which exists in every country, arrived at the practical
conclusion that the salvation of society would come, not from a
wider distribution, but from a greater aggregation of capital.
In spite of all high-sounding phrases, he was in his heart a fol-
lower of *laissez-faire*. He foresaw, indeed, that liberalism would
fail : but the policy which he advocated, in its stead, was born
of the same spirit and marred by the same inefficiency : " Should
a change in the manners and habits of our upper and middle
classes be found impracticable . . . the aid of a higher power
might be required, and legal measures might have to be applied
with a cautious hand, and with a careful regard for the wants and
the weaknesses of our social condition. It is obvious, however,
that nothing would, in such a case, tend more to defeat the object
of legislation, than any measure at all approaching to the character of a sumptuary law. . . . It is not, therefore, the force of
prohibition, but rather the winning influences of taxation that
would, in this case, be employed. . . ." (225–7).

Yet what if even these winning influences should be found
unavailing ? Jennings knew the radical cure : but he hardly
advocated its application. In him, capitalist realism had totally
defeated social idealism : " Should it be found that [even]
measures of this character would not suffice, but that the languor
everywhere perceptible in the functions of Distribution, coupled
with a morbid and misdirected activity in the functions of Production, must receive [still] more active treatment, it needs but
little foresight to discern that foremost among the measures for
ameliorating the condition of England would stand measures
affecting the integrity of testamentary and hereditary successions.
But it may be hoped that, without any further change in our laws
than the application of financial measures to specific defects in
our social organization, the opinions of the wealthy respecting the
proper employment of wealth will eventually be so modified as to
effect, though indirectly, a vital change in the condition of the
lowest ranks of our working classes " (227 sq.).

Thus Jennings' scientific investigations end in a hope which
is utterly vain and utopian. His vision of the ideal was dim, his
will to approach it weak. He realized that capitalism with its
class contrast was not the perfect order of social happiness of

which the classical economists had dreamt : but, on the one hand, he saw no way back to the old ideal of an egalitarian society, and, on the other, he did not wish to go forward to the new ideal of a communist community. In this dilemma, Jennings abandoned the quest for the best order of things and preached the reform of capitalism instead. But it is difficult to increase the sum-total of social happiness without changing the distribution and appropriation of wealth : and so all his labours led to a negative result.

It is apparent from Gossen's work, and, to a still higher degree, from the work of Jennings, that in a fully developed capitalist society the consistent pursuit of an idealist theory of action leads to an embarrassing position. The conclusion cannot well be avoided, that capitalism has not fulfilled the high promise with which it entered upon the stage of history. It is not the order of perfect harmony and happiness : for if it is true that it has realized the greatest possible production, it is no less true that it has failed to realize the best possible distribution, without which (if the law of decreasing utility be correct and universally applicable) the maximum of satisfaction conceivable in theory cannot be attained in practice.

The original programme of capitalism, as embodied in the philosophy of classical economics, was clear : liberty and equality : liberty to achieve the greatest possible production—equality to secure the best possible distribution. The industrial revolution realized the one and destroyed the other. But ideals cannot be forcibly suppressed : they die only when they are fulfilled. Therefore the postulate of equality merely changed its form : in a society of artisans it had been the demand for a just division of the national wealth among all ; in a society of proletarians it must be the call for the full concentration of the means of production in the hands of the community.

Under these conditions, the deduction of an idealist theory of action from a realist analysis of the economic system is of necessity a revolutionary act : an act which cannot but be repulsive to all who cherish the present order for reasons cultural or otherwise. To accept the scientific premises, but to escape the practical conclusions, has accordingly become the wish of most economists : a wish which has born the jealously guarded and forcefully defended thesis that there is no link between them. In Gossen and Jennings the programme of action deduced from economic analysis is so modest that it cannot imaginably be more harmless. But even this was too much for their followers. " Gossen's book ", said Edgeworth, speaking for all, " contains two elements of unequal value : a somewhat narrow and pedantic application of utilitarian philosophy to politics and ethics, and a very original formulation of the principle of final utility in economics ". And, although it is an obvious fact that Gossen's plan of social reform was the logical outcome of his analysis of economic reality, Edgeworth adds the following verdict : " Gossen is guilty of a fallacy "—he is guilty of " what may be called the ' illicit process ' from the principle of utility in economics to utilitarianism in the philosophy of conduct." Much the same indictment can be brought to bear against Jennings (Palgrave's *Dictionary of Political Economy*, ed. 1923, II, 231 and 474).

Here, then, we have reached the end of the way. We see the grand ideal which had filled the classical economists finally abandoned and, indeed, repudiated by their modern successors. The imposing edifice of economic science still stands erect : but the sacred fire within it is extinct.

The generation which followed upon Gossen and Jennings laid the foundations on which economic science has built ever since. Their names therefore mark the threshold of the present, which it is not for the historian to overstep. Of the four great thinkers who first formulated the theory of marginal utility, two still preserved something of the old idealistic spirit : Walras and Marshall. The attitude of Jevons and Menger, however, was already purely positivistic, or, to use the term which the self-love of devoted disciples has made fashionable, purely scientific. It was the more modern attitude, and therefore the attitude which won the field. Walras was eclipsed by Pareto, and it is only at Cambridge that the great tradition of Locke and Leibniz still survives.

The development of political economy from a doctrine that was at once realistic and idealistic, to a purely realist theory is commonly hailed as a glorious progress. Yet it can only appear as such if the standards of the present are uncritically taken for granted. Whether the great change was for the better or for the worse, is a question which the economist, as economist, can hardly decide : the answer can only come from the science of sciences, philosophy. If there be no difference between nature and society, then, indeed, modern economics, consciously shaped as it is on the model of mathematics and physics, is the perfection of reason ; but if the two realms are essentially different because blind necessity dominates the one, while conscious action pervades the other ; because in the one we can only see and learn, in the other also will and act—classical economics must needs be superior because it combined a systematic description and logical analysis of what is, with a normative investigation and ethical doctrine of what ought to be.

One thing, however, is undeniable : the fundamental idea of modern economics, the law of diminishing utility, is not a new invention. It was known to the philosophers of the eighteenth century as much as to the scientists of the nineteenth. The law of Gossen and Jennings is the law of Bentham and Bernouilli in a changed form. And, indeed, it is by a comparison of the two formulations that we perceive the whole contrast between the old school and the new.

Both Bentham and Gossen wished to express the essential fact that an individual unit of a uniform stock has the less importance for the well-being of its possessor, the greater the number of units of which the stock is composed. The difference is only that Bentham thought in monetary terms, while Gossen thought in terms of concrete commodities. The truth set forth is in both cases the same ; but the implications are widely dissimilar.

It is easy to see and can hardly be denied, that, from a technical point of view, Bentham's approach is better than the approach of Gossen. Clearly to explain the whole importance of the law of diminishing utility it is necessary to choose as an example a commodity whose supply is infinitely divisible and whose demand is infinitely extensible. The fathers of modern economics implicitly acknowledged this by uniformly referring to the commodity which most nearly fulfils these postulates : by uniformly referring to water when they developed their idea and exemplified their theory. But, in reality, material goods can neither be supplied in infinitesimal quantities nor is the demand for them ever without limitation. It is only purchasing power, the abstract embodiment of all concrete commodities, of which the maximum amount is desired and the minimum fraction can be transferred.

More important than this purely technical advantage of Bentham's point of view is, however, its greater realism. Bentham started from the concept of an unfolded exchange economy with full division and integration of labour, which is possible only where money is in use ; Gossen from an isolated individual who, severed from all social connections, is envisaged exclusively as a physical entity. Yet such a self-sufficient man never did, nor ever could, exist. Because the modern nation has developed from smaller social units, the rash inference is sometimes drawn that in the end the individual emerges as the ultimate historical reality. This conclusion is purely speculative. Even before the dawn of history, man must have been a gregarious animal, and all records of the past confirm the famous dictum of Aristotle, according to which he is by nature a *zoon politikon*. If, then, isolation must be, let it be realistic isolation ; if isolated man is to be the starting-point of economic analysis, let it be a man who— part and parcel of a larger whole—sells his work and buys his food. Money, however, is in essence a social bond : a man with a monetary income is in essence a social creature. And so

Bentham's approach is based on concrete reality, the approach of Gossen on an abstract fiction.

Lastly, the third and most important difference between the classical method and its modern substitute consists in the fact that the classical method not only created a tool for the analysis of economic reality, but at the same time afforded an instrument for its judgment and critique. If the marginal utility of money decreases with the increase of wealth, it follows [1] that an equal distribution of property is the best, and any other the farther from the ideal the greater the inequality of riches it entails. Many modern economists have, in open defence of the existing social constitution, asserted that a statement of this kind is unscientific. Since the knowledge of every individual is naturally and necessarily confined to his own experience, they argue, interpersonal comparisons of value and utility are impossible and, consequently postulates based on them untenable. This reasoning, however, is weak. We know enough of our neighbours' heart to be perfectly certain that, like we, they long for happiness and flee from misery. The great commandment : do unto others as you would that they should do unto you, has been acknowledged by all mankind as the best guide to social harmony and happiness. It is built on the principle of equality. It must indeed be admitted that no exact interpersonal comparison of psychic magnitudes is feasible : but it is very poor logic to conclude that for this reason all comparison is out of the question. Science and exact science are not identical : around the narrow circle of the one stretches the wide field of the other. Certitude may be physical or moral. Economic thought will always be of either kind : some of the truths it brings to view will resemble mathematical propositions in precision and rigidity, others, though equally valuable, will not. It cannot be denied that a rich man loses less satisfaction than a poor man gains if a penny or a pound is transferred between them—even though the loss and the gain and their difference cannot be expressed in figures and measured in grain. Social justice, assuredly, will ever be imperfect : but so is all justice : so is all that is human. We may be unable to create perfect equality of enjoyment : but we are able

---

[1] This logical connection marks the great difference between the classical and the historical schools. The ideal of the classics was deduced from their scientific findings : the ideal of the historians (if indeed it may be called an ideal) was preconceived and superimposed upon their scientific findings. The historical school was ethical rather than scientific ; the classical school was scientific rather than ethical : but it was scientific and ethical at the same time, logically connecting the scientific premiss with the ethical conclusion.

to grant equal chances of happiness. This must be enough. Who will argue that we should not approach the ideal because we are unlikely ever fully to attain it?

In the last analysis, then, the decision between the social and ethical approach of the classical, and the individualist and scientific approach of the modern, economists depends upon the question whether it be desirable or even possible to divide the search for the true from the quest of the good. To me it seems that the vital link between them should not be severed : that the great mission of human meditation is only fulfilled when either task is accomplished. For of all creatures which we know, man alone has the privilege, and the duty, to raise his face towards that Infinite Perfection, in whose image he has been formed.

INDEX

For Product Safety Concerns and Information please contact our EU
representative GPSR@taylorandfrancis.com
Taylor & Francis Verlag GmbH, Kaufingerstraße 24, 80331 München, Germany